Dynasties

Dynasties
The NOBLE FAMILIES of ENGLAND

PATRICK COLEMAN

AMBERLEY

All badges are used under the Creative Commons Attribution-Share Alike 4.0 International unless otherwise stated. Howard badge courtesy of Saltspan. Seymour badge courtesy of Sodacan. Thynne badge courtesy of Wikimandia. Stanley badge courtesy of Thom.lanaud. Somerset badge courtesy of Sodacan. Percy badge courtesy of Wikimandia. Grosvenor badge courtesy of JMvanDijk. Cecil badge courtesy of Tinynanorobots under Creative Commons Attribution-Share Alike 3.0 Unported. Russell badge courtesy of Tech King465. Cavendish badge courtesy of Jonas Magnus Lystad. Lascelles badge courtesy of Wikimandia. Manners badge courtesy of Wikimandia. Herbert badge courtesy of Tinynanorobots under Creative Commons Attribution-Share Alike 3.0 Unported. Wellesley badge courtesy of Sodacan under Creative Commons Attribution-Share Alike 3.0 Unported. Spencer badge courtesy of Ipankonin under Creative Commons Attribution-Share Alike 3.0 Unported.

First published 2026

Amberley Publishing
The Hill, Stroud
Gloucestershire, GL5 4EP

www.amberley-books.com

Copyright © Patrick Coleman, 2026

The right of Patrick Coleman to be identified as the Author of this work has been asserted in accordance with the Copyright, Designs and Patents Act 1988.

ISBN 978 1 3981 2367 0 (hardback)
ISBN 978 1 3981 2368 7 (ebook)

All rights reserved. No part of this book may be reprinted or reproduced or utilised in any form or by any electronic, mechanical or other means, now known or hereafter invented, including photocopying and recording, or in any information storage or retrieval system, without the permission in writing from the Publishers.

British Library Cataloguing in Publication Data.
A catalogue record for this book is available from the British Library.

1 2 3 4 5 6 7 8 9 10

Typesetting by SJmagic DESIGN SERVICES, India.
Printed in the UK.

Appointed GPSR EU Representative:
Easy Access System Europe Oü, 16879218
Address: Mustamäe tee 50, 10621,
Tallinn, Estonia
Contact Details: gpsr.requests@easproject.com, +358 40 500 3575

For my mother and father, le grá agus buíochas.

Contents

Preface	9
Introduction	12
The Howards of Arundel Castle	51
The Seymours of Bradley House	77
The Thynnes of Longleat	95
The Stanleys of Knowsley Hall	109
The Somersets of Badminton House	123
The Percys of Alnwick Castle	137
The Grosvenors of Eaton Hall	151
The Cecils of Burleigh and Hatfield	163
The Russells of Woburn Abbey	181
The Cavendishes of Chatsworth	197
The Lascelles of Harewood House	217
The Manners of Belvoir Castle	225
The Herberts of Wilton and Highclere	239
The Wellesleys of Stratfield Saye	253
The Spencer-Churchills of Blenheim Palace	265
Bibliographical Note	279
Index	281

Preface

Fascination with the aristocratic dynasties that helped shape the country we know today has only grown in the decades since their eclipse as the ruling class. The houses they built as their monuments have never been more popular with the public. As a student studying England's political and social history – histories strewn with names like 'Russell', 'Seymour' and 'Wellington' – I was continually frustrated by the lack of any single volume designed for the general reader that gave some genealogical and historical context to the *names* that seemed to occur generation after generation, century after century. Given that many of the figures seemed to be in the positions of power they were, precisely *because* of their name (and an ancestor's deeds), this seemed an oversight.

Dynasties is an attempt to provide the book I wish I'd had while intrigued by questions about the origins of figures like the Duke of Wellington and Lady Diana Spencer, and places like Longleat, Blenheim and Woburn. The book aims to guide the reader through the history, and sometimes arcane rules, governing the hereditary nobility (provided in the introduction) and then through the individual histories of the greatest of the noble dynasties. The book devotes a chapter to each dynasty, exploring their origins, notable personalities, titles, houses and achievements. Needless to say, there is not space to cover every family that has ever been granted titles of nobility (the number is in the thousands, and guides such as *Burke's Peerage* exist for comprehensive reference). So, I have chosen a selection whose names seem to appear most frequently in the annals of English history, have made the most significant contributions to the country's governance and culture, that hold the best-known titles, and – crucially – that have *endured*. All the families in this book survive to the present day with their titles intact.

The choices made are, nevertheless, subjective, and I have tried to redress this by including sections in each chapter exploring families that are related to the main dynasty in some notable way. Though one thing that becomes clear when studying the family trees is that all of these dynasties are related to each other many times over anyway (intermarriage was how the nobility retained its exclusivity) and most members alive today have ancestors lurking in all the other trees, whatever their patrilineal 'House' may be.

Nevertheless, the surname of the dynasty remains at the heart of its identity, usually remaining attached to the noble title granted to the original dynast, in some cases the best part of a millennium ago. Every family within has at its head a 'peer of the realm', the hereditary holder of a title conferred by the Crown in the *Peerage* (a type of 'order' or 'fellowship' of legally recognised nobility) of England, or of Great Britain or the United Kingdom that are, nonetheless, seated in England. Members of these noble orders were each other's 'peers' in the sense that they had an equal right to vote in their council – the House of Lords – despite holding different ranks such as duke, earl or baron. Historically, all hereditary peers were members of the upper chamber of Parliament, working alongside the non-titled 'commons' in the lower chamber, to make the laws of the land. In this way, noble dynasties differed from those of gentry (untitled landowning

Preface

dynasties) the baronets (hereditary knights) or knights themselves, all of whom were commoners, with no right to sit in the Lords as peers did automatically.

The birthright to a seat in the House of Lords ceased in 1999, and today members of the Lords are appointed as 'life peers', unable to pass their title or membership on to their heirs. As a result, no new noble 'dynasties' are likely to be created in England again, and those dynasties that survive today are no longer the governing families of the nation. In most cases they would not want to be, though many are proud of their family's historic achievements. This book takes a look at some of the greatest.

Note on Family Trees

The genealogical charts given here are simplified to illustrate dynastic lines of succession. The information provided in each chart is selective and designed to provide the clearest guide to descent from the first to the present peer, rather than comprehensive (but impenetrable) family trees. Bold text highlights the senior line of succession. Dates are given sparingly to keep the charts as uncluttered as possible.

Introduction

The power behind the throne: a brief history of the English nobility

For most of its history, England has not been a democracy. Nor has it – despite public perception – been ruled as a Monarchy. Across ten centuries, from its Anglo-Saxon origins until the turn of the twentieth century, England was, in practice if not in theory, an Aristocracy. The country was dominated politically, economically, and socially by families whose wealth and influence often surpassed that of the kings and queens they nominally served. Though sometimes subject to the whims of individual monarchs, many aristocratic families outlasted the royal one. While reigning dynasties like the Tudors, the Stuarts, and the Hanoverians each gave way to the next in succession, aristocratic families like the Howards and the Cecils, tended to stick around. By tradition, the landed families lay claim to be the true embodiment of the realm, boasting pedigrees longer, and histories more illustrious, than upstart 'foreign' clans like the German Hanoverians. Families like the Cecils held onto their influence far more successfully than the royals; one of their number was chief minister to Elizabeth I in the sixteenth century, while his descendant was Prime Minister to Queen Victoria 300 years later.

Introduction

Some, such as Edward Seymour, served as official regents, ruling as monarchs in all but name on behalf of minors or imprisoned kings. Others like William Cavendish and William Russell were responsible for deposing monarchs they didn't approve of and installing new ones they did. Many a noble title was granted by a monarch who owed their crown to the recipient. Even as monarchical power waned in the eighteenth and nineteenth centuries, the power of the hereditary aristocracy actually continued to grow. Landed magnates used the 'democratic' institutions of Parliament to dominate national government. From the House of Lords, they directed a House of Commons made up largely of members of their extended families, or individuals that they hand-picked to be MPs for the counties they ruled from their stately piles as mini kingdoms. Only in the mid-twentieth century, with the upheaval of two World Wars, was the political influence of the patrician class finally broken. Yet even then, and still today well into the twenty-first century, a certain air of glamour and status clings to the 'old nobility'. The great country houses which are their monuments are among the nation's most celebrated and visited attractions. The houses' former owners – now often custodians – have successfully reinvented themselves as guardians of the nation's heritage in an age of mass tourism. Thrown open to the public, their houses showcase the extraordinary contents amassed by their ancestors over centuries, forming some of the most important collections of art and antiquities anywhere in the world. Although their power and much of their former wealth may have gone, the noble dynasties of England have survived as they always did, by adapting as the times dictate.

Medieval dynasties

Some of England's surviving noble dynasties can trace their origins as far back as the Norman Conquest. William the Conqueror brought with him from France many of the warriors who went on to establish astonishingly long-lasting family lines. The prime example is perhaps that of Gilbert le Gros Veneur, the Conqueror's chief huntsman, and ancestor to today's Duke of Westminster, Hugh Grosvenor.

Along with such family-founders, the Normans also imported the very system of feudal nobility that would keep those families like the Grosvenors in positions of power for generations after the Battle of Hastings. In the years after 1066, most of the defeated Saxon nobility was supplanted by the Norman invaders. Following his coronation, the victorious King William installed hundreds of the men who had been his vassals across the Channel onto new estates all over England. These fortunate Norman, Breton and Flemish knights were to act as the king's regional strongmen. To defend their positions, they built formidable castles – a new architectural feature in England – as bases from where they could enforce the king's laws and collect the taxes owed to him. Notable dynasties founded at this time played famous roles in the national and personal dramas of the Middle Ages, though many have since died out in the male line. Extinctions include the Bigods (Earls of Norfolk), the de Veres (Earls of Oxford), and the de Warennes (Earls of Surrey). Other Houses that failed in the male line saw their inheritance and very names adopted by successor families that could claim descent from them through the female line. These included the Percys of Northumberland and the Nevilles of Westmoreland, as well as Fitzalans (Earls of Arundel).

During the reign of the Norman kings, the only titles granted to vassals were those of 'baron' and 'earl', but these were not yet the positions of *rank* that they became as part of the Peerage, which had yet to develop. A baron was any man who held land given to him by the monarch. In return for that land, the baron provided military service to the king whenever it was required to fight internal or external enemies. The 'barons' actually *included* the earls, who were simply those who held additional administrative roles in their county. Seeds of the Peerage were being sown at this time. Firstly, the greater barons were each summoned by the king

Introduction

to his Great Council of advisors. This began the tradition whereby landowners, who also served as the feudal military, expected to be consulted by the monarch on issues of state. The monarch was, after all, reliant upon the barons to defend the realm in time of war, so the vassals certainly had leverage to demand a say in governing. Secondly, the 'writ of summons' (the legal document issued by Norman kings to their landowner-soldiers, commanding them to attend the Great Council) were usually reissued to the sons and heirs of those landowners after their death. This created an expectation that inheritance of land and wealth paralleled by inheritance of political influence. Thus, membership of the king's Great Council became hereditary alongside the title of baron.

From these beginnings the aristocratic system of government grew. The historian of the British aristocracy David Cannadine explains that the astonishing success of England's noble dynasties was founded on their ownership of land: 'Land was wealth: the most secure, reliable and permanent asset. Land was status: its ownership conferred unique and unrivalled celebrity. And land was power: over the locality, the county and the nation.'

From these foundations, England's landed dynasties would evolve into the most powerful aristocracy in Europe. They steadily eroded the power of the monarch to become the unquestioned governing elite of the nation. It was because of the insistence of the 'Great Families' that they should have their say in national affairs that England never came under the rule of an 'Absolute Monarch' of the type that appeared in France under the *Ancien Régime*. The aristocracy's most emphatic early declaration of their right to limit the monarch s power was the Magna Carta rebellion of 1215. Debate continues as to how important this document, which the barons forced King John to agree to, was in curbing the power of the Plantagenet regime. But the barons who acted as enforcers of the 'Great Charter of Freedoms' – and who included a Bigod, a de Vere, and a Percy – successfully established the basic principle that the monarch was subject to the law like everyone else, and that the nobility – self-appointed guardians against royal tyranny – had the right to hold monarchs to account.

The nobility could pursue these ends because they were military leaders, in command of legions of knights who lived on their lands. The nobles of the Middle Ages were battlefield warriors by necessity, in a time when the right to rule was determined by force, and those who commanded the loyalty of men with swords were those who ultimately controlled the realm. This military route to influence would slowly but steadily decline after the Great Councils evolved into a more powerful Parliament, giving the aristocracy a means other than warfare to exert political influence.

In the thirteenth century Parliament revealed its true potential as an organ of aristocratic rule, though still backed and buoyed by the threat and reality of force. A few decades after Magna Carta, the barons went to war with the Crown to ensure their rights to govern through Parliament. Their leader, Simon de Montfort, Earl of Leicester, was hugely successful in his pursuits. Having become the *de facto* ruler of England, reducing the king to something like a ceremonial head of state for the first time, he summoned the barons to a Parliament unlike any before. It was 1265 and de Montfort summoned the usual noble council (a body that would become the House of Lords) but also a council of commoners: knights from the counties chosen by the landowners, and burgesses, or officials, of the boroughs (towns). This then was the first Parliament recognisable to us today, consisting of representation from the commons (in a council that would become the House of Commons) as well as the Lords. De Montfort's parliament was groundbreaking in creating a body that commanded a form of 'democratic' legitimacy – representing all the people of the realm – something which kings could not ignore, even if many tried. It was a body in which the Great Families held a hereditary right to sit, and through their control of the counties they could also control the commons who sat alongside them.

Introduction

Parliament was, true enough, often dismissed or sidelined by the Crown. But over time it became the body through which the nobility exercised its dynastic rights as the ruling class. monarchs became complicit in their own subjugation to Parliament; seeing the institution as useful for their designs, summoned to sanction the raising of the taxes needed to fund foreign wars. Parliamentary approval gave their actions a form of legitimacy in the short term, but of course meant that similar approval was deemed necessary for future monarchs. It ensured that Parliament's input was required before a monarch could act.

The barons came to believe they had the right not only to advise and give consent to monarchical plans, but also the right to remove a monarch from power altogether if they did not govern successfully and with due respect to Parliament. King Edward II was seen as a particularly poor administrator, not to mention a military failure, and faced baronial rebellions and then overthrow by his queen, Isabella, and Roger Mortimer, Earl of March. Mortimer then ruled England as de facto regent during the childhood of Isabella's son King Edward III. A king had not been dethroned since 1066, and that had been at the hands of a foreign invader. By contrast, Edward II was deposed by his own nobles who ruled in his stead. The nobility had flexed their 'kingmaker' muscles and would do so again with Edward III's grandson, Richard II, deposed by a coalition of noble dynasties, including the Percys, in 1399.

Dynasties, it should be remembered, were always far more than just the men who technically owned the land and made up the membership of the House of Lords. The women of the family might not have appeared in the proceedings of parliaments or in political offices reserved for men, but as family matriarchs they could drive events in subtle and in overt ways. There is a clear distinction to be made between the *theory* of lordly government consisting of noble*men* who just happened to have families, and the *practice* of government which was under the sway of family groupings – wives, sons, daughters, brothers, sisters – who exerted enormous influence over their patriarch.

The rules of the peerage game were, it is true, firmly stacked against women. In several ways they still are. In almost all cases women were not permitted to inherit land or title. Their status depended upon that of their father or of their husband. The coat of arms was passed down the male line with few exceptions. The name of the dynasty was the surname transmitted from father to son and from husband to wife; married noblewomen left their birth dynasty to join their married one. Yet, even with all the legal and conventional rules restraining them, female dynasts had an incalculable impact on national events. This was certainly on show during what was otherwise a catastrophic period for aristocratic dynasties towards the end of the Middle Ages, the so-called Wars of the Roses (1455–1485).

The thirty-year conflict for the throne between two competing branches of the Plantagenet family – the House of York and the House of Lancaster – saw the noble dynasties of England pick their side, then live and die by the choice made. Great swathes of the old nobility were decimated in these wars that had a far greater immediate impact on the aristocracy than those previous medieval military campaigns, the Crusades to the Holy Land (which began in 1095) and the Hundred Years War with France (1337–1453). Those conflicts were, in reality, multiple campaigns against foreign enemies that took place over much longer time spans. Neither saw fighting take place on English soil. English nobles were killed on Crusade or in battle against the French. But even the most famous battle of the Hundred Years War – Agincourt in 1415 – saw few patrician casualties (the Earl of Suffolk is known to have been killed but hardly any other notables are recorded). The Wars of the Roses by contrast saw battles that ended the lives of the heads of the Percy family and of the Nevilles and the Beauforts. The wars came to an end in 1485 in no small measure thanks to the manoeuvring of Margaret Beaufort. Her son Henry Tudor, a member of a minor noble dynasty, became king.

Introduction

Intrigue and betrayal: the Tudor courtiers

The crowning of Henry VII traditionally marks the dividing line between England's medieval and 'early modern' eras. The 300-year rule of the Plantagenets yielded now to the Tudors, who would witness the Renaissance and instigate the Protestant Reformation. Those twin cultural and religious revolutions were what in fact shook the country out of the Middle Ages rather than a change of royal House. But the rise of the upstart Tudors did genuinely mark a dividing line for the noble dynasties of England. A few had risen during the Wars of the Roses (the Howards had first made their mark under the Yorkist kings). But many had been wiped out, leaving openings for new families to take their place. As 'new men' themselves, the first Tudor monarchs Henry VII and Henry VIII, did not stand in awe of the 'ancient' Norman families who had ruled the roost since Hastings. Instead, the Tudors liked to advance ambitious individuals like themselves; individuals who would be loyal first to the Tudor regime that had handed them power, rather than believing their positions to be their age-old birthright.

Dynasties that came to the fore in the sixteenth century were promoted to the Peerage from the ranks of the gentry and the merchant class. They included families like the Russells (former wine merchants), the Cavendishes (civil servants) and the Cecils and Thynnes (landed gentry). At this time, 'new men' like Thomas Cromwell worked to concentrate power into the hands of the king's closest personal advisors. Since Norman times there had been a 'small council' of magnates closest to the monarch, as well as the larger Great Council. But now, this exclusive 'Privy Council' became an institution in its own right, with formal powers akin to Parliament. (Here we have the origins of what we now call the Cabinet, still technically a committee of the monarch's Privy Council.) Ministers like William Cecil used the council to exercise their power, though membership was no guarantee of safety. The Tudor courts were notorious vipers' dens of intrigue and betrayal.

For every new dynasty that rose and endured – like the four mentioned above – there were very many more that fell, losing fortune, position, and often heads.

Parvenu families that managed to survive the perilous reign of Henry VIII, enriched themselves greatly during the Reformation. King Henry's decision to separate the Church of England from Rome, and make himself its Supreme Governor, had profound repercussions for all his subjects, not least his nobility. Those magnates who accepted the Reformation were granted vast new estates on which to found their future success, lands that had belonged to the Catholic monasteries, shut by Henry from 1536 onwards. Former monastic estates were carved up and granted to the loyal nobility in what has been described as the greatest redistribution of land in England since the Norman Conquest. Among the dynasts to profit were William Cavendish who helped oversee the Dissolution of the Monasteries in-person, and John Russell who was given the lands of the former abbey at Woburn where his descendants live today.

The older feudal families didn't go unrewarded either. The Percys and the Howards each received new estates from monastic spoils. Those two families did, however, find the change of their religion more difficult to stomach, even as they gained materially from the Reformation. Some of their members followed their religious conscience, stayed loyal to the Catholic faith, and paid with their lives. Both the Percys and the Howards were famous recusants whose members sometimes openly rebelled against the new Protestant religion – an act considered treasonous by the Tudor Crown. Only during the reign of the Catholic Queen Mary Tudor did the recusant nobility sleep safely in their beds. Afterwards, families who did not join the Protestant ranks were consigned either to destruction or at least to political insignificance for centuries to come.

Introduction

Stuarts and Georgians: from Cavaliers and Roundheads to Tories and Whigs

Under the Stuart monarchs (1603–1714) the nobility continued to be torn by the religious and constitutional conflicts unleashed by the Reformation. While the original impetus for England's break with Rome had been the personal ambitions of Henry VIII – for a divorce, and for freedom from the 'foreign' power based in the Vatican – by 1600 English society was composed of genuine, true believers in the new Protestant religion, as well as passionate adherents to the old Catholic faith. It was a conflict that had split all of Europe. In England, recusant families like the Howards maintained their traditional belief in the Catholic Mass and its rituals and stayed wedded to the idea of a Church hierarchy of bishops, cardinals and Pope chosen by God to lead them to salvation. Protestants – especially the extremist 'Puritan' kind – believed in the centrality of the Bible and each individual's personal relationship with the scriptures. They wanted to see all the distracting ceremonials and the needless (and corrupt) hierarchy of the Roman Church swept away to better focus on the Word. By the early 1600s, the now British Monarchy – since the accession of James VI of Scotland to the English throne – had settled on 'Anglicanism', a sort of halfway-house between Catholicism and Protestantism; Protestant in its administrative independence from Rome and its core doctrines, but maintaining a hierarchy of bishops and at least some of the old church ceremonials. In an attempt to please all, however, the State ended up creating angry factions to either side: Catholics who wanted a full reunion with Rome, and Puritans who wanted a more radical Protestantism than they saw in the Church of England.

Most noble families represented in the House of Lords were generally loyal to the Anglican Church or were secret (or open) Catholics. The House of Commons by contrast was increasingly dominated by the Puritan faction. The Stuart monarchs themselves were nominally heads of the Anglican Church but often displayed

Catholic tastes which antagonised both the Anglican Protestant peers and the Puritan MPs in Parliament. King Charles I not only favoured Catholic practices in religious matters, but the practice of Catholic kings like those of France and Spain of ruling as Absolute Monarchs without the need for a parliament to check their power. It was these tendencies that led Parliament to declare war on King Charles in what is still commonly referred to as the English Civil War, but which in fact extended across the entire British Isles.

The noble families once again found themselves divided on how to proceed. Many of those who had Catholic sympathies declared themselves Royalist, showing loyalty to a king who they saw as a religious ally. Anglican nobles found it more difficult to take a side. In the traditionalist view of their own history, the nobility was supposed to be the guardian against absolutist monarchs. The Anglican dynasties who had grown rich and influential at the expense of recusant families, also feared they would be sidelined by a king more likely to favour those old Catholic dynasties. In the end, most of the nobility did ride to the Royalist cause, fearing the overthrow of the king might lead to the overthrow of the entire social hierarchy of which they were the senior part; survival mattered more than historic principles. Nevertheless, there were a few notable 'Noble Roundheads' who saw their parliamentary role of resisting royal dictatorship as their chief duty. William Russell, 5th Earl of Bedford, was a general in the parliamentary army and fought against King Charles's Cavaliers at the Battle of Edgehill in 1642. He was later to convert to the Royalist cause, but other peers stayed in place to witness the victory of Parliament and the founding of Oliver Cromwell's republic.

After the execution of the king, the hereditary nobility found itself in the perilous position many had feared. Most of them having been Royalists, they were now a defeated enemy of the state. The House of Lords was abolished by Cromwell, which removed the nobility from Parliament and stripped them of their ancient lawmaking powers. Yet despite some radical revolutionary

Introduction

calls to go even further, and for landed estates to be taken into the ownership of the common people, little else ended up changing for noble families under the Commonwealth. They lost their political power, yes, but were allowed to keep their lands and even their titles. Most of them retreated to their estates and kept themselves to themselves, waiting patiently to retake their positions of power, which they did when the Monarchy and the House of Lords were restored in 1660, the republican experiment finally over.

The religious and constitutional issues that had led to the Civil War in the first place were, however, far from settled. The restored Stuart Monarchy in the form of Charles II and his younger brother (and heir presumptive) James, Duke of York, was just as 'Catholic' in its sympathies as that of Charles I, if not more so. The nobility once again found itself split along the lines they had before the Civil War, and they now coalesced into two groupings within Parliament: the 'Whigs' as they would eventually be named, believed strongly in parliamentary supremacy and Protestant supremacy. The 'Tories' believed in a strong Monarchy and, though they did not much like the King and his brother's Catholic predilections, they feared the destabilising effect of removing a Monarch – or their heir – far more. The whole legitimacy of hereditary succession would, they thought, be thrown into question once monarchs were routinely removed from power whenever they caused tension.

The Whigs and Tories were the forerunners of modern political parties and would see the nobility fight each other on the floors of the Houses of Parliament rather than on the battlefield. But that situation did not reach maturity until later in the eighteenth and nineteenth centuries, and the age of habitual political violence was not yet quite over. The founding fathers of the Whig movement included members of the great Protestant dynasties established a century and a half before at the Reformation, including the Cavendishes and the Russells. In 1683, William, Lord Russell (son of the 'Roundhead' Earl of Bedford) was convicted of trying to assassinate the king and the Duke of York in the so-called Ryehouse Plot. Russell was executed. Matters would not be settled until 1688, after the Duke of York had succeeded to the throne as James II.

The openly Catholic king began to advance Catholics at court at the expense of the Protestant magnates who had been long used to power, and without consulting Parliament. Catholic Absolutism was once again threatening the established order. So it was that the great Whig families conspired to remove James from the throne and install his Protestant daughter along with her husband as joint Monarchs (Mary II and William III) under a constitutional settlement that ensured parliamentary supremacy thereafter.

Following this aristocratic coup – or 'Glorious Revolution' as it was termed – Parliament became the undisputed instrument of power through which the nobility would govern. The eighteenth and nineteenth centuries were the era of an aristocratic oligarchy. Parliament was supreme, but far from democratic. Although a recognisable political system featuring a 'Prime Minister', and organised party oppositions and governments, was taking shape in the early 1700s, it was a system over which landed dynasties held total control. The right to vote for MPs was based on property ownership. Prime Ministers and cabinet ministers were often unelected members of the House of Lords. Noblemen's extended family members dominated the House of Commons in any case. The Lords had the power to veto nearly every initiative that came from the Commons. Other national institutions such as the army and the church were also dominated by the landed classes. In local government and in society, the same dynasties also ruled. By now – in less warlike times – the greatest of them lived in country houses that were really palaces, set within genteel landscaped estates over which they reigned as demi-royals. The local dynasty ran the judiciary. Their sons and daughters wielded immense influence over local affairs often simply through an automatic deference shown to them by members of the working and middle classes towards titled 'superiors'. There was a popular belief – right up to the turn of the twentieth century – among the great majority of the people that the landed aristocracy simply had the 'right to rule'. Very few questioned that landowners were the people whose job it was to govern the country through their superior education and inherited expertise. And – given the fact of their wealth and their lack of any need to work – how else were they to fill their time? It was the natural order for the aristocracy – the professional governors – to govern, and the rest of society looked to them to fulfil their obligations.

To be sure, they found time for a lot more besides politics. Great houses like Chatsworth and Blenheim were the scene of sumptuous society gatherings: balls, garden parties, hunts and banquets, all attended on by armies of butlers, footmen, housemaids and cooks. The wealthiest dynasties also owned mansions in London where they would stay during the society 'Season' in late spring and summer, attending Parliament and allowing their younger members to mingle with potential suitors.

Decline and rebirth

This serene golden age of the leisured aristocracy lasted to around the 1880s when cracks began to appear in every facet of landed life. The 'crisis of the aristocracy' was probably sewn in the Industrial Revolution that had begun as early as the 1760s and which created a new class of self-made business and finance magnates whose growing wealth began to challenge the landed class. Although many nobles had begun to make money from industrial enterprises themselves, diversifying into everything from mining to railways, this did not make up for the losses in their traditional income from the land, which came under significant strain from the 1880s. An agricultural depression which hit all of Europe sent rentals plummeting, severely impacting family finances.

Furthermore, the aristocracy's right to rule was increasingly being questioned. A family's age had once been enough to legitimise their power (a reason dynasts had hired pedigree-makers to trace their bloodlines back to Hastings and justify their positions). But the new middle classes now thought that their wealth also entitled them to a say in national affairs. Since the Great Reform Act of 1832, the number of people eligible to vote for their MPs had slowly increased. In 1882 a further parliamentary reform act extended voting rights to two thirds of men across the United Kingdom. The age of mass democracy had begun that would lead to all men and women over the age of twenty-one having the vote by 1928. As this process unfolded, the automatic right of unelected nobles to be lawmakers seemed increasingly anachronistic. The last Prime Minister to lead a government from the House of Lords was Robert Cecil, Marquess of Salisbury, in 1902. In 1911, the Parliament Act drastically reduced the powers of the House of Lords, meaning it could no longer veto the wishes of the Commons. The aftermath of the First World War brought major challenges for country house communities that included higher taxes and a shortage of domestic servants – many lost in the war – which the old way of life had depended upon.

The difficulties of country estates became a huge drag upon their owners. But the situation was not much worried over by the population at large. This was before great houses were seen as national 'heritage', and the plight of the aristocracy drew little sympathy from a public who were shaking off the sense of deference they had previously felt towards the nobility. Hundreds of country houses were sold off, many demolished, and their estates broken up. Dynasties that had been at the heart of rural communities for centuries found themselves packing up and shipping out.

There were some families, however, who stayed. Those featured here are examples of dynasties who not only managed to weather the storms of taxation, death duties and changing societal attitudes (which only grew more pronounced after the Second World War) but also to prosper again in a new way. Public opinion may have gone against the nobility in the first half of the twentieth century, but soon a flickering nostalgia for the peculiarly English world of the country house and its

Introduction

characters began to creep into the popular imagination. Fortunately for the aristocracy, it was just at the same time that mass tourism was bringing day trippers to the countryside. The heritage movement began to recognise the artistic and architectural achievement of the country house, and its importance as a site of major historic collections. The public wanted to see these places, and it provided the houses' owners with an opportunity to bring their country estates back to life. The doors were thrown open, the houses placed under the formal ownership of a charitable trust with some agreement reached to allow the family to remain living there in a private wing.

The aristocratic 'way of life' never re-emerged in the form it had before the nobility lost its position as the governing class. Most families who continued to live at and run their estates could not afford to live in the lavish way that they had before the wars. But the glamour of the great dynasties did not quite disappear. Pioneers of the 'new' country house way of life like Deborah, Duchess of Devonshire, became centres of a high society that now included film stars and artists, fashion designers and models. Duchess Deborah entertained glittering gatherings at Chatsworth, complete with butler, footman and housekeepers (not as many as in the past, maybe, but the real thing nonetheless). Even as she opened farm shops and gift shops to keep the house afloat, she fulfilled the ancient duties of her class, attending state events from the Coronation of Queen Elizabeth II in 1953 to the investiture of her husband Andrew Cavendish, 11th Duke of Devonshire, as a Knight of the Garter in 1996. The Duke also fulfilled his traditional role, from his accession in 1950 to his death in 2004, he administered his estates in the old paternalistic way. Like his ancestors, he became a patron of artists, including Lucien Freud.

These dynastic mansions are once again economic powerhouses, often employing many hundreds of staff. In the twenty-first century, nostalgia for the old world symbolised by country houses shows itself in our culture, in television series like *Downton*

Abbey, documenting the melancholy story of aristocratic decline, and countless films, not to mention the huge numbers of visitors who wander the halls of stately homes every year.

'My Lords and Ladies': the English peerage and the titles system

Some knowledge of the workings of the titles system is necessary for any understanding of the dynasties who held and still hold them. Some of the arcane rules surrounding peerage titles seem outdated today, but it all mattered a great deal in theory and in practice for many centuries.

A dynasty does not of course require a title in order to endure. The Grosvenor family survived as landowning gentry across six centuries before 'Lord' was first attached to their name. And in republican constitutions like the United States, families including the Kennedys have managed to sustain political influence without the trappings of nobility. 'Aristocracy' and 'nobility' are not synonymous. Yet it remains true that in England, a hereditary title conferred by the Crown was the ultimate goal of any ambitious dynast until quite recently. Noble titles bestowed unrivalled status, while their inheritable nature ensured the continued social prominence of a family generation after generation. The dynasties in this book all hold titles that developed in England from the early Middle Ages onward, and which coalesced into a legal system of recognised nobility known as the Peerage.

Until November 1999, when the hereditary nobility lost its right to sit in Parliament, a 'peer of the realm' was an individual who was a member of the upper chamber, the House of Lords (sometimes called the 'House of Peers') and held a noble title. The peers helped make the laws of the land. This had been the case since kings summoned parliaments in the Middle Ages. 'Writs of Summons' and later, 'Letters

Introduction

Patent', were the official documents issued by the Monarch to grant a noble title to an individual. (Titles could also be withdrawn by a Monarch using an Act of Attainder, and they frequently were.) A 'Letters Patent of creation' would declare exactly what title was being granted (baron for example) and to whom, its territorial designation if applicable, and how it would be inherited by future generations, usually by descent through the male line. Each generation would be enumerated upon inheriting; the original grantee would be known as the '1st Baron' (or whatever the title was) and upon his death, his son and heir would become the '2nd Baron', and so on.

Peers – like soldiers or police officers – come in ranks. There is a hierarchy with dukes at the top of the ladder and four rungs below them. In descending order of precedence, the five ranks of the Peerage are Duke, Marquess, Earl, Viscount and Baron. In the upper ranks, the titles usually have a territorial element. For example, the head of the Percy family is the Duke *of Northumberland*; the head of the Thynne family is the Marquess *of Bath*. This tradition began under feudalism when titles were linked to the lands a nobleman controlled. In the lower ranks, titles generally do not have a territorial element. Instead, the title is based upon the family surname; for example, Baron *Davison*. In the middle rank – earl – there are plenty of examples of both forms: there is no difference of precedence between the Earl *of Derby* and Earl *Spencer*.

Most of these titles have a shorter form that can be used informally: the word 'Lord' can replace many of the ranks for ease of conversation. For example, the Marquess of Bath can be referred to simply as 'Lord Bath', the Earl Spencer can be called 'Lord Spencer'. Doing this disguises the rank of a peer, so it may be done only with the four lower ranks. It cannot be done with dukes; they enjoy special privileges as the top rank, and are always referred to by their full title, the 'Duke of... wherever it may be'. Similarly, the lower four ranks are addressed by others as 'My Lord', while dukes alone are addressed as 'Your Grace'.

The five ranks of the peerage

A dynasty's precedence is based upon the title rank which the head of their House holds. Ducal dynasties, like the Howards and Seymours, take precedence over baronial dynasties for example, even if a particular baron's family has a longer noble lineage and an older title. The five ranks developed over several centuries as new titles were adopted.

Duke: the highest rank has its origins as a royal title. William the Conqueror was himself the Duke of Normandy (technically a vassal of the French king, though in practice a sovereign ruler of the duchy) and the English kings long continued to style themselves as Dukes of Normandy. The Plantagenet kings first granted the title of duke to other men only in the form of their own sons. The first ever English duke was Prince Edward, son of King Edward III – and better known as the Black Prince – who was created Duke of Cornwall in 1337 (alongside his position as Prince of Wales). The word derives from *dux*, the term for a Roman general. Dukedoms were first granted to non-royals from 1448 when William de la Pole was created Duke of Suffolk. The title of duke was the highest honour that the Crown could bestow on a non-royal person. There are just twenty-four non-royal ducal dynasties in the UK today, of which fourteen hold titles pertaining to English territory. The 'Premier Duke' (holding the oldest surviving dukedom) is the Duke of Norfolk (created 1483). Today, the granting of dukedoms has once again become a royal-only affair; sons of monarchs are generally granted dukedoms, and all Princes of Wales are Dukes of Cornwall.

Marquess: The second rank of the Peerage was first awarded in 1385 to Robert de Vere who was created Marquess of Dublin by King Richard II. At that time there were only dukes, earls and barons in the Peerage; King Richard decided to insert a new rank of marquess below dukes but above earls and barons, an act which caused outrage among the 'demoted' ranks (de Vere's title was soon revoked). Originally, the term 'marchio' or 'marcher lord' had been an informal reference to any earl or baron whose lands sat on the borders with Wales or Scotland. These men were perhaps seen as more important than their inland colleagues because they would have to defend England in the event of invasion by Welsh or Scots. In several other European countries, nobles who guarded the realm's borders – or 'marks' as borders were commonly known – were given official titles deriving from the word. In Germany they were 'margraves' and in France they were 'marquis'. It was therefore natural that the new English rank of marquess would stand above the earls and barons. Marquessates were later awarded simply as this 'second tier' of nobility to men whose lands were not necessarily near borders. The Premier Marquess in England is the Marquess of Winchester (created 1551).

Earl: The third rank of the Peerage is the oldest linguistically, an Anglo-Saxon word equivalent to the French 'Compte' or 'Count', referring to a landowner whose territory formed a county. The word earl derives from the Saxon 'ealdorman' the name given to the administrator of a county (or 'shire' to use the old Saxon term) in the days before the Norman Conquest. The ealdormen were not initially 'nobles', nor did they pass their titles down to their heirs. They were the king's officials in the provinces. After 1066, the Norman kings kept the position of earl intact, gave the office to many of their own barons, and made them hereditary titles. Soon they became a rank of the Peerage above other barons, and many of their old administrative duties were taken over by the shire reeves (sheriffs). The Premier Earl in England is the Earl of Shrewsbury (created 1442).[1]

Viscount: In 1440, King Henry VI decided to create a new title directly below that of an earl. This new 'deputy earl' would be

---

1. The Earl of Shrewsbury is the Premier Earl 'on the roll' of England; his earldom is the oldest surviving held by a peer who holds no higher-ranking title. The earldom of Arundel is actually older but is held by the Duke of Norfolk.

known using the French form 'vice count' or viscount. A strange choice perhaps, but this was during the Hundred Years War, when the English king claimed France as his kingdom. Henry's new peerage rank was designed to mirror the *viscomptes* already in France. The first English viscount was John Beaumont, Viscount Beaumont. The oldest surviving, and therefore Premier Viscount, is the Viscount Hereford (created 1550).

Baron: the lowest rank of the Peerage has a Norman name from c. 1066, referred to a tenant-in-chief, a landowner under the king. Introduced by William the Conqueror, the barons held a feudal land tenure gifted by the Monarch, were summoned to attend his Great Council, and bound in feudal obligation to provide military assistance. The feudal barons evolved into the Peerage rank created by Letters Patent under the Monarch's Great Seal, but in earlier times all nobles bore the title of baron, even those of greater status (many of the 'Magna Carta Barons' were in fact earls). The Premier Baron of England is the Baron de Ros (created in 1264 through writ, summoning the first holder to attend the Parliament of Simon de Montfort).

The peer and their family

A key feature of the English Peerage which effected the whole noble dynasty, and one the reader needs to bear in mind, is the legal distinction between an individual peer (the formal titleholder; the baron or duke for example) and the peer's close family members (their spouse and children, uncles and aunts). For while the titleholder himself – and it is usually a male who holds that legal position – is a 'nobleman', historically entitled to a seat in the House of Lords, his family members all technically remain 'commoners' with no such rights. To give an historical example: Hugh Grosvenor, the 1st Duke of Westminster, was created a peer by Queen Victoria. His wife, who became Duchess of Westminster, was not. Her 'title'

Introduction

was, in effect, an honorary one, recognising that her husband was now a duke. But in purely constitutional terms she remained a 'commoner'. The Duke took his seat in the Lords as a lawmaker with all the legal privileges that afforded. His wife did not. She was a 'duchess' in name only. The same was true for the duke's children. It remains the case today that even the eldest son and heir of a peer remains legally a commoner until such time as his father dies and he inherits the Peerage in his own right. He may hold an honorary or 'courtesy' title to use the correct terminology – until that time comes (the Duke of Westminster's eldest son is known as 'Earl Grosvenor').

The courtesy title used by an eldest son and heir is usually one of his father's lesser titles; peers in the upper ranks generally have more than one title to their name. A duke is usually also a marquess, an earl and so on, although in practice they only ever use their highest-ranking title. The Duke of Westminster also holds the title of Earl Grosvenor, but 'lends' it as a courtesy to his eldest son and heir. Only the three top ranks of the Peerage give courtesy titles to the eldest son. Such a peer's collection of titles might have been amassed by their ancestors over several centuries as the family climbed the ladder of nobility. The Cavendish family for example started out with the relatively lowly title of Baron Cavendish in 1605, before being 'upgraded' to earls of Devonshire in 1618, then gaining the marquessate of Hartington and dukedom of Devonshire in 1694. The lesser titles were not replaced by these elevations, so the full title of today's Duke of Devonshire is actually His Grace the 12th Duke of Devonshire, the 12th Marquess of Hartington, the 15th Earl of Devonshire, the 7th Earl of Burlington, the 15th Baron Cavendish of Hardwick, the 7th Baron Cavendish of Keighley.

For obvious reasons, he goes simply as 'the Duke of Devonshire'.

Primogeniture and prejudice

When it comes to inheriting titles, there is no avoiding the patriarchal rules governing the Peerage. It was born in the most patriarchal of ages and its governing principles have barely changed since. Although dynasties have been shaped every bit as much by powerful women as by men, the inheritance of titles themselves is almost always a male privilege. The overwhelming majority of hereditary peerages were not just created for a man, they were designed to be held only by his heirs through the male line of descent. The title remained fastened to the dynasty's surname – also traditionally transmitted through the male line – and serving to define dynasties as a very male enterprise.

In the formal language of a Letters Patent, and with few exceptions, the text creating a new title stipulated that it would be inherited by 'heirs male of the body' of the first titleholder. This was the principle of male primogeniture, or the 'male firstborn'. In such a system, the line of succession works as follows.

A peer's eldest son is automatically the 'heir apparent' to his father's peerage. He will inherit the peerage upon his father's death. *His* eldest son then becomes the next heir apparent, and so on, passing the peerage down the generations, father to son. Simple enough, but for the obvious question arising: what if a peer has no son? In the case of a brand-new peerage, the title would simply die out with the first holder; there have been many cases of a 'first and last' duke or earl of somewhere-or-other, the title becoming extinct for lack of a male heir.

In the case of older peerages, however, a titleholder who has no sons of his own may be able to look elsewhere in his extended family for a male. This is because the older a title is, the more chances there are that some previous title holder produced *younger* sons in addition to an heir apparent, and who may then have spawned 'cadet branches' (junior branches) of the family. Such branches could include male cousins with the same surname, meaning that they descended in the male line from a previous title holder, and therefore, from the *first* titleholder. And that is the criteria demanded in a Letters Patent: that titles may descend to 'heirs male of the body' of the first holder. In such cases, a peer who has no sons may be succeeded in his title by a male cousin – sometimes a very distant one – whose descent can nevertheless be traced patrilineally back to the first titleholder. Such a case occurred in 1975 when the 16th Duke of Norfolk, Bernard Howard, died. He had no sons, but was succeeded by a cousin, Miles Howard, who became the 17th Duke. Miles was a great-grandson of the 13th Duke's younger son! A convoluted claim perhaps, but he was nonetheless an 'heir male' of the 1st Duke, John Howard, who lived 500 years before him.

The more generations that a dynasty persists, the more chance its peerage title has of surviving, for it is likely that an indirect male heir – known as an 'heir presumptive' – will be available to continue the line. Such *presumed* heirs cannot use a courtesy title before they succeed however, because their status as heir could always be overturned if the sitting peer suddenly produced a son and heir of his own.

There are very few instances in the English Peerage where the ban on female inheritance of titles does not apply. A number of the more ancient earldoms have passed through the female line when a family died out in the male line, and this was usually due to quirks of feudal tradition. The earldoms of Arundel and of Warwick, for example, both depend on a medieval custom whereby the title belongs to whoever owns the great castles which are their respective seats. If the owners had a daughter, the castle – and so the earldoms – would pass into the possession of that daughter's husband *jure uxoris* (by right of his wife). *Their* son could then inherit it *jure matris* (by right of his mother). Woman became peeress in their own right – *suo jure* – for various reasons – usually because they were royals – or when special provision was made in a Letters Patent to allow a woman to inherit in certain specific cases where there was no male heir available. Such a 'special remainder' was written into the patent creating the dukedom of Marlborough.

Generally, however, a title will become extinct for want of male heirs. Upon extinction, it may be created anew by the Monarch for another family. A title may go through several separate 'creations' over time, granted to different families if the title keeps dying out. If a title is recreated, it is often granted to someone descended from the previous family through a *female* heiress. For example, the first creation of the earldom of Burlington was granted to the Boyle family in 1664. When the 3rd Earl died in 1753 without a male heir apparent or presumptive, the title became extinct. The last earl did, however, have a daughter: Charlotte Boyle. Her son later received the second creation of the earldom and became the '1st Earl of Burlington' in this second incarnation of the title. This earl was not of the House of Boyle (his father was a Cavendish) but he had Boyle blood through his mother. This process of 'recreating' titles is the usual way that female ancestry has been recognised in the Peerage.

Historically, the wives and daughters of peers have had very few rights beyond the social status that membership of their family brought them. The same has usually been true for any younger sons of a peer. Under primogeniture, the eldest son inherits title and estate, while younger sons inherit nothing save what provision their father chooses to make for them.

It is status that that has been the key benefit for the family members of peers. Throughout their lives, the wives, daughters and younger sons of peers are able to hold honorary titles that distinguish them as members of a noble House. Wives use the feminine form of their husband's title: Duchess, Marchioness, Countess,[2] Viscountess or Baroness. Unlike their husbands, peeresses by marriage are not enumerated as a '1st', '2nd', '3rd' peeress; for as long as they are married to the living peer, they are simply 'The' Duchess or 'The' Countess of wherever. In all other ways, however, their titles

---

[2]. The use of 'countess' for the wife of an earl is the result of no Saxon equivalent ever having developed.

mirror those of their husbands. The peeresses of the four lower ranks can have their titles camouflaged by a shorter generic one: 'Lady'. For example, the Marchioness of Bath can be referred to as 'Lady Bath', the Countess Spencer as 'Lady Spencer' (and they are addressed as 'my lady'). Duchesses, like their husbands, are always known by their full title and addressed as 'your grace'.

The daughters and sons of lower ranking peers (the viscounts and barons) do not receive courtesy titles. Even the eldest son does not. They are all known simply as 'the Honourable...' followed by their full name. Daughters and sons of the higher-ranking peers (the dukes, marquesses and earls) do receive courtesy titles. As mentioned above, the eldest son is given one of his father's lesser titles to use. Daughters and younger sons of these peers do not get quite so grand a style: daughters are known simply by their full name with the honorary prefix 'Lady'. A daughter of the Earl and Countess Spencer might be 'Lady Sarah Spencer'. In conversation she could be referred to simply as 'Lady Sarah' (not as 'Lady Spencer' as that would be to confuse her with her mother, the Countess Spencer). Similarly, younger sons of these peers are known by their full names with the honorary prefix 'Lord'. hence 'Lord Robert Spencer'. In conversation he could be referred to as 'Lord Robert' (not as 'Lord Spencer' as that would be to confuse him with his father, the Earl Spencer).

The widow of a peer receives a rather curious new prefix upon her husband's death, that of Dowager. Upon the death of the 11th Duke of Devonshire, his widow the duchess became the 'Dowager Duchess of Devonshire'. This was to prevent any confusion between herself and the *new* Duchess of Devonshire (wife of the newly succeeded 12th Duke of Devonshire). In cases where two or more widows of previous peers are alive, only the earliest surviving uses this title of 'Dowager'. The others simply use their forename to distinguish them. This was the case with the Devonshires in 1950, when the 11th Duke succeeded to the title. His wife became

'The Duchess of Devonshire', but the widows of both the 10th and the 9th Dukes were still alive. The 9th Duke's widow was 'Dowager Duchess of Devonshire', while the 10th Duke's widow was known as 'Mary, Duchess of Devonshire'. (When the Dowager died in 1960, Mary then became known as the Dowager Duchess.) Dowagers do take 'precedence'. over the new peeress.

Precedence and the 'trimmings' of nobility: coats of arms and ceremonial dress

Precedence, according to *Burke's Peerage* – the 'who's who' register of UK hereditary peerages – 'concerns itself with such matters as the order in which people go in to dinner, leave the dinner table, march in procession ... or are listed in an official description of some ceremonial function'.

The orders of precedence in England are complex to say the least and can change depending on whether peers hold certain other additional roles. They may perhaps be one of the 'Great Officers of State', one of the traditional Ministers of the Crown with titles like 'Lord High Constable' or 'Lord Privy Seal'. These were once powerful posts in government, usually granted to peers, though today they are largely ceremonial like the other trimmings of nobility. Many such offices became hereditary in noble dynasties. The office of Earl Marshal has been hereditary in the House of Howard for centuries. Precedence can also turn on any number of other archaic rules. Generally, however, precedence within the Peerage of England is determined first of all by rank, and then by the age of the peerage title, with the oldest, or 'premier', peer of the rank coming first followed by the others in order of creation.

Rank and station have been enthusiastically shown off by peers using similar methods to other hierarchical institutions. Like the armed forces and the church, the Peerage has its ceremonial dress, forms of rank insignia, and uses emblems to identify peers and their status. For nearly 900 years the coat of arms has been the essential

Introduction

'logo' of any self-respecting dynasty. And although the robes and regalia of peers and peeresses are now worn only on ceremonial occasions (and maybe not even then anymore) these 'uniforms' of rank remain the entitlement of all members of the Peerage.

The coat of arms is usually referred to as a 'family crest'. This is incorrect on two counts. Firstly, a coat of arms does not technically belong to a *family* at all but is the personal emblem of an individual peer. Secondly, a 'crest' is only one component part of a coat of arms, (as any exasperated expert on heraldry will tell you when provoked).

Coats of arms originated in the mid-twelfth century when knights and lords took part in tournaments. The joust and melee events were the Premier League matches of their day, and the competitors in these tournaments wore 'strips' just as footballers do. Their surcoats were decorated with personal colours and symbols, their 'coat' of arms. These were repeated on the competitor's shield and subsequently became convenient identifying symbols for use on personal flags and seals.

In 1484, King Richard III established the College of Arms – or College of Heralds – to regulate English coats of arms. The heralds had once been the 'announcers' of royal courts, declaring victories or war for example. In the age of chivalry, they also made announcements at tournaments, which is how they came to be experts in describing coats of arms. They were charged with keeping written records of arms so that they remained unique to a dynasty. They blazoned (described) them in detail and produced beautifully detailed painted representations. The heralds gained the right to design and grant coats of arms, which became increasingly complex and symbolic, referencing everything from events in family history to places associated with the dynasty. For this reason, heraldry is more than just a frivolous, if beautiful art. It can tell us a lot about a family, how members saw themselves, and how they wanted to present themselves to others.

The elements of an Achievement of Arms represent accessories worn or used by medieval combatants (for illustrations, see plate 1):

Shield: The key component of the Achievement of Arms, representing the real shield. The symbols used on them are known as 'charges' and range from simple bands and crosses to animals – real or mythological – buildings and weapons.

Crest: Usually an animal – this represents the leather or wooden figurine often worn atop a knight's helmet.

Mantling and **wreath:** Represents the plumage that flowed from the helmet and was kept in place by a wreath of twisted silk.

Helm: Represents the helmet itself.

Supporters: These appear only on the coats of arms of nobles or royals. They are usually animals or mythological beasts, and stand to either side of the shield, supporting it. They are thought to represent the uniform worn by a peer's page.

Coronet of rank: Coronets as insignia of the nobility started to appear in the 1300s. Initially, only dukes and marquesses were granted them. In 1444, they were given to earls too. The Stuart monarch James I then granted coronets to viscounts and, finally, Charles II allowed barons to wear them at his coronation in 1661. In the medieval age, coronets did not have a standard design, but Charles II instructed his barons to wear a circlet of gold with six pearls. Since then, each Peerage rank has its own particular coronet design, signifying its status.

Motto: The family motto – usually given in Latin – is thought to derive from battle cries.

Garter: Many high-ranking peers – though far from all – have the Garter symbol surrounding their shield. If they do, it indicates that the peer has been inducted into the Most Noble Order of the Garter, the oldest and most illustrious order of knighthood in England. Founded around 1350 by King Edward III (in emulation of the legendary Knights of the Round Table) it is limited to twenty-four non-royal members at any time. The origin story tells how at a Windsor Castle banquet, the garter of one of the ladies fell off. To save the lady embarrassment, the king himself picked up the garter and fastened it to his leg saying, 'Shame be to him who thinks evil of it.' These words appear in Latin around the ribbon, 'Honi soit qui mal y pense.'

Marshalling of Arms: Sometimes, peers will present their coat of arms alongside those of their wife's family by marshalling, or dividing the shield in half. The peer's arms appear on the left (from the viewer's standpoint), the wife's family's on the right. Peers may also present their coat of arms alongside those of their mother's family, or of multiple female ancestors. They do this by 'quartering' the shield, dividing it into four (or more) parts, with their own dynastic arms appearing in the top-left quarter, and those of families they descend from through female ancestors in the other quarters. Heraldic terminology can be confusing: a shield is said to be 'quartered' however many parts it is divided into. When describing a shield, heralds refer to it as though it is being held by its owner, so the left and right sides – dexter and sinister – are inverted.

These 'dignified' accessories of the nobility are now all that remain of the privileges of rank. Much as Monarchs today stand as a figurehead without the political power of their predecessors, the peers of the realm retain their titles and their place in the pomp and circumstance of national life, without any of the influence over affairs that they once enjoyed. A few peers have regular duties in state ceremonial. As Earl Marshal, the Duke of Norfolk must process at the annual State Opening of Parliament. But in modern times the coronets and ermine robes that each peer and peeress is entitled to have only been dusted off to attend a royal coronation.

It was tradition for all peers of the realm to attend Westminster Abbey when the Monarch was being crowned. At the moment of crowning, the peers would place their own coronets on their heads, creating a sea of gold through the abbey transepts. However, the last time such a show of noble glitz was seen was at the coronation of Elizabeth II in 1953. For the most recent coronation, King Charles III requested that any peers attending not wear robes or coronets (and many peers were not invited in any case). Officers of State and heralds wore them, but it now seems unlikely that we shall see the hereditary nobility parade *en masse* in ceremonial dress again.

Castle and country house: the dynastic seat

Evelyn Waugh, author of the celebrated novel of country house life, *Brideshead Revisited* (1945) once remarked that such buildings were England's 'chief national artistic achievement'. The architectural historian Christopher Hussey was even more effusive when he described the country house as 'England's most characteristic visible contribution to the richness of European civilisation'.

It's certainly true that England's great houses are an impressive – world famous – icon of a certain type of Englishness. Today they evoke a bygone age of fealty and aristocratic paternalism, what the historian A. P. Thornton described in 1966 as a nostalgia for a lost tradition of hierarchy, deference and obligation. Romanticisation is only part of the story, of course, for it was the people who lived in these buildings – people with all their capacities for good or ill – not the buildings themselves, who affected the lives of those lower down the social scale.

Evolving from the castellated manor houses of the Middle Ages, the country house became not just a major architectural form, but a political and social centre in both local and national life. As the seats of England's aristocratic elite, stately homes became the

Introduction

governing powerhouses of the nation. Today, they are monuments, museums and, in the case of most in this book, still family homes. As a more recent commentator observes:

> The English Country House is an imposing record of aristocratic wealth, innovative architecture and fashionable interior design; a glorious museum of world art and personal history bottled up in one unique building. More than this, it reflects the whims of its owners, their family's ancestry, and the lives of the countless staff who helped develop the house, its gardens and estate.
> (Trevor Yorke, *The English Country House Explained*)

There are critics however, who – understandably – cannot get past what these extravagant palaces say about historic societal inequality, and about an aristocratic class who chose to build such lavish monuments to excess, to *themselves*, and to personal luxury, in ages when the general population lived brief and precarious lives. There's a temptation to compare such obsessive builders as Bess of Hardwick – who vainly placed her own initials atop the towers of Hardwick Hall – to a Donald Trump, who similarly emblazoned his name onto Trump Tower. The super wealthy of centuries past, who hoarded the nation's wealth and used it for self-promotion, may be said to have been motivated by the same base impulses as the plutocrats of our own time.

Such criticism is quite justified, and a lot of the interest in visiting country piles today is like that of a tourist to the Pyramids: a desire to understand how an historic society operated, and how members of its ruling class chose to memorialise themselves. (For country houses are monuments to England's ruling dynasties, just as the Pharaoh's tombs were to Egypt's. They were built to reflect and to mythologise the owner's 'god-given' right to rule.)

Yet besides gaining a better understanding of our history, many of us today also thoroughly enjoy the experiences that country houses offer, something which serious academics have tended to feel sheepish about. Princeton and Oxford Professor David Cannadine felt it necessary to make a confession in the introduction to his classic work *The Decline and Fall of the British Aristocracy* (1990):

> I must also declare my belief that some of the most attractive and abiding features of life in Britain today are the legacy of [aristocrats], a view that some may find intrinsically distasteful and implausible, and that others may feel makes the general tone [of the book] far too indulgent and uncritical.

But while it is correct to question the motivations behind building these extravagant homes, it is disingenuous not to observe in them – as we do in the great cathedrals and basilicas – what these buildings reveal about human ingenuity. The sculpted stone, exquisite ceiling paintings, carved wood and decorative arts are statements of the heights to which human imagination and skill can reach. Though their purpose may have been to flaunt wealth, stately homes provided a canvas for works of sublime artistic and architectural genius, allowing the greatest talents of their age to create works that most of us can only marvel at.

The evolution of the family seat

English aristocrats were always a fashion-conscious breed, as well as rich, and their homes reflect their desire to keep up with contemporary architectural trends and to show off that enormous wealth.

The dynastic seat was really an invention of the Renaissance. In the Middle Ages, nobles had possessed family homes, usually where the family had first emerged. But the medieval nobility (like medieval monarchs) were never 'seated' anywhere in particular; rather, they moved around between far-flung castles, hunting

Introduction

lodges and manor houses. They took most of their possessions with them as they went, so the idea of a family seat filled with finery did not describe the medieval castle.

It was the great Tudor and Jacobean courtiers who first went all out building themselves palaces. The building frenzy was driven by the desire of these new dynasts to launch themselves and their families as forces to compete with the 'old' nobility. Their sumptuous mansions and innovations in design were made possible by the relative absence of civil warfare after the accession of Henry VII. The new nobility who rose under the Tudors used grand houses as foundations on which to establish their dynasties.

Those like Bess of Hardwick and William Cecil, who basked in the favour of Elizabeth I, were also responsible for introducing Renaissance architecture to England. Unlike in Italy where the Renaissance had begun, there were very few royal or ecclesiastical commissions in England in the sixteenth century (certainly nothing to compare to the palaces of Florence or to St Peter's Basilica in Rome). By contrast, the new aristocracy of Elizabeth's court began building monumental houses through which Renaissance styles first appeared in England. The architectural historian Sir John Summerson dubbed these buildings 'Prodigy Houses', designed with a view to entertaining Queen Elizabeth and her entourage in lavish style on her annual progresses through the country.

Great Elizabethan houses were designed to show off the status and wealth of their owners. With less need to build defensively, architects were freed to create ornamental facades. One of the best-known architects of the period, Robert Smythson, is popularly said to have used 'more glass than wall' at his great masterpiece, Hardwick Hall. The vast windows were a statement of his employer's disposable wealth, the high cost of glass being no issue for Bess of Hardwick. Smythson's extravagant Prodigy Houses are known for their conspicuous symmetry, and they represent a fusion of Renaissance styles and medieval influences. Hardwick, for example, may not have been a defensive fortress (not with all that glass) but its towers are still reminiscent of a castle. Wollaton Hall, another of Smythson's designs, has a central raised block which looks very like a medieval keep. Renaissance ideas were not received directly from Italy, but through the filter of other European countries, especially France. Smythson would have read architectural treatises on design and decor across the Channel; Wollaton's intricate, ornamented facades show the influence of Italian architects like Serlio (d.1554) who helped build the vast royal chateau of Fontainebleau south-east of Paris. Nevertheless, elements of medieval tradition were retained, with Great Halls for banqueting and entertaining remaining a feature.

The Renaissance in English architecture continued into the 1600s under the first Stuart monarch. And, as under Elizabeth, it was the aristocracy who drove developments with Prodigy Houses fit to receive and entertain King James I. Although Jacobean houses did not differ greatly from Elizabethan, they did develop a distinctive style imported from the Netherlands by Dutch craftsmen, employed in numbers by the nobility. The Jacobean house is recognised by its decorative curved 'Dutch gables' and turrets, on display at Blickling Hall.

The possibility of accommodating the monarch would continue to be a preoccupation for nobles and their architects for more than a century. In the later 1600s, the rise of the baroque house saw the creation of 'State Apartments' built to lodge a royal guest. These were a set of interconnecting rooms, usually leading from a Great Chamber through a series of state drawing rooms, state music rooms, and any number of other 'state' rooms, to a state bedroom and closet.

The first baroque house in England was Chatsworth in Derbyshire, which William Cavendish began in 1686 to replace one of his ancestor Bess of Hardwick's manors. The baroque style is often said to have appeared in England as a direct result of the Civil War and its aftermath. The outbreak of war in 1642

Introduction

interrupted the burgeoning taste for the ancient Greco-Roman classical architecture typified by designer Inigo Jones (1573–1652). Many of the Royalist aristocrats who fled to France after Oliver Cromwell's victory then came into contact with the ornate baroque splendour of Louis XIVs Palace of Versailles. After these nobles returned to their English estates, and particularly following the Glorious Revolution of 1688, the nobility began to imitate that style, but with adaptation that established a noticeably English Baroque. William Cavendish (Earl and later 1st Duke of Devonshire) designed much of Chatsworth's new facades himself and employed French artists like Louis Laguerre (born at Versailles) to decorate the interior.

No country house was designed by the greatest of English baroque names, Sir Christopher Wren, though the dome he built at St Paul's Cathedral could be said to have influenced the domestic architecture of his follower Sir John Vanburgh. The lantern dome Vanburgh designed for Castle Howard in Yorkshire was an innovation in the stately home silhouette. Vanburgh went on to design the most extravagant of all expressions of English Baroque: Blenheim Palace near Oxford, often described as England's Versailles.

The baroque did not stay popular for long, partly because of that association with Versailles and Absolutist royal power. The 1700s was the age of the Whig Supremacy. The aristocracy did not want a return to the Stuart monarchs' authoritarian ambitions, which the baroque seemed to symbolise. Under the Georgian regime, the nobility wanted a new style, and they favoured those architects who started looking back to Inigo Jones's nascent neo-classicism. The flowering of English Neo-Classical houses came largely through the reinterpretation of Greco-Roman design pioneered by the Italian Renaissance architect Andreo Palladio (1508–1580). Palladian houses are epitomised by Chiswick, a villa in London, completed in 1729. The aristocratic owner and architect was one Richard Boyle, 3rd Earl of Burlington. The 'Architect Earl' placed statues of Palladio and Inigo Jones on Chiswick's steps in honour of his twin inspirations. Other followers such as William Kent and Henry Flitcroft were responsible for Palladian high points: Devonshire House in Kent's case; Woburn Abbey and the grand east front of Wentworth Woodhouse (the longest private house façade in Britain) in Flitcroft's.

It was not just the buildings but the surrounding grounds that saw a shift away from the baroque in the eighteenth century. Gone were the formal gardens and parterres of the type that can still be seen at Versailles. In their place were naturalistic landscapes, rolling lawns and deer parks. The doyen of the English Landscape Garden was Lancelot 'Capability' Brown. He not only created grounds for newly built neo-classical houses but was employed by many fashion-conscious owners of older piles to update their grounds for Georgian sensibilities. The 4th Duke of Devonshire employed Brown to create parkland around baroque Chatsworth; the Marquess of Bath chose him to landscape the grounds around Elizabethan Longleat.

Updating and embellishing to suit current tastes was not restricted to the grounds. The Dukes of Northumberland completely renovated the interiors of their medieval Alnwick Castle to turn it into an Italianate palace. Alnwick acts as a symbolic bridge between the different periods of dynastic homes: feudal castle from the outside; Georgian and Victorian country house on the inside.

Great late Georgian and Victorian houses are a product of a fascination with much earlier styles. Architects enamoured with medieval chivalry began creating fantastical 'gothic revival' castles (which, like the renovated Alnwick Castle, had comfortable modern interiors). Belvoir Castle in Leicestershire is a beautiful example, created for the Manners family. Elizabethan and Jacobean houses were also much admired by the Victorians, resulting in 'Jacobethan' pastiches like the Earl of Carnarvon's Highclere Castle, TV's Downton Abbey.

Introduction

In the twentieth century, the fear that such houses – and their contents – might be lost, became a preoccupation of public bodies. That fear was made the more pronounced by the loss of so many country houses in the early part of the century, when the hereditary nobility found itself unable to maintain the vast palaces built by their ancestors. From the end of the First World War and accelerating in the 1950s, hundreds of country houses were demolished. Few groups or individuals were interested in helping to save the private houses that were not yet seen as the emblems of English national identity that they are now. It was only in the later century that the desire to conserve these buildings started to emerge.

In 1974 a major exhibition at London's Victoria & Albert Museum entitled 'The Destruction of the English Country House' drew attention to the demolitions and was influential in fostering a new sense of nostalgic affection for those that remained. The concept of heritage (and its attendant industry) emerged on a large scale in the second half of the twentieth century and provided many owners with a new role to compensate for their loss of political power. Today, many of the latest representatives of centuries-old dynasties are the heads of visitor attractions. Some oversee unexpected additions to their ancestral seats; Knowsley, Longleat and Woburn have each opened safari parks on their lands. But however they adapt, the houses and grounds are today internationally significant collections, amassed as private individuals but now available for public education and enjoyment. This is a state of affairs which the nobles of today welcome. In the twenty-first century there are none who would wish to close their doors and live lonely in their vast marble halls. They recognise in particular how their ancestral collectors (even if they had collected for personal pleasure) managed to assemble, and save for posterity, items of immeasurable historic importance. Like the houses they built, the collections help tell the stories of the extraordinary dynasties that created them.

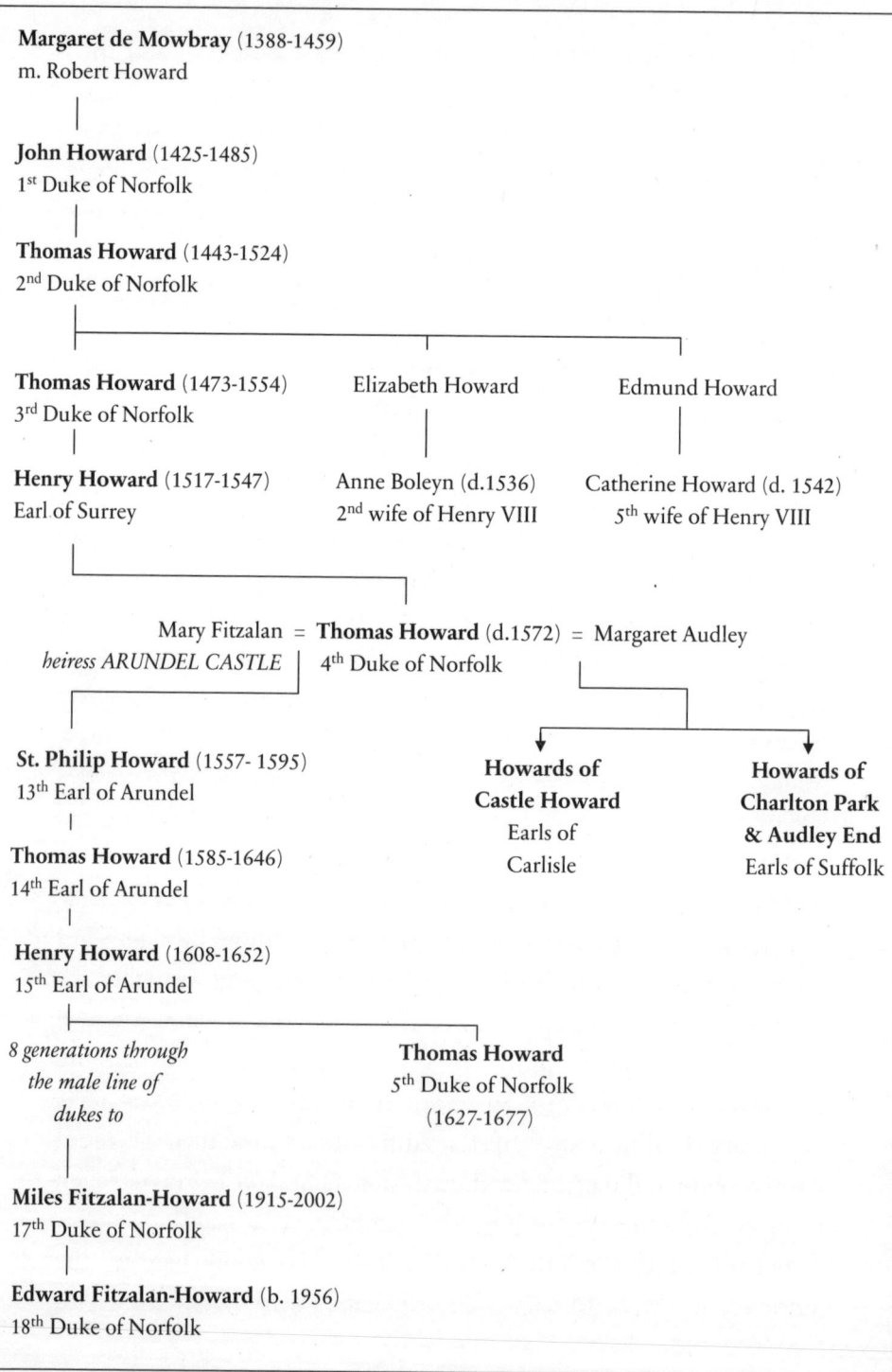

The Howards of Arundel Castle

Duke of Norfolk

Dukedom created	1483
Monarch	Richard III
Subsidiary titles	Earl of Surrey, Earl of Arundel, Earl Marshal of England
Junior branches	Earls of Carlisle (Castle Howard) Earls of Suffolk (Charlton Park)

The Howards' status as the 'first family' of the English nobility has long been unrivalled. The head of the House holds the only medieval dukedom surviving in England (Norfolk, bestowed upon John Howard in the closing years of the Wars of the Roses). He also holds the oldest earldom (Arundel). In addition, he is hereditary Earl Marshal of England – head of the College of Arms – with influence over the ennoblement and heraldry of all subjects of the Crown.

The Howard family's power reached its zenith during the Tudor period when they produced two of Henry VIII's six wives;

Catherine Howard and Anne Boleyn were nieces to the 3rd Duke of Norfolk. Both came to untimely ends at Henry's hands, and the Howards' star then faded owing to their allegiance to the Catholic faith. They were deprived of the dukedom for nearly one hundred years from 1572 to 1660, when they were known instead by their secondary title, Earl of Arundel. Nevertheless, as Earl Marshal, the present duke remains responsible for organising State ceremonials, including Openings of Parliament and the latest royal Coronation.

The pride of the Howards

'It runs in the family' is a saying that proves itself true again and again in any number of personal characteristics. Family traits are, some say, passed down in our DNA, or else learnt from parental example in our childhood. However it occurs, there's no doubt that generation after generation of any family may display uncannily similar behaviour, for good or for ill. Such is the case with the Howards who, from the very start, exhibited natures that made them very difficult to be around, or even to like. Successive Howards were each consumed by extreme arrogance born of vanity and pride in their ancestry. It showed itself in everything from a comical – if somewhat pathetic – class snobbery, to a more dangerous, vicious – even murderous – hatred of anybody who was deemed to have slighted them, or stood beneath them in nobility of blood (which, in the Howards unhumble opinion, was pretty much everyone)

That pride, and the lengths the Howards would go to defend their ego, backfired often, and was responsible for some spectacular falls from grace, which included the deaths by execution or in battle of numerous Heads of the House. Indeed, when the story of the first Howard duke is related to its violent end, the existence of a *second* duke (never mind an eighteenth, as at the current count) seems to require some serious explanation. The 1st Duke of Norfolk, John Howard, was after all, slain in battle; defeated alongside his liege lord, the last Plantagenet king, Richard III. Their mutual enemy Henry Tudor lost no time in arresting Norfolk's son and heir, Thomas Howard, and consigning him to the Tower, an Act of Attainder depriving him of title and estates. All seemed irretrievably lost for the House of Howard when its foundations had barely been laid.

Their remarkable survival was founded upon another family trait, one more useful than pride, that emerged whenever required to bring the Howards back from the brink: *adaptability*. Some would call it cold calculation or duplicity, but the Howards were nothing if not flexible. They learned to follow the political winds whichever way they blew, and barely four years after being attainted by Henry VII, Thomas Howard (who himself had fought Henry at Bosworth Field) was standing in the presence of his old enemy, a free man once again, swearing fealty to the Tudor Crown, and well on his way to having his title of 2nd Duke of Norfolk restored.

The need to adapt to circumstances was learnt from bitter experience by Thomas, having witnessed the demise of his father who had failed to switch sides when the time had come, and had died fighting for a lost cause. Yet it was John Howard whose ambition for himself and his family had taken the Howards from relatively humble knights of the shires into the inner circle of the Plantagenet court in its sunset years.

King Richard III and his loyal servant, Norfolk

The man who became 1st Duke of Norfolk (in the third creation of the title) was born John Howard around 1425. He was a member of a military line that until then had little to boast of. A myth later circulated claimed romantic origins for the family springing from Hereward the Wake, the Anglo-Saxon nobleman who led the English resistance against William the Conqueror. This lineage made the Howards heirs to the Dark Age chieftains in whose veins ran the blood of Hereward (from whom the family name supposedly evolved). The truth of their origin was rather less colourful. The first historic Howard of any note had been a lawyer by the name William of Wiggenhall (c. 1225–1308). William was from Norfolk and distinguished himself enough in law to be knighted. His direct descendants also made names for themselves in Norfolk, becoming Sheriffs and MPs. But none rose to the heights of John, whose ambitions far surpassed those of any of his forbears.

Some of John's self-belief stemmed from a sense of entitlement – the brewing Howard pride – deriving from his mother's noble bloodline. John's father Robert had boosted his family's position by marrying a duke's daughter, Margaret de Mowbray (of a storied family that had been present at the signing of Magna Carta and whose members appear frequently in Shakespeare's character lists). Through his mother, John Howard was also descended from Thomas of Brotherton, a royal prince no less, younger son of King Edward I. John Howard thus had a splash of royal blood, and he acted like it. He seized every opportunity his mother's connections afforded him and was able to advance his military career by following his Mowbray relations into the Wars of the Roses on the Yorkist side.

One of Howard's earliest escapades – and one that made his name – came on Palm Sunday, 1461. On that day he rode with his cousin John de Mowbray to Towton in Yorkshire, and straight into the largest and bloodiest battles ever fought on English soil. In the midst of a snowstorm, Howard fought to place Edward of York on the throne and depose the Lancastrian Henry VI. Howard's part in the decisive Yorkist victory brought him to the attention of the triumphant Edward IV, who by some accounts knighted Howard right then and there on the battlefield.

There was, to be sure, a degree of luck involved in Howard's choice of allegiance to the Yorkist cause; had his Mowbray cousins been Lancastrians, he might not have risen quite so swiftly in royal favour! A knighthood was, however, but the start of Howard's ambitions. Given that he was related to the new king, Howard thought himself squarely in line for a much more significant title.

By the 1470s, Howard had grown so self-confident in his nobility, he believed himself the natural heir to the recently extinct dukedom that had belonged to his mother's family. This was the dukedom of Norfolk, a title first created for Thomas de Mowbray – Howard's maternal grandfather – in 1397. The dukedom died out in 1476, and Howard immediately had his eye on obtaining a new Patent of Creation. It was not only ducal status that made the Norfolk title attractive; the estates that came with it were also highly appealing. They centred around the sprawling Framlingham Castle in Suffolk, with lands amassed centuries before by the old Norman Earls of Norfolk (the Bigods). Framlingham itself had been gifted to Prince Thomas of Brotherton before passing to his Mowbray descendants. *Their* descendent, John Howard was thus an obvious candidate to assume the grand inheritance.

Howard's inheritance of the Norfolk legacy was not to be, however. At least not yet. For there were other heirs to the property who were higher up the pecking order. These included the infant Prince Richard, younger son of Edward IV. At just four years old, Prince Richard had been married to another Mowbray heiress (Anne de Mowbray, aged five). John Howard could not hope to compete with the king's own son who was created 1st Duke of Norfolk in the second creation of the title. The pathway by which the dukedom eventually ended up with John Howard was suspicious to say the least, and forms part of the story of that most infamous episode in royal history: the disappearance of Prince Richard, Duke of Norfolk, and his brother Edward V – the so-called 'Princes in the Tower' – as their uncle Richard III usurped the throne.

Related family: The Mowbrays

John Howard's maternal grandfather Thomas de Mowbray was a man famed throughout medieval Europe as a champion of the tournament circuit. He was a childhood friend of King Richard II who eventually created him Duke of Norfolk despite a difficult relationship in adulthood. The pair fell out spectacularly when Mowbray grew jealous of the king's new favourites at court. He rebelled in 1388 with a group of nobles and formed a council of regency known as the Lords Appellant. Later, Richard regained his royal authority and banished Mowbray to the Continent. There, while on his way by pilgrimage to Jerusalem, the exiled duke found himself in the romantic surroundings of Venice, unfortunately for him during a visitation of the Black Death. Mowbray died of plague in the city just days before Richard II was finally deposed.

Even at that time, the Mowbrays were considered an 'ancient' family. They had originated in Normandy and were present for all the major dramas of the Middle Ages: Roger de Mowbray supported King Stephen during the Anarchy; his son, Nigel, was a Crusader, travelling with Richard the Lionheart to battle Saladin, the Sultan of Syria and Egypt. Nigel died at the Siege of Acre in 1191, after which his son went down in posterity as a 'founding father of English liberty' – William de Mowbray was one of the barons who forced Magna Carta on King John in 1215. His direct descendant, Thomas, Duke of Norfolk, followed in these rebellious footsteps, and during the 'Merciless Parliament', had ensured that Richard II's hated favourites were convicted of treason. Clearly a confrontational character, Thomas then fell out with one of his fellow rebels, Henry of Lancaster (the future Henry IV) and vowed to settle the matter in Trial by Combat. It was just before the joust began that King Richard called a halt to proceedings and banished both rebels from his kingdom.

It began in 1483, when Edward IV died unexpectedly, leaving his twelve-year-old son to take the throne. The boy-king Edward V and his brother, the Duke of Norfolk (and of York) were placed into the care of their uncle Richard of Gloucester. No sooner were they in Richard's 'care', then the boys were taken to the Tower of London and declared illegitimate on spurious grounds that their parents' marriage had been unlawful. The Crown of England and the dukedom of Norfolk were therefore vacant owing to the boys' illegitimacy. Next in line for the throne was Uncle Richard, of course, supported in his coup by none other than John Howard. Having once fought to put Edward IV on the throne, Howard now betrayed Edward's children and was richly rewarded. On 28 June 1483, King Richard III dubbed Howard the 1st Duke of Norfolk in the third creation of the title, and the one that survives to the present day. Along with Framlingham Castle and the rest of the Norfolk estates, the Howards also received the earldom of Surrey (bestowed on John's son, Thomas) while John himself was further honoured as Earl Marshal of England, titles which remain allied to the dukedom of Norfolk today.

Given the honours and riches showered upon John Howard, there have been rumours that he was personally complicit in the disappearance, and presumed murders, of the Princes in the Tower. If so, Howard wasn't too concerned about appearances; as Earl Marshal he attended Richard III throughout all the ceremonial aspects of the succession, even carrying the crown at Richard's coronation in Westminster Abbey on 6 July. Whatever the truth, neither King Richard nor his loyal servant Norfolk were to prosper long after wresting their titles from the royal children. Two years later, at Bosworth Field, the pair were killed by the invading army of Henry Tudor. Howard's son, the wounded Earl of Surrey, was imprisoned, and it appeared that the third iteration of the Norfolk dukedom had been snuffed out.

Thomas Howard had, however, learned something valuable from his father's experience; the 1st Duke's loyalty to the flailing Richard III had cost him his life. If his son was to regain the family honour, he would need to adapt as his father, in the end, had not.

Earl Marshal of England

The Earl Marshal is one of England's 'Great Officers of State', one of very few feudal-era officials still performing duties today. The role grew from one of marshalling the king's horses into a key minister responsible for organising ceremonials such as royal funerals and coronations. The office itself is not a peerage, but by tradition is hereditary. The 'Lord Marshals' of the thirteenth century were of the Marshal family whose name actually derived from the office.

Since Richard III made John Howard Earl Marshal, the office has presided over the College of Arms, the corporation created by Richard to regulate coats of arms in England. Today, the Earl Marshal remains custodian of some peculiarly medieval customs and concerns. As the only judge of the High Court of Chivalry, the Earl Marshal has the right to decide any disputes over the use of arms. This authority was tested as recently as 1954 when the then Earl Marshal, the 16th Duke of Norfolk, heard a case brought by Manchester City Council to prevent its heraldic arms from being used by private companies. (The council won.)

Although the Earl Marshalcy has sometimes been confiscated by the Crown and given to other families, it has most often descended through dynastic lines associated with the Norfolk estates. Way back in 1245 it passed through the Marshal heiress to Roger Bigod, Earl of Norfolk. It was also part of the inheritance gifted to Thomas of Brotherton and the Mowbray dukes of Norfolk. When the dukedom was revived for John Howard in 1483, the Earl Marshalcy accompanied it, and since 1672 every Duke of Norfolk has held it. The baton of office is represented today on the ducal coat of arms.

The 2nd Duke of Norfolk: from prisoner to war hero

Behind the bars of his Tower cell, Thomas Howard began plotting the first of what were to be many spectacular Howard comebacks. His first step was to switch his allegiance – very loudly – from the Plantagenets to the new Tudor regime. He justified this cynical manoeuvre by proclaiming that his loyalty was – and had *always* been – to 'the Crown of England', rather than to the person wearing it. He told King Henry that he had fought for Richard III because Richard had been the 'crowned king, and if the parliamentary authority ... set the crown upon a stock, I will fight for that stock. And as I fought then for [Richard], I will fight for you.' Unsurprisingly, Henry was not immediately convinced by this argument, so Howard's next step was to prove this fealty. He did so by refusing multiple opportunities to escape his prison cell. He could have fled overseas, but his ambition to return to the high table of England – his birthright as he saw it – was greater than his desire for freedom. It did, eventually, do the trick; Henry released Howard in 1489, restoring him initially as the Earl of Surrey, though not as Duke of Norfolk. Howard would have to wait twenty-five years and until he was nearly seventy years old for a chance to win back the top prize his father had lost.

Henry VII was dead and Henry VIII was away fighting in France when the Scottish king, James IV, suddenly invaded England. The Earl of Surrey saw his chance and took command of the situation, leading his troops to challenge the Scots in Northumberland. On 9 September 1513 at Flodden Field, Howard won a genuinely astonishing victory. 10,000 Scots were killed in the battle, while English losses were only around 400. Scotland's most powerful leaders, including King James himself, perished in the slaughter.

Surrey returned to London and to a grateful king. Having regained his family's honour, he died as the 2nd Duke of Norfolk in 1524

The heights of power: Anne Boleyn, Catherine Howard and their uncle, Norfolk

Under Henry VIII the Howards played their most memorable roles in English history. The tenure of the 3rd Duke of Norfolk Thomas Howard (1524–1554) overlapped with the religious upheaval that no dynastic family could ignore: the Protestant Reformation. The Howards – far from ignoring it – were intimately involved from the start. Thomas Howard's part in the events leading up to the break with the Roman Catholic Church was, however, as complex and contradictory as King Henry's own part, both being driven towards reform by a desire for power rather than by spiritual concerns. The king and the duke were actually both staunch Catholics in their beliefs and practices. But both were also willing to cast aside the institutions of the Roman Church in order to remove the interfering influence of that 'foreign power' from English affairs and secure personal power for themselves and their families. The catalyst for both men's embrace of Protestantism was the Duke of Norfolk's niece, Anne Boleyn.

She may not have borne the Howard name (it was her mother who was a Howard) but Anne was very much a part of the Howard clan. For most of her life she was the willing ally and accomplice of her uncle Norfolk. Born in 1501 or 1507 (there is some confusion over this) Anne entered court in 1522 as a maid of honour to Henry VIII's first wife, then queen consort, Catherine of Aragon. The story of the king's growing obsession with Anne and his desire for a male heir which Queen Catherine seemed unable to provide is the subject of countless studies, not to mention period dramas. When the Pope refused to grant an annulment of Henry's marriage and allow him to marry Anne, the king was incensed. Increasingly infatuated with Anne – who refused to be his mistress – Henry grew determined to overrule the Pope. The break with the Catholic Church became for Henry a governmental principle which today we would probably call 'nationalism'; Henry believed that an English king should be master of his own affairs in his own realm and not be subject to decrees by an 'international authority' like the Papacy.

Both Anne Boleyn and her uncle Norfolk had much to gain from the Act of Supremacy, which made Henry VIII supreme governor of the Church of England in 1534. The Duke of Norfolk was able to engineer the dismissal of the king's chief minister Cardinal Wolsey (a 'lowborn' upstart who'd long been an obstacle to Norfolk's ambitions). The independent Church of England having annulled King Henry's marriage, Anne Boleyn then became Queen of England, joining the Howards by marriage to the Tudor Crown. That crown, in its literal sense, now always included the golden arches of 'imperial' authority. The Reformation in England was always as much about political as religious authority, with adherence to Protestantism demonstrating a patriotic loyalty to the Monarch against threats from Catholic foreign powers like France and Spain.

Thomas Howard, Duke of Norfolk was able to support Henry and Anne's marriage despite being a Catholic at heart, precisely because the early Reformation was largely a political rather than religious affair: the Pope's power in England was gone, but little changed at the level of religious belief or observance. The English Reformation under Henry was nothing like the radical Reformations seen in Germany, for example, where Martin Luther sought to do away with all the ceremony and ritual of the Catholic Mass. In England Henry kept much of the old ceremonies intact, including the core belief in transubstantiation and the use of Latin in church services. For the Duke of Norfolk, it was the best of both worlds: his cherished religion coupled with the political influence he believed to be the Howards' birthright.

Unfortunately for Norfolk's continued contentment, there were those at court who *were* true Reformers, those who wanted to go much further in the journey to Protestantism, and who did not stand in awe of the Howards' status as an ancient feudal family. The arch-Reformers who now emerged included chief minister

Thomas Cromwell and the Archbishop of Canterbury Thomas Cranmer, and they were no friends to the Howards. These two began to exploit Anne Boleyn's inability to produce a male heir for King Henry. When the king set his sights on a new wife, Cromwell swooped, moving against Anne and having her arrested on trumped-up charges of incest and adultery. The Duke of Norfolk now displayed that ability learned by his father while in the Tower of London and quickly adapted to survive. Sensing that the king was done with his niece, Howard ruthlessly deserted Anne, saving his own reputation in the king's eyes by presiding as judge at the queen's trial and standing by as she went to the executioner's block in 1536. He had shown loyalty to the Crown before loyalty to his own niece. It saved him from the king's wrath, but the Howard's were still weakened, as were all Catholic adherents at court.

The Protestant faction now rose to power at the expense of the Howards. Cromwell and Cranmer began undermining the old religion, aided by another keen reformer, Edward Seymour, brother to the new queen, Jane. The Duke of Norfolk loathed all three; low-born upstarts all, who had the audacity to usurp his rightful place at the king's side and who dared to sweep away the ancient nobility's religious practices. Howard did, nonetheless, benefit from some of his enemies' actions; he deigned to accept many new estates confiscated from the monasteries being dissolved by Cromwell.

It was around now, as the religious divide deepened, that the Howards became – along with the great northern dynasties, the Percys and Nevilles – the self-appointed guardians of the Old Faith. Howard led this conservative faction at court. His greatest success came when, seething with wounded pride at being sidelined by the 'new man' Cromwell, he managed to bring the chief minister down. The chance had come after Cromwell made a spectacular error in judgement, arranging a fourth marriage for King Henry to the Protestant princess Anne of Cleves. The king famously did not find the choice of bride attractive, and Cromwell slipped from

Henry's favour. Howard seized the opportunity, leading a coup – personally arresting Cromwell on charges of promoting radical theology – and ensuring Cromwell's execution.

Following this episode, the Howards and their Catholic faction were once again ascendant. It was Howard, alongside the conservative bishop Stephen Gardiner, who drafted a set of laws that affirmed traditional Catholic doctrine in England. King Henry was pleased to sign the Six Articles that enshrined, among other things, transubstantiation and clerical celibacy. Now, pressing his advantage, Thomas Howard proposed yet another of his nieces as a potential fifth bride for the king. This poor unfortunate was Catherine Howard, the teenage daughter of the Duke of Norfolk's brother Edmund. Norfolk shamelessly paraded Catherine before the king, hoping her youthful charms might entice Henry into another union with the House of Howard. It did not take long for the aging king to succumb. Norfolk had the pleasure of seeing a Howard sitting in the queen's throne in July 1540, and he took his place again in the royal family.

The downfall of the 3rd Duke and the 'Poet Earl' of Surrey

It was perhaps the Howard pride that made the 3rd Duke of Norfolk risk wedding another of his nieces to the tyrannical Henry VIII. History very soon repeated itself when, like Anne Boleyn before her, Queen Catherine Howard was accused of adultery, tried and executed. This was the most dangerous moment for the House of Howard since Bosworth, with members of the wider family accused of concealing evidence of Catherine's affair with courtier Thomas Culpepper. The Duke of Norfolk himself escaped direct implication in the scandal but was severely weakened politically. He limped on for a time. But his absolute fall from grace came soon afterwards due not to his poor niece's actions but those of his son and heir, the Earl of Surrey.

It was an unavoidable weakness of dynastic aristocracy that any one member of an extended family could, through miscalculation, arrogance, accident, or sheer stupidity, bring the whole House crashing down around them. The Earl of Surrey, Henry Howard, possessed all of the Howard vanity in abundance, and it was this that cost his family its position and Surrey himself his life.

Like his father, Henry Howard was deeply offended by the appearance at court of 'new' families like the Seymours, and their influence over the king. Jane Seymour had been the most beloved of Henry VIII's wives and had produced the longed-for son, Prince Edward. This had cemented the position of Jane's brother Edward Seymour in the king's inner circle, much to the Earl of Surrey's fury. Members of old feudal families like the Howards were incensed by the presence of parvenus like Seymour (or Wolsey or Cromwell, both of whom had been cast down by the Duke of Norfolk). Now, in a fit of boiling pride, Norfolk's son attempted to assert his own superiority of breeding. In order to show off his antique ancestry, Surrey decided to have the Howard coat of arms impaled alongside those of the Saxon king, Edward the Confessor. The Confessor actually lived before the age of heraldry, but his attributed arms were often used by members of the Blood-Royal to denote their status. Henry Howard was flaunting his descent from King Edward I, aiming to remind people like Seymour just who they were dealing with. Instead, however, the Howard-Royal arms only succeeded in reminding the Tudors that they themselves were a 'new' family, and that key relations of the Plantagenets were looking down on their like, while, possibly, plotting to replace them.

The Earl of Surrey was arrested and confined to the Tower on charges of treason. The Duke of Norfolk was also imprisoned thanks to the impulsive actions of his son. The earl was later beheaded, and the duke would have been too, but for the timely death of Henry VIII, who passed away the night before the planned execution. The duke's life was pardoned but Thomas Howard remained a prisoner, just at the very moment that King

Henry's death had created a power vacuum at court. So it was that the Protestant party under the despised Edward Seymour was able to seize control of the kingdom and unleash a radical Reformation in the name of the boy-king Edward VI. Not for the first time, it seemed the House of Howard had crumbled into oblivion.

The legend of Surrey and the Fair Geraldine

Today, the executed Earl of Surrey is chiefly remembered not for his peculiar 'martyrdom' to heraldic vanity, but for his pioneering poetry. Regarded among the greatest of English Renaissance poets, he was responsible for introducing the sonnet to England, the favoured verse form for love poetry of William Shakespeare.

Surreys own love poems also became the stuff of legend, thanks partly to their subject, the courtier Lady Elizabeth Fitgerald. Surrey was in his twenties when he first noticed Elizabeth, who was then only ten. Historians debate whether Surrey later fell in love with the girl he called the 'Fair Geraldine' or merely wished to burnish her status at court by addressing his romantic poetry to her. Surrey's apparent infatuation nevertheless became a favourite subject in the Romantic imagination of later centuries. In 1805, Sir Walter Scott told a dramatic tale in verse recounting Surrey's journey to Renaissance Florence where he fought in a dazzling tournament to revenge himself on any challenger daring to deny that Lady Elizabeth was the most beautiful creature on Earth. Onward through Italy, Surrey sings of his lady's beauty beneath twinkling stars in the olive groves, until finally the earl seeks out the alchemist Cornelius Agrippa, in whose magic mirror Surrey beholds the object of his desire.

> ... Dark was the vaulted room of gramarye
> To which the wizard led the gallant knight
> Save that before a mirror, huge and high,
> A hallowe'd taper shed a glimmery light ...

> ... but how passing fair
> The slender form, that lay on couch of Ind!
> O'er her white bosom strayed her hazel hair
> Pale her cheek, as if for love she pined;
> All in her night-robe loose, she lay reclined
> And, pensive, read from tablet evernine
> Some strain that seemed her inmost soul to find
> That favoured strain was Surrey's raptured line
> That fair and lovely form, the Lady Geraldine...

Scott's hypnotic verse is based on a myth that grew up around the Earl of Surrey's poetry. There is no actual evidence that Henry Howard travelled to Italy, let alone met the renowned occultist Agrippa. Though belief in forms of alchemy was widespread among scholars of the Renaissance, Surrey is unlikely to have been convinced of the power of magic mirrors. He was a believer, however, in the power of poetry. Surrey not only brought the Petrarchan sonnet to England but was the first to use blank verse in English when he translated Virgil's epic tale of the Trojan hero Aeneas.

The 4th Duke of Norfolk and Mary, Queen of Scots

Fortunes could change very quickly in the sixteenth century. The 3rd Duke of Norfolk had been sent to the Tower, his son the Earl of Surrey beheaded, and his Protestant enemies were ruling the kingdom unopposed. But then, in 1553, the sickly young King Edward died suddenly, to be replaced by his Catholic sister Mary I. The new Queen knew exactly who her allies were; upon news of Edwards death, she headed straight to Framlingham Castle, the seat of her friend, the imprisoned Duke of Norfolk. There, Mary summoned the Catholic gentry to her cause in the face of Protestant attempts to keep her from the throne. Once Mary had seen off her hapless Protestant rival, Lady Jane Grey, she released Thomas Howard from prison and did away with many the duke's enemies, including Archbishop Cranmer, who was burnt at the stake. The tables had decidedly turned. The Duke of Norfolk was restored to his titles, serving as Earl Marshal of England for Queen Mary's coronation. And though he had lost his impulsive son Surrey to the executioner's block, Norfolk still had a living heir to continue the family line: Surrey's son, another Thomas Howard.

This Thomas succeeded as the 4th Duke of Norfolk when his grandfather died (unusually for a Howard, of natural causes) in 1554. The new duke's tenure was equally as turbulent as his predecessors, for he soon witnessed the religious tables turn again when Queen Mary died in 1558, to be replaced by her Protestant sister Elizabeth I. Once more a Howard was left aghast at a Tudor's disregard for his religion; once more a Duke of Norfolk was taunted by the promotion of new men (this time in the form of the Queen's chief minister William Cecil) in violation of his ancient right to rule. In response, the slighted Howard allied himself with other great Catholic families in a dangerous plot to overthrow Elizabeth and replace her on the throne with her cousin, the Queen of Scotland, Mary Stuart. Not only that, but Norfolk apparently planned to marry the Catholic queen himself, securing a Catholic succession to the throne and a *Howard* succession, too. Norfolk had already ensured a ducal heir by his marriage to Mary Fitzalan, daughter of his arch-Catholic ally, Henry Fitzalan, Earl of Arundel. After Mary's death, he fathered more Howards with his second wife Margaret Audley and his third, Elizabeth Leyburn. Three times a widower, the duke could, with Mary Stuart as a wife, produce a Howard heir to all of England.

The wily William Cecil was, however, far too shrewd an operator for Norfolk. The plot was quickly uncovered and Howard was sent to the Tower. While there, his sister Jane Howard – who had married the head of the Neville family – took command of the Catholic faction and pushed the northern dynasties to outright rebellion. The Nevilles and Percys led the Northern Rising of

1569-70, demanding the restoration of the Roman Church, hoping for military support from Catholic Spain. That support never materialised, resulting in the execution of many a Catholic earl. Howard himself was only spared because of his familial link with Queen Elizabeth (her mother was, of course, Anne Boleyn). Elizabeth released her cousin from the Tower in an act of good faith in 1570, only for Howard to try his luck a second time. Cecil – less trusting than the queen – soon foiled the 'Ridolfi Plot' to assassinate Elizabeth and put the Queen of Scots on the throne. With a sense of *deja vu*, the Duke of Norfolk was arrested and committed for trial. During the proceedings, and under examination by one of those new men whom Howard so despised, Francis Russell, Earl of Bedford, it emerged that the duke's exceptional recklessness might have been inspired by one of the many bizarre prophecies then circulating concerning the fall of Elizabeth I. Such prophesies had abounded among northern Catholics ever since the queen's accession. This one foretold that 'a lion and a lioness' were destined to ride to power in England, figures which the duke interpreted as referring to himself and the Scottish queen. It would certainly explain the duke's self-destructive actions and is possibly why his younger brother penned a treatise entitled *The Poison of Supposed Prophecies*.

This time the sentence was final. Howard was attainted and executed on the direct orders Queen Elizabeth. The dukedom of Norfolk was forfeit and would now be withheld from the House of Howard for the better part of a century.

Saint Philip Howard and the Earls of Arundel

From the moment the 4th Duke of Norfolk was beheaded in 1572, the power of the senior Howard line declined markedly. The first four dukes of Norfolk had become key characters in the national psychodrama of the Tudor Court. But the family was never to regain the status and influence it once 'enjoyed'. Deprived of the dukedom, the next Head of the House, Philip Howard, would be known primarily for his uncompromising religious conscience, and as a martyr to the Catholic cause. Philip, son of the 4th Duke, spent ten years locked in the Tower of London following the execution of Mary, Queen of Scots. There, he was accused of praying for the success of the Spanish Armada, which was launched against Protestant England in 1588. Any hope that Spain might overthrow Queen Elizabeth and re-Catholicise England sank with the armada's ships in the tempestuous North Sea and Philip languished in his cell, communicating with other prisoners (including the Catholic priest Robert Southey) by means of a pet dog who carried messages between their cells! Philip died in 1595 from dysentery. Considered a martyr by the Catholic Church, he was canonised in the twentieth century by Pope Paul VI and is now known as 'St Philip Howard'. His shrine is in Arundel Cathedral where a statue of him – and his faithful dog – are carved in marble.

St Philip Howard was never a duke owing to the Act of Attainder against his father. But he inherited through his mother the ancient title of Earl of Arundel by which he, his son and grandson would each be known in turn. Despite their fall from royal favour, the Howards were now heirs to a still greater legacy stretching back further in time than their confiscated dukedom. It included the fabled Arundel Castle previously owned by his mother's family, the mighty Fitzalans.

Related family: the Fitzalans

The marriage of Mary Fitzalan to the 4th Duke of Norfolk in 1555 had been designed to further enrich the Howard estates. The Fitzalans had been Earls of Arundel since 1243, a title that came with possession of the synonymous castle. Their extinction in the male line in 1580 meant that Mary's son, Philip Howard, became the genealogical successor to one of the most revered of all medieval dynasties. (This was a fact not lost on subsequent generations of Howards; in 1842, the 13th Duke of Norfolk went so far as to adopt 'Fitzalan-Howard' as the surname of his children, a name still used by the Howards of Arundel Castle.)

The Fitzalan pedigree was indeed impressive. They descended from Alan Fitz Flaad (*fl. c.* 1090), a Breton mercenary in the service of King Henry I. Alan spawned not one, but two, illustrious lines. One of his sons went to Scotland where he became hereditary High Steward. This branch later changed its surname to Stewart – or Stuart – and became Scotland's royal House. Meanwhile, another son settled in Oswestry in Shropshire. It was this branch that succeeded as Earls of Arundel through marriage to the great castle's heiress.

The names of these earls weave themselves through the blood-stained tapestry of medieval power-plays. The 2nd Earl was executed by Queen Isabella, the 'She-Wolf of France', following her coup against her husband, Edward II. The 4th was executed for treason by Richard II. (A friend and fellow rebel of Thomas de Mowbray – another Howard ancestor – he had been among the Lords Appellant opposing the king). The 5th Earl, only a teenager at his father's execution, was then given as a domestic servant by the king to his brutal half-brother, the Duke of Exeter. The boy was terribly mistreated by Exeter but eventually managed to escape to the Continent. There, he met up and conspired with his father's old Appellant ally, Henry of Lancaster, to overthrow King Richard. After Henry succeeded in seizing the throne, Fitzalan took grizzly revenge on Exeter, pressing for the execution of his former tormentor.

Given the storied – if bloody – history, it's not surprising that the Howards were eager to embrace the identity of the Fitzalans. In becoming Earls of Arundel, the Howards were entwined with the mythology of a once great House whose passing inspired poetic works even into modern times. Philip Larkin's famed meditation on love and mortality 'An Arundel Tomb' (1964) captures some of the melancholy atmosphere at a crumbling monument to the Fitzalans in Chichester Cathedral.

Growth of the junior branches: the Howards of Castle Howard and Charlton Park

Despite their Fitzalan inheritance, the senior line of the Howard family seemed destined to remain in the shadows of state affairs, only stepping into the limelight to fulfil their obligatory ceremonial duties. In such circumstances, it was left up to the saintly Philip Howard's younger brothers to restore the family's reputation with Queen Elizabeth. Two of these brothers succeeded admirably in that regard, founding junior lines that survive intact to the present day, and which were both honoured with their own earldoms: Suffolk and Carlisle.

The elder of these brothers – yet another Thomas Howard – made a good start in winning over the Queen. In 1588, while his elder sibling Arundel was praying for the success of the Spanish Armada, Thomas was taking up arms against it. In marked contrast to his Catholic forebears, Thomas Howard proclaimed himself to be a good Protestant, took command of the Queen's great warship, the *Golden Lion*, and sailed to meet the forces of Spain in the English Channel. Howard was knighted on the deck by the grateful Elizabeth, who referred to him affectionately as 'Good Thomas' thereafter. After the Queen's death, Thomas was advanced still further, King James I granting him a peerage as 1st Earl of Suffolk. Thomas seated himself at Audley End (his inheritance through his mother Margaret Audley), which he rebuilt in lavish style. Later, he settled at Charlton Park, a residence he also rebuilt as a magnificent Prodigy House, and which came to him through his marriage to the fascinating and mysterious courtier Katherine Knyvett.

Katherine was the daughter of Sir Henry Knyvett (whose London home, incidentally, stood on the site now occupied by 10 Downing Street). In 1605 Sir Henry and his son-in-law, Suffolk, were personally responsible for helping to foil the Gunpowder Plot to blow up Parliament, King James and all. Lord Suffolk had made a search of the basement of the House of Lords, noting something awry; Knyvett then uncovered the powder barrels laid by Guy Fawkes. Marrying Knyvett's heiress had brought huge wealth to Howard, but also enormous trouble thanks to his wife's duplicitous behaviour. Lord Suffolk may have been considered a loyal Protestant – especially after his part preventing the Catholic gunpowder conspiracy – but Lady Suffolk was a different matter.

Rumours swirled around Katherine Knyvett all her adult life. She had entered court to rapturous acclaim, celebrated as one of the great beauties of her age. She married Thomas Howard aged eighteen, but her looks continued to captivate an army of besotted admirers. Katherine took starring roles in many of the court entertainments performed for King James, her devotees packing into the banqueting halls to watch her dance in a series of magnificent Jacobean masques. In one noted performance she played the Roman goddess Juno. In another, premiering on Twelfth Night, 6 January 1605, she performed before a stage set designed by Inigo Jones, playing the mythical sea nymph Kathare. Katherine was dressed to dazzle in silver and azure, adorned with strings of pearls. She entered upon a great seashell, accompanied by Mermen torchbearers, alongside the primordial sea god, Oceanus, astride his seahorse, while a storm raged.

Katherine's power at the Stuart court was soon the subject of scrutiny, however. She was suspected not only of Catholic sympathies, but of being recruited as a spy for the Spanish Crown. The Countess was considered dangerous by much of the establishment, a Jacobean *femme fatale* who used her looks to devastating effect to seduce court officials and extract information. Possibly on behalf of her Spanish spymasters, or possibly for her own ends, Katherine enriched herself by demanding hush money from those who had succumbed to her charms. It wasn't until her later life that Katherine's behaviour was officially censured, and a scandal ensued. She and her husband Lord Suffolk were tried, found guilty of embezzlement, and confined to the Tower. They were eventually released, but were forced to retire to their country seat, Katherine now scarred by a bout of smallpox.

Their successors at Charlton Park were no less notorious. Thomas and Katherine's daughter, Lady Frances Howard, inherited her mother's criminal streak, and just like her ended up in the Tower, in this case for her part in the murder by poisoning of a court enemy, Sir Thomas Overbury. Lady Frances was, like Katherine Knyvett, a ravishing beauty. But the man she had settled on for a husband was warned off her by the aforementioned Overbury. Furious and seeking revenge, Frances enlisted the help of a hunch-backed apothecary who supplied her with a variety of sinister and exotic poisons including 'Powder of Diamonds' and 'Great Spider' as well as white arsenic. Frances then arranged for food laced with these toxins to be delivered to Overbury. After the murder was uncovered, the twenty-six-year-old Frances was arrested. At her trial there were whispers of witchcraft, sorcery and even of demonic possession. Lady Frances was conveyed to the Tower, the Howards of the Charlton Parks infamy now assured.

A less controversial Howard cadet was cultivated by Lord William, another of St Philip Howard's brothers. Unlike the Suffolk branch which was known for its rogues' gallery of spies and murderers, the Carlisle branch (it received its earldom in 1661) are noted for contributing to England one of its most iconic country houses.

Castle Howard in Yorkshire is not a castle in the architectural sense, but rather a baroque palace built on the site of a medieval fort. It was begun by the 3rd Earl of Carlisle in 1699, working to the designs of architect John Vanburgh. Today it is widely recognisable thanks to its use in numerous film and TV dramas. It has played Brideshead in two adaptations of Evelyn Waugh's 1945 novel *Brideshead Revisited*. In that story Brideshead is home to the Catholic Flyte family. Castle Howard makes a fitting double as the seat of a branch of England's pre-eminent Catholic dynasty.

Catholicism, and the dukedom restored

As we have seen, not every member of the House of Howard has been an avowed Catholic. At times many members found it expedient to – nominally at least – embrace Protestantism. It was part of that Howard adaptability and the impulse to survive. It remains true, however, that recusancy was the default position for Howards, sometimes at enormous personal cost. Adherence to Catholicism cost the family dearly politically. Even after St Philip Howard's heirs were restored to the dukedom of Norfolk by Charles II in 1661, they faced exclusion from the corridors of power.

It had been eighty-four years since the execution of the 4th Duke of Norfolk, when his great-great-grandson was at last proclaimed as 5th Duke. The restoration did not begin well. The new duke was an expatriate, confined under a doctor's care in Padua, where he had lived since contracting a brain fever that rendered him insane. His brother and successor, the 6th Duke, was a sincere Catholic at a time of anti-Catholic hysteria, whipped up by the Anglican priest Titus Oates who spread falsehoods of a Popish Plot against Charles II. The 6th Duke was barred from taking his seat in the House of Lords in 1678 for refusing to take the oath recognising Charles as head of the Church of England. The expulsion of Catholic peers from the Lords was formalised in law, Catholicism remaining a suspect 'foreign' religion into modern times. Only with the Catholic Relief Act of 1829 were subsequent Dukes of Norfolk allowed to return to Parliament. Many of them, however, still chose to seclude themselves at Arundel, the fortress retreat of their ancestors. The 15th Duke, Henry Fitzalan-Howard (1847–1917) spent his time building the church of St Philip Neri at Arundel, as well as beautifying the castle.

The Howards of Arundel Castle

Family seat: Arundel Castle
Overlooking the River Arun in West Sussex, the Howard family seat stands like a storybook vision of the bygone age of chivalry. Although the Howards only inherited it in 1580, their ancestors of the Fitzalan line had held it since 1243. It dates from earlier still, built by the Norman, Roger de Montgomery soon after the Conquest. Roger built the motte and gatehouse which still survive, constructed in 1068 and 1070 respectively. After the Montgomerys, the castle reverted to the Crown until Henry II confirmed William Aubigny as its owner. Since then, Arundel has passed down family generations, twice through heiresses from the Aubignys to the Fitzalans, and finally the Howards. The castle has altered significantly over the centuries, being badly damaged in the 1600s by Civil War hostilities. Henry, 15th Duke of Norfolk, was responsible for most of the romantic castle we see today. His Victorian gothic creation is a fitting monument to the medieval Earls of Arundel.

Survival: into the twentieth century
Though their political power had long since passed, the dukes of Norfolk, like the rest of the nobility, managed to retain an aura of superiority into the twentieth century. Even after the First World War they exercised an extraordinary hold on the collective imagination of their local communities. At Arundel in the 1920s, the 16th Duke of Norfolk was treated like a mini-monarch by the townsfolk, with events marking his coming of age looking for all the world like a royal coronation. There were marching bands, crowds and a three-day 'public holiday' for tenants and staff. Beacons were lit on the Howard estates across the kingdom, just as they might have been by the pagan Saxons long before the duke's supposed ancestral link to them – Hereward the Wake – had haunted the Isle of Ely. Even far to the north, in estates like Sheffield, the Howards still captured the imagination. Sheffield was

one of umpteen properties the Howards had gathered to themselves over their long history (in this case plucked from the hands of the Talbots of Shrewsbury). The family was commemorated throughout the city, from Norfolk Park – where celebrations for the 16th Duke's birthday were joyous – to Arundel Gate, Surrey Street, Fitzalan Square, and beyond.

The collective folklore clinging to the 'Fitzalan-Howard' family, senior line of the House of Howard, is enough to lend a mystic medievalist glow to Arundel today. The great Catholic Cathedral which stands in the town is now dedicated to Our Lady and to St Philip Howard, the family's revered Catholic martyr. In 2016, the present heir to the dukedom, Miles Fitzalan-Howard, Lord Arundel, was married in Arundel Cathedral. In 2023, his father, the 18th Duke of Norfolk, organised the Coronation of King Charles III. It remains a constitutional curiosity that this Catholic peer acts as Earl Marshal to the head of the Church of England.

The Seymours of Bradley House

Duke of Somerset

Dukedom created	1547
Monarch	Edward VI
Subsidiary title	Baron Seymour
Junior branch	Marquess of Hertford (Ragley Hall)

Until the reign of Henry VIII, the Seymours were a relatively obscure family of Wiltshire gentry. Fate stepped in when the king visited the Seymour estate in 1535 and his eye is said to have been taken by the beautiful daughter of the house, Jane. Henry was to take Jane Seymour as his third wife, propelling her family from their quiet life in Savernake Forest into the highest circles of court. The new queen's brothers – Edward and Thomas Seymour – had never imagined such status, and when their sister produced the king's sought-after male heir, the position of the family was secured. Or so they believed.

As 'new' nobility and champions of the new Protestant religion, the Seymours were despised by many of the old Catholic families

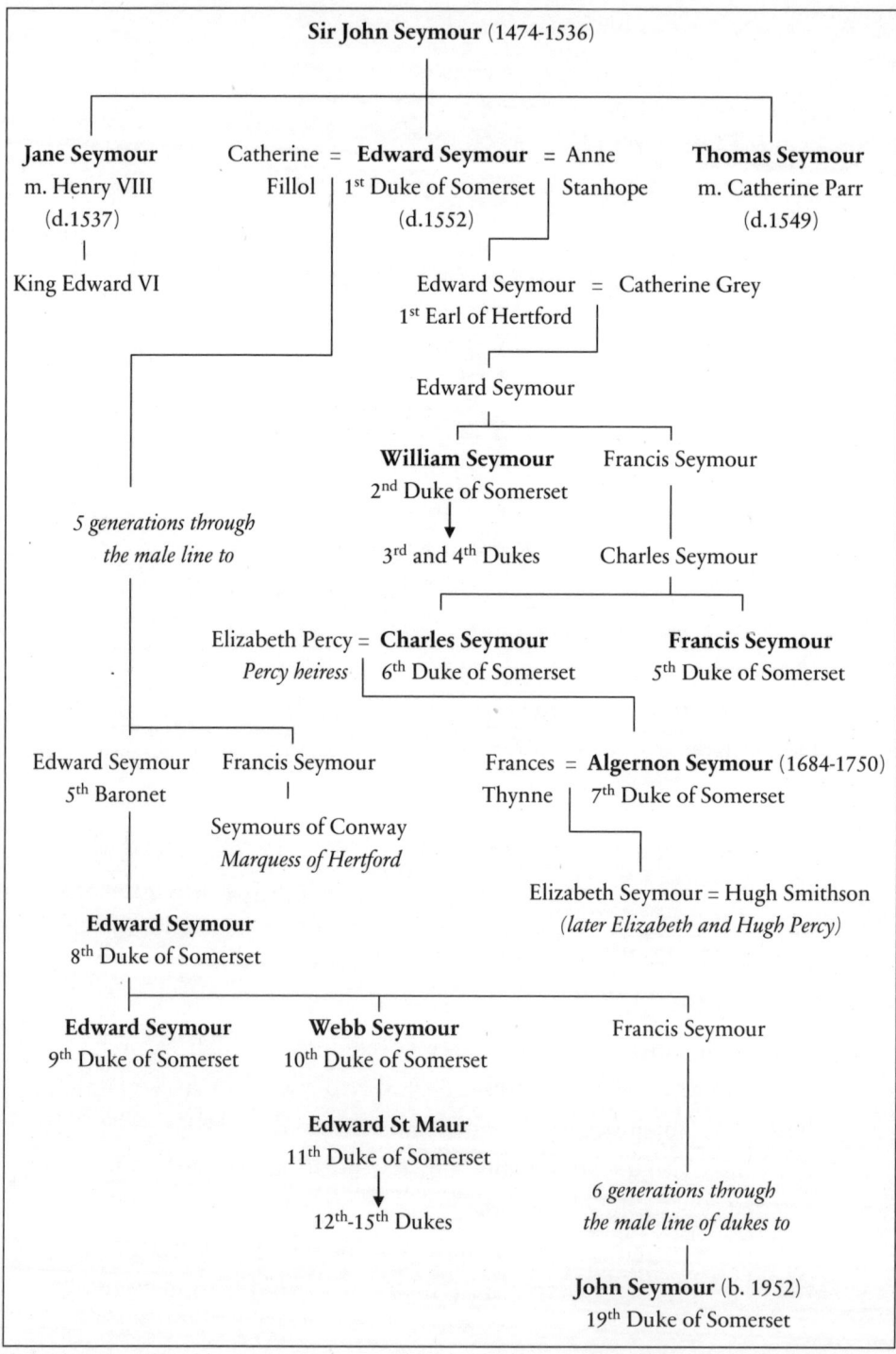

at court. Yet upon the death of Henry VIII, it was Edward Seymour, as 1st Duke of Somerset, who was able to wield power in the name of his nephew Edward VI, and – as Lord Protector – govern England as its first genuinely Protestant ruler. He unleashed a radical Reformation never contemplated in the days of King Henry. Seymour's fall would come just as rapidly as his rise. But he had laid the groundwork for a lasting dynasty by obtaining land from the dissolved monasteries on which was built Bradley House. There, his descendants would reemerge, and there the 19th Duke of Somerset resides today.

The Forest Lords: origins of the Seymours

Despite being sworn enemies for much of the sixteenth century, the House of Seymour shared much in common with the House of Howard. Both families provided brides for King Henry VIII. Both thought themselves as good (or better) than the royal family. And both were deprived of their highest titles through Acts of Attainder and executions, only for their respective dukedoms to be restored to their heirs – in the same year, 1660 – and then endure, though never again achieving the remarkable power that they had under the Tudors.

The pride that both families took in their ancestry might be seen as amusing aristocratic eccentricity, if not for the viciousness of the feelings unleashed. And yet, for all that vanity, just like the name of Howard, the name of Seymour had itself not been of any particular renown in antiquity.

The early history of the Seymours is bound up not with the halls of Renaissance palaces, but the forests of southern England. In 1491, a man named John Seymour (1474–1536) was Warden of Savernake Forest. He was the master of the manor of Wolf Hall, a scion of provincial gentry who, through military service against a popular rebellion in Cornwall in 1497, was knighted by Henry VII and went on to serve the king at court. The opportunity to move from woodsman to warrior and catch the attention of Henry VII had come as a result of the king's desperate need to raise funds from his subjects, which made him deeply unpopular, particularly in Cornwall where the famous tin mines were burdened with unprecedented taxation. The Scots were threatening invasion in the north, and Perkin Warbeck was claiming to be one of the missing Princes in the Tower (supposedly Richard Plantagenet, Duke of Norfolk and York) and the rightful monarch. The Cornish Rebellion metamorphosed into the Warbeck Rebellion when, later in 1497, Perkin landed on the Cornish coast and occupied St Michael's Mount, the fairytale-like fortress protected by the sea which cuts it off at high tide. The rebels declared Warbeck to be 'Richard IV'. Henry VII was in need of men he could trust, which was why John Seymour was rewarded with a knighthood.

Sir John was not the first of his family to distinguish himself (a William Seymour had attended the Black Prince in Gascony at the opening of the Hundred Years War), but before Sir John, the family had largely avoided celebrity, keeping themselves to themselves in the forest that had been their domain for over a century. Savernake had been carved out of primeval woodlands by William the Conqueror and granted to a Hastings knight, Richard Estury. The land was passed down, sometimes through the female line, eventually landing with the Seymours in the early fifteenth century. The Seymour family (originally known as 'St Maur', and said to derive from Normandy, though that claim is unproven) had been established as landowners in Monmouthshire in the mid-thirteenth century. The St Maurs were in the orbit of the great Marcher lords of the Welsh borders, and in the fourteenth century, a Roger St Maur made a lucrative marriage to Cecily de Beauchamp of Somerset. This was their first link to the Beauchamp barony that one day would become their first peerage, and to the county whose dukedom would be their greatest.

The Seymours' acquisition via marriage of Savernake Forest brought them rich new land. The manor house there, Wolf Hall, has today been made famous by the title of Hilary Mantel's Booker-winning novel, but little is actually known about what the building looked like. It probably had castellated towers in the late medieval style and served as a comfortable though modest seat for a gentry family yet to have its big break into historical stardom. Savernake took up much of the time of its squires, for it came with some peculiar responsibilities, duties that were the province of any warden of a Royal Forest.

Royal forests and their wardens

Savernake was one of several royal hunting forests that were established by William the Conqueror and his heirs. The Norman kings had set aside vast tracts of England for the private use as hunting grounds by the king and his favoured nobles. These forests were administered by officials known as forest wardens, positions that often became hereditary in the local landowning family.

The creation of royal forests caused bitter resentment among the local peasantry. Under the Saxon kings, the forests had been classed as common land. Whole communities had lived in and from them. Its resources – everything from wood for building and burning, animals for hunting, berries, wild herbs and honey for eating – were the property of everyone who dwelt there. The forests did not consist only of woodland; within their borders were grasslands and heaths, clearings and pastures for livestock. All this ended after the Norman Conquest when the forests became the personal property of the monarch and were made subject to the hated 'Forest Laws'. Henceforth the king's wardens would deal out harsh punishments to anybody trespassing or poaching the king's deer and game.

The 'Norman yoke' made outlaws out of ordinary people seeking a living from the wild woods. Among the peasantry, a folklore of the forests grew, lamenting the idyllic sylvan societies that had been stolen by the Norman tyrants. Individuals who rebelled were romanticised in legend (Robin Hood, outlaw of Sherwood Forest, appeared in medieval literature which drew from this folk-hero tradition).

In real life, the right of access to the forests by all 'free men' was restored by the signing of the 'Carta de Foresta' or Charter of the Forests, by King Henry III in 1217. This was a companion document to the Magna Carta, sealed two years before by Henry's father John.

As 'Forest Knights', the Seymours had to enforce the laws in their domain, but the powers of the Wardens of Savernake had been significantly curtailed after the Carta de Foresta. They now had to ensure the rights of local people to gather wood and graze their animals there, and they could no longer deal out arbitrary punishments for poaching or minor offences. However, they did still have to maintain the forest for royal use, making sure it was well stocked with deer for the king and his party, should they wish to hunt.

There is good evidence that King Henry VIII hunted at Savernake in 1535 and that he visited the Seymour family at Wolf Hall. It's not known for certain that Sir John Seymour's daughter Jane was actually present, though local tradition – and much historical fiction – has Henry and Jane's first meeting taking place at the house. If the pair did not first set eyes on each other at Savernake, they had ample opportunity to do so in London, where Jane was in the service of Henry's first and second queens, Catherine of Aragon and Anne Boleyn. It was Jane who was to propel her family into the historical spotlight by becoming Henry's third.

Jane Seymour: from waiting on a queen to queen-in-waiting
Jane Seymour became a lady-in-waiting to Queen Anne Boleyn around 1533, the year the queen gave birth to the future Elizabeth I.

Jane had her father's position to thank for her place in court where she witnessed the downfall of Queen Anne at extremely close quarters. The king seems to have had his eye on Jane for at least several months before Anne's execution, and his growing devotion was probably another contributing factor in his wish to be free from Anne.

Jane was, according to those who knew her, a compassionate, gentle and charming young woman who, though not highly educated, had a practical mind which proved valuable when dealing with the minutiae of court affairs. John Russell, Earl of Bedford, thought Jane the most beautiful of all the king's wives, and it is generally agreed that Jane was Henry's favourite. This was perhaps partly because she gave him his male heir (the future King Edward VI was born in 1537), but the relationship between Henry and Jane is also considered a genuine love-match. It's thought the king fell for Jane as early as 1535, meeting her through secret passageways at Greenwich. His desire for Jane was clearly urgent. Without a shred of respect for his former love and consort, Henry VIII married Jane Seymour the same month Anne was beheaded in May 1536.

Sixteen months after her wedding, Jane gave birth to a boy who was grandson to both Henry VII and his defender Sir John Seymour. Tragically, Jane died just days later from complications of childbirth. King Henry was said to be inconsolable. Jane became an almost saintly figure in the king's memory, shown by the fact that when Henry himself died, it was only Queen Jane buried beside him.

Jane's memory also ensured that the position of her family was assured under Henry VIII. At the christening of the Prince of Wales, Edward Seymour carried the infant Princess Elizabeth (Anne Boleyn's daughter) and returned to court as the uncle of the future king, and a royal himself in all but name.

Edward Seymour, 1st Duke of Somerset

The rise of the House of Seymour to the ranks of the Peerage was directly related to Jane Seymour's marriage and progeny. It was just after Jane's wedding to the king that her brother Sir Edward Seymour (he had been knighted in 1523) was granted his family's first peerage title, being created Viscount Beauchamp in June 1536. Then, on the same day that his nephew was christened – 15 October 1537 – the king elevated Seymour further as the 1st Earl of Hertford.

It is unlikely that Seymour would have gained such a central position at court and been ennobled in this way without his familial relationship to a queen consort. Nevertheless, Edward took the opportunities he was given to prove his abilities, and he was marked out by King Henry as man of promise. In 1541, the king made Seymour a Knight of the Garter, a sure sign that was rising in royal favour. A skilled political operator, Seymour was soon being entrusted with the running of government during the king's absences from London.

Lord Hertford possessed the exact combination of talents still required of premier noblemen at the time of Henry VIII: political skill, yes, but also military effectiveness, if not savagery. In 1542, he was entrusted with the defence of the northern border as Warden of the Scottish Marches. When in 1545 the Scots insulted the English king by breaking off the betrothal of the infant Mary, Queen of Scots to Prince Edward, it was Seymour who was despatched to make Edinburgh pay. Lord Hertford sailed into Leith, captured and raided the Scottish capital, then marched back to England burning everything before him: castles, monasteries, towns, and more than 240 villages. Today, we would call this targeting of civilians a war crime. In the age of the tyrannical Henry VIII, Hertford's actions only enhanced his reputation in the king's eyes.

By the time Henry had married his sixth wife, Catherine Parr, Seymour had been made lieutenant of the realm and was serving as Regent of England while the king was away campaigning in France. Seymour was to serve Henry in battle again both in Boulogne and once more in Scotland, where he repeated his earlier brutality, leaving town after town burnt and in ruins.

All this, coupled with the self-inflicted downfall of his enemies the Howards, meant that with the death of Henry VIII in 1547 it was Edward Seymour who was the natural, and more than willing, Regent for a kingdom headed by a boy-king, his nephew.

The seizure of power was orchestrated with precision. Seymour ensured that the ten-year-old Edward VI was immediately taken into his care. With complete control of his nephew, Seymour proclaimed himself Lord Protector of the Realm. It was also clearly important to him that the Regent of England should be more than simply an earl in rank, so Seymour also created himself Duke of Somerset for good measure. This was of course done in the name of King Edward whose signature appeared on the Letters Patent, and who probably had Seymour watching over his shoulder as he scribbled.

What followed was one of the clearest examples of sovereign-nobleman rule, for the Duke of Somerset was king of England in every practical sense. He acted like a king too, building himself a new palace in London's Strand, Somerset House. Even the title that he chose for himself had a royal flavour to it. The old medieval dukes of Somerset had been the Beauforts, the family of Henry VII's mother Margaret Beaufort.

The government of the Duke of Somerset is chiefly remembered for its religious reforms, which were far more radical than those undertaken under Henry VIII. A true Protestant in his dogma – a follower of Jean Calvin – Somerset enforced the use of the English language in place of Latin in church ceremonies. He also allowed priests to marry and decreed that icons should be removed from church buildings. Seymour's successes were aided and abetted by his dynastic supports including his younger brother Thomas.

Yet just as the Howards found out, close relations could be a hazard as much as a help, and as time went on it was a growing personal rift between the two Seymour brothers that would lead to a fall as spectacular as any of the Howards.

Thomas Seymour and the fall of Protector Somerset

Upon the rise of his brother to the Protectorship, Thomas Seymour (1508–1549) was made Lord High Admiral and given his own peerage as Baron Seymour of Sudeley (he was, after all, also uncle to the boy-king). Cementing his links to royalty, Thomas then married Henry VIII's widow, the queen dowager Catherine Parr (with whom he'd had a romantic dalliance before the king had set his sights on her). Thomas Seymour was consumed by ambition, every bit as much as his brother. But where Edward was shrewd in his machinations, Thomas was reckless and impulsive. Before he married Catherine, he had first suggested an even more regal match: he wanted to marry the Princess Elizabeth (then only fourteen years old). The Duke of Somerset was aghast and expressly forbade the plan. He made it clear to his brother that he was overreaching himself in imagining he was a match for the potential Queen Regnant. It was probably around then that Thomas began to be consumed not only by ambition, but by jealousy. He grew resentful of his brother's supreme leadership, believing he had just as much right to, at the very least, a share in the regency. Thomas withdrew to his seat of Sudeley Castle in Gloucestershire, taking with him his wife Catherine and, for good measure, the Princess Elizabeth.

Lord Seymour's actions were near treasonous, as was his behaviour towards the princess. Elizabeth was to spend many months under the care of Thomas and Catherine, where her treatment by Lord Seymour raised eyebrows. Soon after the death of his wife Catherine in childbirth in 1548, Seymour renewed his scheme to marry Elizabeth. He also began plotting to replace his brother as Lord Protector, hatching an audacious plan to kidnap his nephew, King Edward, and thus take possession if the kingdom. It proved a fatal error, for Thomas was not the careful orchestrator his brother was; impetuous as always,

Thomas took some henchmen late one night and stole through the palace corridors on a kidnap mission. As he reached the king's bedchamber, however, his nephew's pet spaniel began to bark loudly, raising the alarm. Thomas Seymour was quickly arrested and transported to the Tower, where he was charged with many treasonous designs including planning to wed Princess Elizabeth.

The ensuing trial of the Protector s brother produced an avalanche of scandalous details. Evidence was presented by the Princess Elizabeth s governess, Kat Ashley, that Thomas Seymour had been amorously familiar with his teenage charge while he and Catherine Parr had been her guardians. Thomas would, Kat testified, come into the princess's bedchamber early while she was still in bed. He would slap her on the behind and then strive to kiss her, while in his own nightshirt. It was revealed that Catherine Parr had once come across Thomas with Elizabeth in his arms and had admonished them both. The princess was also questioned, admitting that she was aware of Seymour's intentions to marry her, but that it was not her own wish and that she had never sought it.

Thomas could not count on any fraternal bond to save him. Lord Seymour of Sudeley was executed in March 1549 on the orders of his own brother. The fratricide marked the beginning of the Duke of Somerset's own downward spiral. Long disliked by factions of the court for what was seen as enriching himself by his position, Somerset was accused of inciting rebellion by the common people against their landlords. It was true the duke had spoken up on behalf of the poor and dispossessed. His policies on controversial issues like land enclosure also tallied with his rhetoric, and he cultivated an image of the 'Good Duke', a friend of the people. The anti-landlord rebellions were easy to blame on Somerset, and this allowed a cabal of his enemies to mount a coup. The duke was arrested, attainted and sent to the Tower like his brother before him.

That the duke was indeed popular with the 'common people' became clear upon the day of his execution. When Edward Seymour was led to the block in 1552, sorrowful crowds packed London's streets. As the axe fell, several people leaped forward to dip their handkerchiefs in the duke's blood, keeping them afterwards as a martyr's relic. The people were seemingly far more bereft than their king was at the death of the former Lord Protector; Edward VI recorded in his diary without even a hint of emotion: 'The Duke of Somerset had his head cut off upon Tower Hill between eight and nine o'clock in the morning.'

The fall of the 1st Duke was complete, but his dynasty had a pathway to survival. He had a son, also Edward, whose prospects were inevitably affected by his father's disgrace. He was prevented from inheriting titles, wealth, and much of the family land. For a while he relied on the generosity of his father's former protégé, Sir John Thynne of Longleat, for his survival. But over time Edward quietly and diligently began to ensure that the Seymour line would continue and indeed prosper. He took as his wife Lady Catherine Grey (sister of the 'Nine Days Queen' Lady Jane) giving subsequent generations of Seymours a link to the Blood-Royal through descent from Henry VII. Other members of the family began to reassemble the Somerset empire. At the Dissolution of the Monasteries, the duke had obtained the lands in Maiden Bradley, Wiltshire and had purchased the castle at Berry Pomeroy. Though confiscated at his execution, these estates were later granted to another of the duke's sons (and are both now ducal seats).

Perhaps the greatest insurance against oblivion for the dynasty remained, however, the hallowed name of Jane Seymour. Her alliance with the Crown had more than tangible results; it lent an aura to her family name which persists even today, thanks to a continued fascination with the six wives of Henry VIII. Upon his marriage to Jane, the king granted her brother Edward a special augmentation to his coat of arms. Henceforth, the golden wings of Seymour were quartered with a personalised arrangement of the royal three lions of England and the fleur-de-lis. The House of Seymour may have come close to the precipice, but it always had its royal past to fall back on.

The 2nd Duke and Lady Arbella Stuart

For 108 years after Edward Seymour's execution, there was no Duke of Somerset in the House of Lords. The title was forfeit until 1660 when Charles II restored it to the Lord Protector's heir. The 2nd Duke was William Seymour, great-grandson of the 1st. He was only to be duke for a month, not living long enough to attend Charles II's coronation.

Seymour's life before the dukedom was returned had been one of romantic tragedy. At fifteen he had fallen in love with the twenty-two-year-old Lady Arbella Stuart. Arbella was a cousin to the king of Scotland and a descendant of Henry VIII's sister, Margaret Tudor. She had thus been considered a prime candidate to succeed her cousin Queen Elizabeth I. Though Arbella appeared to reciprocate the feelings of the teenage Seymour, as a Blood-Royal, she was not permitted to marry a boy from a disgraced family. The pair were kept apart for seven years, but their affair was rekindled in 1610 and they secretly married without the knowledge of Arbella's cousin James I.

When the illegal marriage was discovered, Arbella and Seymour were imprisoned in separate locations. They were permitted to visit each other, however, and during their visits cooked up a plan to escape. Both of them managed to walk straight out of their cells in disguise (she as a man, he as his own barber). The plan was to flee to the continent where they would meet up and live out their lives free of royal and aristocratic rules. Seymour made it, but the unfortunate Arbella was caught and taken straight to the Tower. There she slowly went mad, dying in 1615. Her lover Seymour returned to England where he would eventually remarry.

The Proud Duke

Later dukes of Somerset failed to make much impact in political or in social circles, perhaps because many tended to look backwards instead of to the future. More than one Seymour spent his days brooding over the importance of their illustrious ancestry and obsessing about a glorious history. The 6th Duke, Charles, (1662–1748) was described by a contemporary as 'a man in whom the pride of birth and rank amounted almost to a disease'. He was labelled as the Proud Duke and roundly mocked for his vanity. His ego only inflated when he married Lady Elizabeth Percy, last of the famous line of the Earls of Northumberland and sole heiress to a fortune that included Alnwick Castle, Northumberland House and several lesser estates and baronies. The inheritance underscored not only the duke's pomposity, but also his coldness and cruelty. When his grandson, Viscount Beauchamp, died tragically at the age of nineteen, the Proud Duke considered it a dynastic disaster rather than a human one. The boy's poor father and mother (later the 7th Duke and his Duchess, Frances Thynne) had to endure the fury of the duke who was more concerned about the division of the Somerset properties that would occur as a result of the death. The heir to the Percy properties was now the dead boy's sister – the duke's granddaughter – Elizabeth Seymour, while the next in line to the dukedom of Somerset (which could not descend on a female) was a very distant cousin. With breathtaking spite, the duke blamed his son for Lord Beauchamp's death. Though the cause had in fact been smallpox, the duke told his son that the loss was a judgement sent against him for his many failings. Even in an age when the aggrandisement of titles mattered far more, such behaviour was seen as callous in the extreme, and the duke became even more despised.

Part of the Proud Duke's fury rested upon his hatred of the new heir. Sir Edward Seymour, Baronet, was in a male line of descent from the 1st Duke, a line which, by the usual rules of the Peerage, would have inherited the dukedom from the start, for it descended from the eldest son of Lord Protector Seymour by his first wife Katherine Fillol. The 1st Duke had disinherited the children of his first marriage, stipulating on the Patent of creation that his titles should pass instead to his younger son by his second marriage to Anne Stanhope. (The cause of his preference may have been a suspicion of infidelity on the part of Katherine.) The dukedom was only to revert to the elder line if the male descendants of Anne Stanhope became extinct, which they now would, given that George, Lord Beauchamp, had been the last. The new heir to the dukedom was therefore technically of the *senior* branch of the family, a fact that infuriated the Proud Duke further. Unsurprisingly, his only surviving descendant, his granddaughter Elizabeth, had no loyalty to the Seymour name. Upon inheriting the Percy properties, she changed her surname to Percy and re-established the Northumberland dynasty as a dukedom along with her husband Hugh Smithson (who also became a Percy. The Proud Duke's only legacy was his ridiculous pride rather than his dynastic hoard, which was dismantled upon his death.

The eccentrics

Some later Seymours were infamous for reasons other than pride. The 5th Duke was shot dead while on the Italian Riviera by a Genoese man named Horatio Botti, whose wife he had insulted. The 12th Duke (who was perhaps afflicted with a little pride, petitioning for the additional title of Earl St Maur) married a woman famed during her lifetime for her eccentricities. Some of Jane Seymour's pastimes were only seen as eccentric because they were progressive for her time. The 'Sheridan Duchess' – she was born Jane Sheridan – was, along with her two sisters, more than simply a society beauty. Between them they were social reformers, poets, feminist pioneers and authors. Some of Duchess Jane's ideas were undeniably eccentric, however: she tried and failed to introduce guinea pigs to the English diet, believing them delicious.

The Sheridan Duchess's son, Ferdinand (known as Ferdy) was not a typical ducal heir, but a young man obsessed with military adventure who went wandering the globe in search of conflicts where he could make his name. When the Indian Mutiny broke out against the rule of the British East India Company in 1857, Lord St Maur volunteered to fight. He was there at the relief of Lucknow and as Britain took direct control of India the following year, beginning the period of the British Raj, or Crown rule.

St Maur's soldiering spirit could not be sated. Next, he was volunteering in Italy, joining Giuseppi Garibaldi's forces in 1860 as they fought the Wars of Italian Unification. Ferdy made his way to the banks of the River Volturno where he distinguished himself in battle. Garibaldi made him a captain.

For all those military achievements, Ferdy was clearly a self-absorbed man, eager for fame and indifferent to his parents' love and fear for his safety. Both the Sheridan Duchess and the 12th Duke were tormented by their son's constant absence and the knowledge that any moment they might hear of his demise in wars he did not need to fight. Ferdy's younger brother Edward was similarly beset by worry. Far more studious and gentler than his brother, Edward would write to St Maur, begging him to return home, to settle and marry. Edward had a career in diplomacy, serving in the British Embassies in Vienna and Madrid. Finally, he followed his brother's footsteps to India where, in a cruel twist of fate, it was he rather than St Maur who was killed. In the jungle he was set upon by a bear. Doctors tried to save his life by amputating his leg, but it was no use. He only had time to compose one last letter to his brother, signing it 'your affectionate cripple'.

After this, Ferdy did return to England, only to die himself at the age of thirty-four of heart disease. His parents were devastated. They only had two sons and both were now dead. It seems the duke did not care much about the succession, which would now pass to his younger brother, for he left most of his wealth to Ferdy's illegitimate children. Harold and Ruth St Maur were the offspring of Rosina Swann, daughter of a local builder, whom he had taken with him on many of his adventures overseas. Later, Harold St Maur attempted to prove himself the rightful 13th Duke, arguing that his parents had in fact been married and that he and his sister were therefore legitimate. It was to no avail, and the dukedom remained in the hands of his great-uncle.

The rather tortured succession of the dukedom of Somerset has been a feature since the 1st Duke's attainder all those centuries before. The 15th Duke died childless; once again a distant cousin inherited, and once again a challenge was made to the succession in the House of Lords. The fragility of the House of Seymour is oddly reflected in the fragility of their actual houses. The old seat, Wolf Hall, no longer exists of course. Bradley House, though a very elegant mansion, is today a shadow of its former self after having several wings demolished. The castle of Berry Pomeroy is largely a ruin. Stover, an estate in Devon, was left by the 12th Duke to Harold St Maur, his illegitimate grandson. This elicited the fury of the 13th Duke, who fought vainly with the trustee that the 12th Duke had appointed. This was his son-in-law, Lord Henry Thynne, a son of the Marquess of Bath. The relationship between the Seymours and the Thynnes was clearly still going strong, having been first been established by the Lord Protector and a loyal servant, John Thynne, back in the days of the Seymour ascendancy. The two families are related many times over by marriage. The current Duke of Somerset, John Seymour (b. 1952) has the Thynnes to thank for helping his family survive several turbulent periods.

Family Seats: Berry Pomeroy Castle and Bradley House
Today, the Duke of Somerset is seated at Bradley House, Wiltshire, and still owns Berry Pomeroy Castle in Devon. Both were originally acquired by the 1st Duke in the 1540s. Yet Berry Pomeroy is today uninhabitable, though described by English Heritage who oversee it as 'counted among the most picturesque and romantic ruins in England'. The castle features in the English Heritage book of ghost stories as one of the most haunted castles in the country: 'While many of the ghost stories ... may be attributed to the imagination of the Victorians, there does seem to be something that troubles the place. It manifests itself chiefly in malfunctioning technology: failing cameras and smart phones.' The castle certainly has the potential for ghosts. It was originally the property of the de la Pomeroy family who held the feudal barony after the Norman Conquest. One of the reputed ghosts – the White Lady – is said to be the restless spirit of Margaret Pomeroy, who was imprisoned in the dungeon by a sister jealous of her beauty. There is a Blue Lady haunting the dungeons. She is also said to have been a Norman, daughter of the then lord, who murdered her baby, having become pregnant by her own father. However, no trace of the Norman Castle has been found, with the present ruins dating from the 1400s and from the buildings constructed by Lord Protector Somerset.

Like Berry Pomeroy, the estate at Maiden Bradley (not far from the Thynne family seat of Longleat) Wiltshire, had descended with the line of the Seymour Baronets which succeeded to the dukedom of Somerset in 1750. The current house is just a small part of a gigantic mansion built around 1700 when the family abandoned Berry Pomeroy in favour of Bradley. Much was demolished in the early 1800s. The church of All Saints, just behind it, contains many of the tombs of the dukes of Somerset.

The Thynnes of Longleat

Marquess of Bath

Marquessate created	1789
Monarch	George III
Subsidiary titles	Viscount Weymouth; Baron Thynne

John Thynne (1515–1580) made a spectacular fortune while serving as the steward to Edward, Duke of Somerset. The progenitor of the Thynne (sometimes spelled Thynn) dynasty remained in the service of the Seymours right up to their dramatic fall from grace in 1549. Sir John, as he became, was imprisoned after the coup against his master, but unlike Seymour, managed to escape the executioner's block. Upon his pardon and release, Thynne fled London for Wiltshire where he set about building one of England's most important country houses. In the twentieth century, Longleat became the first stately home to regularly open its doors as a visitor attraction, while remaining home to Sir John's descendants, the sometimes-colourful Marquesses of Bath.

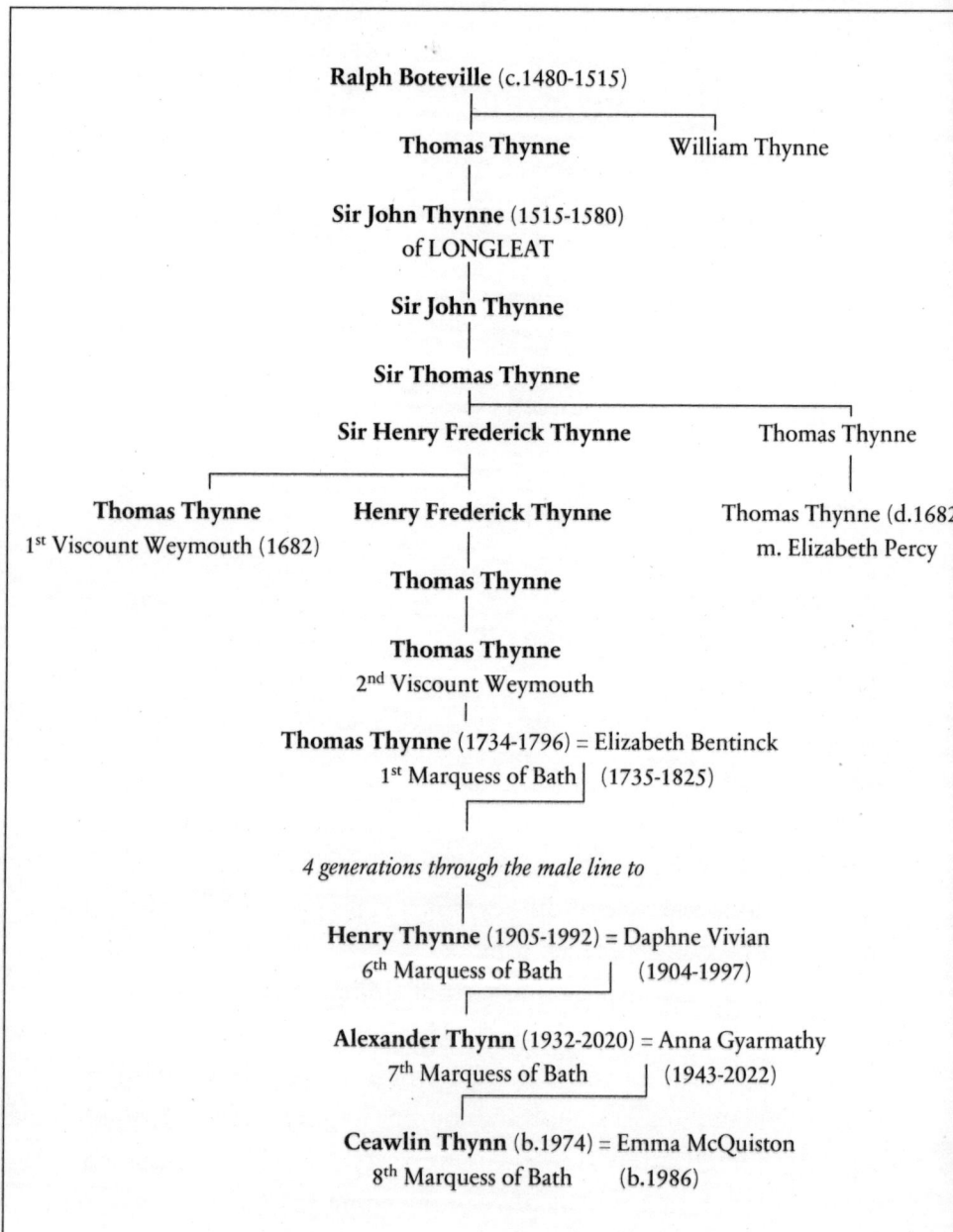

Seymour's steward

In 1538, a shadowy figure by the name of John Thynne – who was apparently also known by an alias, John Boteville – was named in court records as being 'a servant of the Lord Hertford', brother to the late queen consort, Jane. The steward's name (or names) cropped up in a property dispute centring on an estate in Northamptonshire which Thynne believed he had been cheated out of by a former employer. The details of the case are not particularly important, except that they illustrate a key characteristic of this cunning man who founded the noble House of Thynne: an obsessive desire to gather to himself as much land, property, and wealth as he possibly could, as quickly as he could.

John Thynne (the surname is pronounced 'thin', and the 'e' at its end has been used and discarded by members of his family) seems to have been hyper-ambitious from a very young age. He was born into a gentry family in Shropshire, the son of Thomas and grandson of Ralph Thynne or Ralph Boteville, for it seems that Ralph used two surnames. Confusion over the family name remained in the records for several generations.

The Thynnes were not a lowly family – John's father appears to have been an esquire to Henry VII – but they were hardly movers and shakers either. The provincial life was not for John, and as soon as he was old enough, he left Shropshire for London. There, his uncle William Thynne was working as a clerk of the kitchen in the household of Henry VIII. John used his uncle's connections to move from a lowly position in the king's household to a more satisfactory one in the household of Edward Seymour, a man he had identified as similarly ambitious, and a possible passport to the wealth and status he craved.

Thynne soon became Seymour's steward and, like many a would-be dynast, used military opportunities to prove his value to his patron. As Seymour's right-hand man, plenty of such military opportunities arose. Thynne accompanied Seymour on his campaigns against the Scots during the debacle over the on-off betrothal of Prince Edward and Mary of Scotland. In 1547 near Musselburgh, Thynne fought at the last major battle between the kingdoms of England and Scotland before the union of the Crowns. It was there, after the triumphant Battle of Pinckie, that Thynne was knighted for his service. He would be known as Sir John Thynne for the rest of his life; it was his descendants that would rise to the Peerage. But titles were never Thynne's first desire. That was money.

When Seymour became Lord Protector, Sir John used every opportunity it gave to enrich himself. As the *de facto* king's private secretary, Thynne amassed great tracts of monastic land, and took the chance to purchase farms, woodlands, orchards, as well as several houses by which he might ensure his family's future. These houses included one in Wiltshire by a little river called the 'Long Lete'. This he purchased for £53, and it was to be his most important. Sir John remained at Seymour's side throughout the Protectorship, observing his master's grandiose building projects, which included Somerset House. No doubt this helped inspire Thynne's plans for the great house, today known as Longleat.

Over a very short space of time, Thynne became so excessively wealthy that a suspicious Wiltshire neighbour reported him to the Privy Council. The councillors demanded that Thynne account for his riches. Sir John replied to their summons by declaring that it was simply 'a good master the Duke of Somerset', together with his own honest industry, careful management of his property, and an advantageous marriage to the daughter of the Lord Mayor of London, that was responsible for his success.

The times were perilous however, and when the 'good master' Somerset was arrested and attainted, Thynne found himself in a precarious position. Like many of Somerset's circle, he was sent to the Tower. The new regency council seemed unsure exactly what to do with Somerset's ministers, however. Thynne was soon released, possibly in an attempt to calm the political atmosphere after the palace upheaval, only to be arrested a second time and again released. In the end, Thynne decided not to tempt fate. He had escape with his life, but was heavily fined for his part in Seymour's council, with much of his property confiscated. Thynne left court life behind and retreated to his remaining property in Wiltshire. There, he would apply his considerable energies on creating a dwelling that could help him realise the dynastic dream he had for his family. The result was spectacular.

Family seat: Longleat House
'One of the great monuments of the Elizabethan Age, perhaps the greatest', according to Debrett's *Stately Homes*, Longleat was the work of Sir John Thynne and his architect-mason Robert Smythson. There would have been a house on the land of the Augustinian priory at Longleat long before Thynne began building in earnest following a disastrous fire in 1567, but the new house was to be far superior, counting today as one of the pioneering 'prodigy' masterpieces.

Sir John bought an entire quarry of Bath stone to supply the needs of his masons. The construction period would be an unhappy one for his workers, for Thynne revealed himself to be a bad-tempered employer and a typical bully, forcing builders to work on through the night, over winters and often without proper breaks. The result of these years of contention was a house of firsts. Longleat was the first house in England built in the style of the Italian Renaissance, with its harmonious, symmetrical facades and large mullioned windows. It was also the first built specifically to entertain Queen Elizabeth I, with whom Thynne came to be on good terms. In modern times, it became the first stately home to open as a regular visitor attraction, and its estate home to the first drive-through safari park in the world outside of Africa.

The house at Longleat survives very much as John Thynne envisioned it, a huge rectangular block, with Doric, Ionic and Corinthian orders set about two interior courtyards and great screens of exterior glass. No additions were made to the building that would upset the precious balance. But like many a great house that stood into the eighteenth century, Longleat found itself surrounded by a landscaped parkland designed by Lancelot, Capability Brown. And like many that survived into the nineteenth century, the house found its interiors being redecorated by the Victorians. In the 1870s, J. D. Crace, the great gothic and Renaissance revival designer, was employed by the 4th Marquess of Bath. Lord Bath was inspired by his time spent in Italy, both on a Grand Tour through Rome and Florence, and also as Ambassador Extraordinary to Venice, to create interiors that matched the classical grandeur of the facades. Many of the rooms had been altered over the years, leaving little of the originals intact. So Crace created what are now some of the most important Italianate interiors in England for Longleat's suite of State Rooms. The Elizabethan Long Gallery became a saloon. The coffered ceiling was copied from the Palazzo Massimi in Rome, the marble fireplace from the Palazzo Ducale in Venice. Tapestries from Brussels were hung that depicted scenes from the life of Cyrus, conqueror of Babylon, and liberator of the Jews. The treasures amassed at this time make Longleat a fine museum to the ancients housed in a Renaissance English palace.

The Thynne knights

The late Alexander, 7th Marquess of Bath, described the transformation of his ancestor's standing by the time of Queen Elizabeth's reign: 'Sir John may have been an uncouth, domineering, formidable rogue of ill-gotten wealth, shrewdly cunning and essentially ruthless, but he was now emerging as an eminent Elizabethan with a far healthier climate for the development of his own interests.' The magnificent house at Longleat was Sir John's foundation for establishing his dynasty. His son and heir had been born in 1555. Sir John, with his usual self-absorption, wrote to his wife Christian Gresham to instruct her not to let his heir catch cold.

When Sir John died in 1580, his heir was alive and well and able to take over the running of his estates. The Thynnes were now established territorially, but it would be another three generations before they were elevated to the Peerage. Sir John's immediate successors in Wiltshire were little more than the country squires that his immediate ancestors had been in Shropshire. They were knights of the shire and elected MPs and High Sheriffs. Some did gain fame but generally through personal scandal. Sir John's grandson caused a family rift by secretly marrying the granddaughter of an enemy. The match between Sir Thomas Thynne and Maria Tuchet caused consternation. Maria's grandfather had had a fifteen-year dispute with her husband's grandfather Sir John, and the two families had been sworn rivals ever since. Thomas's mother, Lady Joan Thynne, attempted unsuccessfully to have the marriage annulled. The whole saga caused such an uproar that it has been touted as one of the potential inspirations for Shakespeare's *Romeo and Juliet*. The star-crossed lovers' grandson was also known for a famous marriage, and for an untimely end.

The murder of 'Tom of Ten Thousand'

We have already heard the name Elizabeth Percy, the heiress to Northumberland, who was unfortunate enough to marry the Proud Duke of Somerset. Before that marriage, Elizabeth had been wed to another man of questionable character, Thomas Thynne of Longleat. This particular Thomas Thynne (1647–1682) was a notorious libertine. His mistreated wife fled, slipping away from her husband's servants on a shopping trip and retreating to the home of a close friend.

Due to his enormous wealth, Thynne was known as 'Tom of Ten Thousand'. Riches could not protect him from the vengeance of one of Elizabeth Percy's admirers. In February 1682, Thynne was sensationally murdered, shot dead while travelling in his carriage along Pall Mall. The three assassins who had ambushed Thynne were arrested and exposed as hired hitmen recruited by a European nobleman, a Count Karl von Konigsmarck. Karl had wished to marry Elizabeth Percy himself before her marriage and decided to rid Elizabeth of her philandering husband. Any hope that Kongsmarck had to marry Elizabeth afterwards were dashed by the trial which, although officially acquitting him of involvement (due to a corrupt jury) still banished him from England. The three hitmen were hanged. Konigsmarck went to Greece, eventually dying of wounds sustained while serving in the Morean War.

The Weymouths

The first peerages to come the Thynnes' way were presented to the cousin of the murdered Tom of Ten Thousand. Also named Thomas, he inherited Longleat upon his cousin's death, and in the same year was created Baron Thynne and Viscount Weymouth.

The Patents of creation signed by Charles II stipulated a special remainder: in the event that Lord Weymouth left no direct descendants, the titles should pass to his younger brother and thereafter to his brother's heirs. This came to pass, all three of his own children predeceasing him. Nevertheless, the 1st Viscount Weymouth left a considerable mark on his ancestral home. He created extraordinary formal gardens in the baroque style popular in the late 1600s. The parterres, fountains, canals, orchards, groves, cascades, kitchen gardens and labyrinths were all recorded (as they were at similar gardens being created at Chatsworth and Hampton Court) by the Dutch draughtsman Leonard Knyff.

Weymouth was also responsible for expanding Longleat's celebrated library. The family's book collection had been started in Sir John's time by his uncle William, who first secured him his position at court. A manuscript of Chaucer's poetry is still at Longleat inscribed to 'the Clerke of the Kechin'. Lord Weymouth received a significant bequest of books from the former Bishop of Bath and Wells, Thomas Ken, who was a lodger at Longleat for twenty years. Bishop Ken had refused to take the oath of allegiance to William of Orange and Mary after the Glorious Revolution, having already sworn allegiance to the deposed James II. The new monarchs duly deprived the bishop of his see. Luckily for Ken, he had been a friend of Lord Weymouth since they had studied together at Oxford. Ken was given rooms at Longleat and an allowance on which to live. It is said that this devout man had a profound effect on Thomas Thynne, turning him into the sort of generous and benevolent figure which the Thynne family was not exactly famous for producing before then. The 'Lord Weymouth School' was founded in Wiltshire at his behest, and another was built on his estate in Northern Ireland. Weymouth also created a chapel at Longleat, which must have pleased Ken. While in residence, the bishop wrote several hymns that became among the most well-known in the English hymnal, including 'Awake my soul'.

When the 1st Viscount died in 1714, the special remainder was activated and the title passed to his great-nephew, Thomas Thynne, 2nd Viscount Weymouth (1710–1751). He was the four-times great-grandson of Sir John, builder of Longleat, and the son of a Thynne and a Villiers. But it was his second wife who did more for the status of his family than anyone since Sir John. This was Lady Louisa Carteret. A popular legend at Longleat today says that Louisa's ghost haunts the its passageways. The story is that Lord Weymouth grew jealous of his wife's very handsome manservant after hearing rumours of an affair between the two. In anger, the viscount arranged the manservant's murder. He was found with a broken neck at the bottom of a staircase at Longleat. Its said Louisa's spirit still roams here and there searching for her lost lover. There is absolutely no evidence that any such event occurred. Indeed, when Louisa died in childbirth, her husband was devastated and went into deep mourning. Both their sons were elevated further in the Peerage due to Louisa s family connections. The younger son, Henry Thynne, was given a title as 1st Baron Carteret in a recreation of his mother's family's barony. (Henry was compelled to change his surname from Thynne to Carteret, and this cadet line is still extant.) The elder son and heir – who became the 3rd Viscount Weymouth – received a still higher honour on account of his mother's heritage. Louisa had been the great-granddaughter of John Granville, Earl of Bath. That descent was responsible for the creation in 1789 of the Thynne Marquessate of Bath.

The ground-breaking Baths

None of the Marquesses of Bath made much impact in political life. There is certainly no Bath to compare to the name of Salisbury where it comes to prime ministerial marquessates. But the Baths did prove hugely influential in creating the modern-day cultural obsession of the country house. That is probably appropriate, given that Longleat was the pride and greatest legacy of the founder of the House of Thynne.

The 6th Marquess of Bath, Henry Thynne (1905–1992), has been described as the founder of the stately home business. In April 1949 he opened Longleat to the public, charging 2s 6d a ticket, the first great house to be opened on a regular commercial basis. He was criticised in some quarters for what was seen as the vulgar idea of making people pay to come and look inside your house. It was done out of financial necessity. The Longleat estate did not have an income that could cover the massive debts inherited by Lord Bath. Over 1000 similar country seats had been lost in the previous fifty years because their owners could not afford to run them. There was a real danger that the Thynne seat would follow suit.

There was 'a long tradition in this country of housekeepers showing houses to visitors', Lord Bath later explained, suggesting that open-house was not as novel an idea as it appeared. 'So, we decided to develop that and to remain open permanently, on a commercial basis, every day of the year except Christmas Day.' In the early days, the night watchman's wife ran a small cafe in the basement. It was decidedly amateurish in customer-service terms. But business boomed. In the first year of opening, Longleat took the equivalent of £1.5 million. The appetite among the public to explore stately homes was thus revealed. Lord Bath was proved right, and his peers followed his lead. By 1965, at least 600 country houses had been opened to paying visitors.

It is difficult to understate the consequence of the Thynne family's decision to turn their private home into a visitor attraction. The historic houses sector today generates billions for the UK economy, with estates that are often the key employers in their local areas. While there is an argument to say that if Longleat hadn't done it first, some other house would have, it's harder to say the same about the 6th Marquess's next money-making innovation. In 1966, and to an even greater furore, he made the bold and decidedly eccentric decision to open a safari park in the middle of the Longleat grounds. It was eccentric not only because of the bizarre combination of English Elizabethan Country House and African lions, but because, at that time, there had never been such a safari park anywhere outside the African continent. The opening of The Lions of Longleat – as it was first named – made worldwide headlines. It was hugely controversial, even being raised in the House of Commons. But once again Lord Bath was vindicated. Visitors queued for miles to get in. Today, Longleat Safari Park covers 9000 acres and brings in more money that the house itself. There are now safari parks at other country seats: The Russells have one at Woburn, and so too do the Stanleys at Knowsley.

If the 6th Marquess saved Longleat, the 7th made it famous in the TV age as one of the most famed of aristocratic eccentrics. Alexander Thynn (he dropped the e) was a bohemian artist, decorating his private apartments with his own unique works that he sculpted from a mix of oil paint and sawdust. Three-dimensional portraits of his ancestors were his passion. Lord Bath's flamboyant dress sense and famous libido made him a favourite with the tabloid press. While married, Thynn had open relationships with – reportedly – more than seventy mistresses he called 'wifelets'. Many lived in houses on the Longleat Estate.

'The *Loins* of Longleat', as he was dubbed, did have some serious political ambitions, however. As 7th Marquess, he was the last of his family to automatically enter the House of Lords as a hereditary peer, which he did upon his succession in 1992. Sitting as a Liberal Democrat, he argued that 'Wessex', by which he meant the lands once covered by the Anglo-Saxon kingdom of the same name and which included Wiltshire – should have devolved powers within the UK. Devolution to the regions was an official policy of the Labour government after 1997, so this was not as eccentric a position as it might sound. But Labour also acted to remove hereditary peers from the Parliament in 1999, officially ending Lord Bath's political career. Alexander Thynn died aged eighty-seven in 2020.

Today, Longleat is administered by Ceawlin Thynn (b. 1974). The 8th Marquess's unusual name was the choice of his father, Alexander. It alludes to a sixth-century king of Wessex who is mentioned in the Anglo-Saxon Chronicle. Alexander was standing to be an MP on the Wessex Regionalist Party ticket the year of his son's birth. Alexander was able to stand for the House of Commons that year because he was still a 'commoner' in 1974, still heir apparent, using the courtesy title of Viscount Weymouth. Ceawlin Thynn also used the old Weymouth title before his succession to the Marquessate, a title which fell to secondary status following the creation of the Marquessate. In 2019, it was, of all things, *Strictly Come Dancing* that made the name of Weymouth famous again. Ceawlin's wife, Emma Thynn, then Viscountess Weymouth (and known in the aristocratic shorthand as 'Emma Weymouth') became a contestant on the popular TV dancing show.

The daughter of a Nigerian father and an English mother, Emma married the then Lord Weymouth at the age of twenty-seven. A successful fashion editor and model, she also quickly proved adept at developing the business interests of Longleat. Her dual heritage proved a talking point for the media, Emma's marriage to the Longleat heir being yet another example of the Thynne family breaking new ground.

'Meet the Viscountess transforming the idea of the British Aristocracy,' ran the header of a 2018 *Vanity Fair* article centring on Emma Weymouth. 'An extraordinary cook and mother who is positioned to become Britain's first black marchioness, has recast the mould of aristocracy with her stylish, entrepreneurial spirit.' *Vanity Fair* was not the first to note that:

> When her husband, Ceawlin, Viscount Weymouth, assumes the title [of Marquess of Bath], Emma will become Britain's first black marchioness. In the ranks of British peerage, a marquess and marchioness are second only to a duke and duchess. And someday [her son] young John ... will assume his father's title and become the United Kingdom's first marquess of colour.

With the death of the 7th Marquess, Emma Thynn (nee McQuiston) is indeed now the first black marchioness in England, and she has broken fresh ground in the near millennium-long history of the Peerage.

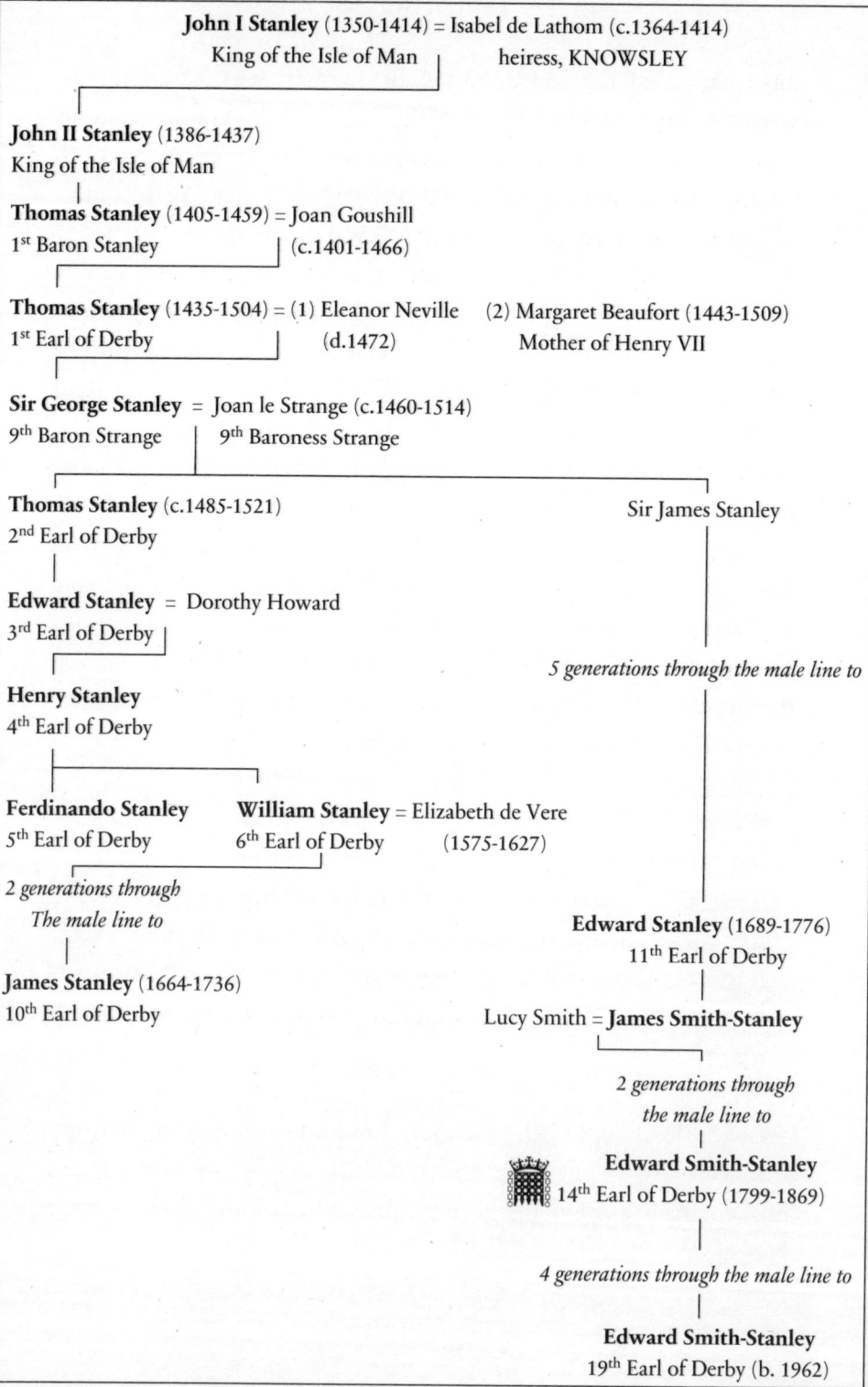

The Stanleys of Knowsley Hall

Earl of Derby

Earldom created	1485
Monarch	Henry VII
Subsidiary title	Baron Stanley
Junior branch	Baron Stanley of Alderley (Alderley Park)

Many legends surround the origins of the Stanleys and their title. Dramatists recount how Thomas, Lord Stanley, wandered the misty battlefield of Bosworth after the fighting had ended in 1485, and discovered in a hawthorn bush the crown of the slain King Richard III. He retrieved the crown and later placed it on the head of his stepson Henry Tudor, who was still clad in armour. The Stanleys were already an old family by the time of Bosworth. They had ruled the Isle of Man for the Plantagenet kings and, though later flaunting their Norman origins, were heirs to a far older Saxon heritage steeped in folk memory and myth. What is historically certain is that Thomas Stanley was created 1st Earl of Derby by his stepson Henry VII, and that his descendants played a central role in the political and cultural life of England: they were patrons of William Shakespeare, became one of the most significant of Tory – and later Conservative – families, and today, just like the Thynnes, run one of the nation's most popular safari parks.

The eagle of the Lathoms

Perched atop the Stanley family home of Knowsley Hall near Liverpool is a huge stone sculpture of an eagle, its wings outstretched. The statue's base is difficult to make out, but the bird seems to be perching on a bundle of... something. To determine exactly what you're looking at, it helps to read the blazon of the Earls of Derby's heraldic arms, which can be found in the pages of *Burke's Peerage*. The eagle is the family's crest: *'On a chapeau gules doubled ermine an eagle, wings extended or, preying on an infant in its cradle proper, swaddled gules, the cradle laced or'*.

The infant upon which the eagle peers down is said to be Sir Thomas Lathom who, in the fourteenth century, was lord of Knowsley and the lands of Lathom. Sir Thomas did exist. So, too, did his daughter and heiress Isabel Lathom (1364–1414) and her husband John Stanley (1350–1414) who – by his marriage – gained ownership of the Knowsley estate that has been in the Stanley family ever since. The great eagle, however, almost certainly did *not* exist. The Stanley crest stems from a legend told by generations of Stanleys about their Lathom ancestor, Thomas. It was said that Thomas was a foundling child, discovered in an eagle's nest in nearby Terlestowe Woods by the aged and childless owner of the Knowsley lands. This old man took the child back to his hall and made him his heir, thus the origins of the last lord of Lathom were never known. It's an interesting story and, like many a family legend, makes up for lack of knowledge about true origins. The Lathoms appear to have owned their estates since at least the 1100s and may actually have used an eagle crest some generations before Sir Thomas's supposed discovery in a nest. The Stanley family, who became their genealogical successors and adopted the crest, are much better documented.

The House of Stanley descends from an Adam de Stanley (c. 1125–1200) born Adam de Audley to a Norman family who gained control of the manor of Stanley during the troubled reign of King Stephen. The place name he adopted is thought to derive from the term 'stoney meadow' (*Stonely*, Stanley). It came to Adam through marriage to Joan, daughter of an ancient Saxon family previously known as Stonely. A few generations down this line of Norman-Saxons, we come to the Sir John Stanley, Knight of the Garter, who married Isabel Lathom. And here, the national significance of the family truly begins.

The kings of man

As a garter knight, Sir John Stanley was clearly a man of consequence during the reigns of Richard II and Henry IV. He is recorded as being Lord Deputy of Ireland and Constable of Windsor Castle. But delve further into the symbolism of the Stanley coats of arms, and an historic title of genuine or at least quasi-royal status is revealed. In many of the quartered achievements, a distinctive, even bizarre, charge is included. The heralds describe it as '*gules, three legs armed and flexed in triangle*'. It is best seen to be understood, and is now displayed on the flag of the Isle of Man.

Stanley's association with the wind-swept island in the Irish Sea began in 1405 when King Henry IV granted him the fiefdom. It was a mark of solemn trust from the king, for the island's location made it strategically important, and gave whoever controlled it had enormous influence on a par with the most powerful marcher lord. For most of the early Middle Ages, the Isle of Man had been fought over by successive rulers from Norwegian Vikings to Scottish and English chieftains, and later Monarchs. The kings of England saw control of the island as vital to the defence of their realm. Henry IV experienced first-hand how dangerous it could be to place its lordship in the wrong hands; its previous holder, Henry Percy, Earl of Northumberland, rebelled against him, leading waves of invasion. The king duly stripped the Percy of his lands and transferred the Isle of Man to John Stanley.

The status of the island was questionable. Today it is a self-governing Crown Dependency, but when John Stanley was granted the fief, it was described as a 'sovereign lordship'. The word sovereign suggests an unusual degree of independence from the kingdom of England. Indeed, the lords of Man at this time have even been described as 'kings' in their own right. Some histories name John Stanley and his namesake son as 'King John I' and 'King John II' of Man. The characters of the two Stanley kings of Man were dubious. John I had been convicted of murder in his youth but was pardoned because of his usefulness in war against the French. John II faced a number of rebellions in his small kingdom and was forced to personally bring order to his angry subjects. He is remembered for putting the laws of the island in writing for the first time.

The Stanleys retained their feudal claim to Man for several generations until it once again became contested between the English and the Scots. Meanwhile, they were concentrating their power more firmly in London. John II's son, Sir Thomas Stanley (1405–1459) was issued a writ of summons to Parliament in 1451, creating him Baron Stanley. The king demanding Stanley's presence in Westminster was Henry VI, the timid Lancastrian whose mental breakdown would trigger the Wars of the Roses. Stanley's son, who succeeded as 2nd Baron in 1459, became a pivotal figure in that conflict and was there to witness its very end.

Stepfather to the king: Thomas Stanley, 1st Earl of Derby

The actions and intentions of Thomas Stanley throughout the Wars of the Roses defy a simple explanation. When the final battle came at Bosworth Field, his position was as confusing as ever. Often said to have 'betrayed Richard III' at the pivotal moment, and handing victory to Henry Tudor, the previous thirty years has seen Stanley flip sides between Lancaster and York so many times that it is difficult to say which House he was betraying at any given moment.

In that respect he was very like his brother-in-law Richard Neville, Earl of Warwick, the notoriously fickle 'Kingmaker'. Stanley had married Warwick's sister Eleanor in 1451, allying himself with the traditionally Yorkist Nevilles. Stanley's son George followed suit, marrying the daughter of a Woodville, sister of the Yorkist Edward IV's wife. By the time Richard III came to the throne, Stanley was such an avowed Yorkist that he was given the great mace to carry at the king's coronation. Yet by the same time, his Neville wife – and mother of his eleven children – had passed away, and Stanley had remarried to an arch-Lancastrian. Margaret Beaufort was the mother of the last Lancastrian claimant to the throne, Henry Tudor. Stanley was in fact highly suspect in the eyes of Richard III. But the king apparently decided to trust this immensely powerful magnate who had somehow found favour with both bunches of warring roses. That trust did not survive news of the invasion of Stanley's stepson Henry Tudor. As the Battle of Bosworth approached, Lord Stanley was viewed by Richard not only with mistrust, but as a significant threat to his throne. When Stanley sought permission to leave court and visit his estate at Lathom, Richard insisted that Stanley's son and heir, George, should remain behind, a hostage to ensure the House of Stanley's loyalty.

There is disagreement about what Lord Stanley did next, after Henry Tudor began his march through England. King Richard ordered Stanley to muster his troops and lead them to meet Tudor's army. It is possible, however, that Stanley and his brother Sir William had already met with Henry, and even settled upon a plan to overthrow Richard. Becoming stepfather to a king must surely have proved far more tempting a prospect than staying loyal to the flailing usurper Richard. In the event, Stanley famously sat and watched the battle unfold from a safe distance, rather than launch in with his troops. His brother Sir William did take part, however – and on the side of Henry Tudor. That intervention proved decisive, bringing the battle to its climax and the Tudors to the throne. Some accounts say that Richard, seeing that he was betrayed, gave a final order on the battlefield to execute the captive Stanley heir. Baron Stanley was said to have retorted with indifference: 'Sire,' he said, 'I have other sons.' William Shakespeare recounts the resolution of the hostage situation at the end of his play, *Richard III*:

Richmond (Henry Tudor): Great God of heaven, say Amen to all!
　But tell me, is young George Stanley living?
Derby: He is my lord and safe in Leicester town...

Strictly speaking, Lord Stanley was not yet 'Derby' at this point, though he is called so throughout the play. In fact, Thomas was only elevated to become the 1st Earl of Derby two months after Bosworth, on 27 October 1485. Still, it was a remarkable feat. In managing to navigate the Wars of the Roses to their conclusion, Stanley was more successful than many of his contemporaries, including the Duke of Norfolk who lay slain, and the so-called Kingmaker, Warwick.

The Kingmaker-in-law

Like Stanley, his brother-in-law Richard Neville had divided loyalties to Lancaster and York. Unlike Stanley, however, Neville was not one to sit out a battle and see which way the wind was blowing. Once Neville pinned his colours to a mast, the 'Kingmaker' led the fight with gusto.

　The ancient earldom that fell to Neville (which dated to 1098) was deemed to be inheritable through the female line and – as with the earldom of Arundel – was associated with the ownership of a great castle. Neville came into possession of Warwick Castle through his marriage to Anne Beauchamp and thus became the 16th Earl of Warwick.

Earl Richard was originally a supporter of the Lancastrian king, Henry VI. Disputes over land then led him to intervene on the Yorkist side, commanding troops at the Battle of Towton in 1461. Later, Warwick changed his mind about his choice of king, enlisted the help of the King of France and sailed into England with an invasion fleet to restore Henry VI, whom he had previously helped overthrow. Warwick died at the Battle of Barnet in 1471 defending the Lancastrian regime. His earldom passed to a minor royal descendant of the Beauchamps before becoming extinct. (The title has been recreated three times since then and has been held by the Greville family since 1759.)

Although Thomas Stanley, as Head of the House, commanded his feudal retainers, it was his brother William whose actions at Bosworth won the day for Henry Tudor. William was rewarded with posts including Lord Chamberlain and Chamberlain of the Exchequer. Like his brother, William had switched sides during the Wars of the Roses. Remarkably, although he survived the final battle of the wars by switching his allegiance to Henry, he was to lose his life ten years later for betraying the Tudor king in favour of the Plantagenet pretender Perkin Warbeck. It is not known just how committed William Stanley really was to the Warbeck Rebellion, even though he confessed to involvement. His execution by Henry VII in 1495 is a bizarre instance of a man snatching defeat from the jaws of a famous victory, a decade after the fact.

The strange baroness

Luckily for the continuance of the Stanley line, 'Young George Stanley,' as Shakespeare called him – the heir apparent who had survived his hostage ordeal – did not follow his uncle William's lead. George was already a baron in his own right at the Battle of Bosworth, thanks to his marriage to Joan, 9th Baroness Strange. Despite Joan being the inheritor of her father's title (one created by writ allowing it to pass through the female line) it was her husband George who was summoned to Parliament, a new writ making him Lord Strange by right of his wife, in 1482.

> ### Related family: The Ferrers
>
> Why 'Derby' for the Stanley earldom? There had been earls of Derby before 1485, dating to the war between King Stephen and Matilda, when a landowner named Robert Ferrers successfully commanded Stephen's troops at the Battle of the Standard (1138), and was duly rewarded for his services. The Ferrers earls of Derby held extensive estates in Derbyshire and Staffordshire in the thirteenth century. Particularly notable was the 3rd Earl, William, who married the heiress of the Peverils of Peveril Castle, Lords of Royal Forest of the Peak. He later went on crusade and died at the Siege of Acre in 1190. The family's undoing came in 1266 when the title and lands were confiscated by the king after an ill-conceived rebellion by the 6th Earl. The Derby title then became a royal possession, passing into the House of Lancaster (and used by Henry IV before his rise to the throne). The Ferrers family had, meanwhile, survived their demotion; the granddaughter of the last Ferrers earl, Alianore, went on to marry Thomas Lathom, the true grandfather of Isabel Lathom and ancestress of the Stanleys. So it is that today's Earl of Derby descends from those who, before 1066, had been Lords of Ferrieres in Normandy.

Joan le Strange's surname does not mean 'peculiar' but rather refers to 'a stranger' or a foreign person. It is apt for Joan, a figure who is a stranger to us today. It's a mark of the patriarchy of the times that so few details are known of the life of Joan le Strange, while plenty are recorded of her husbands. George Stanley, Baron Strange, became a Knight of the Garter and Constable of several strategic castles. He did not, however, succeed as the Earl of Derby, having died before his father in 1503 in somewhat strange circumstances. Lord Strange had been banqueting at Derby House in London (the site of the College of Arms today) where it is believed that he was poisoned. Just who murdered him, we don't know. But with George dead, it was his and Joan's son that went on to succeed as the 2nd Earl of Derby (and 10th Baron Strange). The earls of Derby held the Strange barony until the death of the 5th Earl when it was allowed to fall into abeyance. The title was recreated – strangely enough, by mistake – for later earls when they were summoned to Parliament under 'Baron Strange' in the belief the title was extant! A strange barony indeed.

The artistic earls

In the three centuries following Bosworth, the Earls of Derby were much better known for their contributions to the arts than to warfare. The 5th Earl, Ferdinando Stanley (1559–1594) maintained a company of actors and was a patron to some of the biggest literary names of the English Renaissance. These included the playwright Christopher Marlowe (author of *The Tragical History of Dr Faustus*) and the poet Edmund Spenser (composer of *The Faerie Queene*, a fantastical tribute to Elizabeth I). The earl was a passionate lover of music, dance, poetry and theatre. His acting troupe (known as Lord Strange's Men before his accession to the earldom, and then as Lord Derby's Men) included acrobats and entertainers as well as dramatic actors, but it later settled into a more focused theatrical company. It is possible that the troupe included William Shakespeare. Lord Derby's Men certainly produced many of Shakespeare's plays; *A Midsummer Night's Dream* was likely first performed at the wedding of William Stanley, the earl's son, who had recently succeeded as the 6th Earl.

Ferdinando Stanley died after falling suddenly ill at Knowsley Hall in similar circumstances to Lord Strange. Once again, murder was suspected (in this case the use of poisoned mushrooms, and once again, the identity of the murderer is open to speculation. One theory is that the earl was the victim of a group of conspirators who had tried to enlist his support for their plot to overthrow Queen Elizabeth I. Though the earl was not known to be particularly religious, he was identified by one of the Catholic rebels, Richard Hesketh, as a potential candidate to replace the queen. (Stanley had a trickle of royal blood, descending through his mother from Mary Tudor, sister of Henry VIII.) Lord Derby was not at all interested in deposing the queen or in being king, but he was allegedly threatened with death by Hesketh if he did not go along with the plotters. Derby called Hesketh's bluff and turned him over to the chief minister William Cecil. The question remains as to whether the remaining plotters carried out their threat to kill the earl.

Family seats: Lathom House and Knowsley Hall
Knowsley Hall stands upon the Lathom lands near Liverpool that came to the Stanleys by the celebrated marriage of Isabel Lathom to John I Stanley, King of Man. It was originally a hunting lodge in the grounds of a much larger seat, Lathom House. Although called a 'house', the structure built by the Stanleys at the end of the fifteenth century, was one of the most formidable castles ever seen in England. The old Lathom family undoubtedly had a stronghold on the site before that, but the Stanley building was immense. Its curtain wall was six feet thick, surrounded by a moat. It had eighteen towers, crowned by the central keep which loomed above all others: the Eagle Tower. That name was of course an allusion to the Stanley Legend and crest.

The castle stood for some centuries until the English Civil War proved its undoing. The 7th Earl of Derby, James, was an ardent Royalist, with Lathom House serving as a major Cavalier stronghold. It was besieged twice by the Parliamentarians and its fortifications later demolished. The earl retreated to the safety of the Isle of Man, the Stanleys' old home, which King Charles I had re-granted and ordered to be fortified. As Lord of Man, the earl offered shelter to many fleeing Royalists. Never giving up the cause, he took part in the last major battle of the war at Worcester in 1651. Soon after that, he was captured and beheaded at Bolton. Nothing now remains of the castle.

James Stanley's grandson, the 10th Earl, was responsible for turning what had been the hunting lodge of Lathom into the grand Georgian mansion now known as Knowsley Hall. Its eagle is not a formidable tower, but the statue atop a beautiful house of red sandstone.

In the nineteenth century, the 13th Earl continued his family's patronage of the arts. Something of a zoologist, he kept a private menagerie at Knowsley where he employed the artist and poet Edward Lear to be his draughtsman between 1832 and 1836. Lear famously drew birds from life rather than from taxidermy models and skins, as was the norm. Lear certainly had plenty of live subjects to choose from at Knowsley: nearly 1300 birds (and over 300 mammals) were found to be living at Knowsley upon the earl's death in 1851. Derby and Lear proved quite a partnership. Both have parrots named after them, Lear's Macaw and the Derbyan Parakeet. Much of the earl's natural history collection is today housed at the World Museum, Liverpool. Lear, meanwhile, is best remembered for his nonsense poetry, most famously *The Owl and the Pussycat* (first published 1870).

While the 13th Earl's parakeet may be a rather obscure memorial, the Derby name is more famously commemorated. The annual

Derby horse race run at Epsom each June is named after Edward, 12th Earl of Derby. Edward was the host of the inaugural race on 4 May 1780. The race is now the most prestigious of the five flat racing Classics, and its longevity has meant that the Derby name enjoys international renown (the Kentucky Derby borrows its name from the English race).

Lord Derby's premierships

It was not until the nineteenth century that an Earl of Derby had as significant an impact on national events as the 1st Earl did back in 1485. And when Edward, 14th Earl, rose to the pinnacle of the British government, he proved just as fickle as his ancestor. He switched political parties between Whigs and Tories just as easily as Thomas Stanley had once switched allegiance between Lancaster and York.

Edward Smith-Stanley (his grandfather had added 'Smith' to the surname in honour of his mother) began his career as a Whig, serving in Earl Grey's government, but later joined the Tories. The motives for his party defections are as complex as the 1st Earl's. Seemingly progressive, he set up a board of education for Ireland and oversaw the passage of the Abolition of Slavery Bill. But he left Grey's government due to his opposition to the Great Reform Act, which he considered far too radical in its expansion of democracy. Then, as a Conservative Prime Minister, he is best remembered for the Second Reform Act of 1867.

Rather than a contradictory or capricious figure, however, Derby might be seen as an independent who occupied the 'middle ground' of politics. He rejected what he saw as the radical liberal agenda of the Whigs and the reactionary right of the Tory party, and he attempted to chart a course through the centre. As leader of the breakaway 'Derby Dilly' group of MPs, he would have been remembered as the founder of the modern Conservative Party, except that his achievements were overshadowed by those of his contemporary, Sir Robert Peel. Derby had a plan to moderate the Tories and thus widen their popular appeal, announcing his programme in the 'Knowsley Speech' in December 1834. Unfortunately for him, Peel's 'Tamworth Manifesto' had been issued three days before, gazumping the Stanleyite's effort and becoming the foundation document of modern, moderate conservatism, accepting democratisation and reform where it was needed to correct injustices or abuse

Nevertheless, Derby was a towering political figure, the first person to serve three separate times as Prime Minister. David Cannadine assesses him favourably: 'Although almost entirely forgotten today, Derby was one of the great figures of nineteenth-century British public, social and cultural life: he was a fine debater, a classical scholar of note and a significant patron of the turf.'

'Patron of the turf' is a title that could well be conferred on all subsequent earls of Derby. The current Earl, the 19th in line of descent from the stepfather of Henry Tudor, is a breeder and owner of racehorses. He also runs Knowsley Safari Park, opened by his father the 18th Earl in 1971 in emulation of Longleat's. The menagerie-owning 13th Earl would very much approve of this park, eight miles from Liverpool city centre, home to lions, cheetahs, monkeys, giraffes, zebras, elephants and antelope. Knowsley Hall itself today plays host to weddings, conferences, and guests.

In another uncanny example of history repeating itself, in 1995 the 19th Earl of Derby married the Honourable Caroline Neville, member of the same House as the 1st Earl's wife, Eleanor. This Stanley-Neville couple have three children including the heir apparent, Edward, Lord Stanley. He served as a page of honour for several state events. He attended Prince William during his installation as a Knight of the Garter in 2008.

King Edward III
|
John of Gaunt = Katherine Swynford (m.1396)
(1340-1399)   (1350-1403)
|
John Beaufort
Earl of Somerset
|
├───┐
Edmund Beaufort (d.1455)   John Beaufort
2nd Duke of Somerset   1st Duke of Somerset
| |
Henry Beaufort   Margaret Beaufort
3rd Duke of Somerset   m. Edmund Tudor
| |
Charles Somerset (1460-1526) = Elizabeth Herbert   King Henry VII
1st Earl of Worcester   (1476-1507)
|
3 generations through
the male line to
|
Henry Somerset (d.1646) = Anne Russell
1st Marquess of Worcester
|
Edward Somerset
2nd Marquess of Worcester
|
Henry Somerset (1629-1700) = Mary Capell
1st Duke of Beaufort   (1630-1715)
|
10 generations through
the male line to
|
David Somerset (1928-2017) = Caroline Thynne
11th Duke of Beaufort   (1928-1995)
|
Henry Somerset (b.1952)
12th Duke of Beaufort

The Somersets of Badminton House

Duke of Beaufort

Dukedom created	1682
Monarch	Charles II
Subsidiary titles	Marquess of Worcester; Earl of Worcester; Baron Herbert (abeyance, 1984)

The House of Somerset is the last remaining shoot of the Plantagenet tree surviving in England. Their surname would in theory be Plantagenet, but for the fact that they descend from an illegitimate son of a royal prince born outside wedlock, and by medieval tradition unable to inherit the family name (hence the invented surname 'Somerset'). If not for illegitimacy, the Somersets would have a good claim to the English throne, for they form an unbroken male line from King Edward III of the 'old' royal family. Instead, they have had to make do with peerages. Henry Somerset was created a duke in 1682 'in consideration of noble descent from Edward III'. The choice of 'Beaufort' for his title was a reference to a castle in the Champagne region of France once owned by his royal ancestor, John of Gaunt.

Badminton House is the family seat today, where, in 1949, the 10th Duke established the famous Badminton Horse Trials. This duke was Master of the Horse to Elizabeth II and Master of the Beaufort Hunt for so long that he became known simply as 'Master'. The Beauforts' long association with field sports is reflected in impressive artworks at Badminton, but in the twenty-first century, has become a controversial aspect of their heritage. Politically, they were founding fathers of Toryism and have remained Conservatives to their core.

Before the Somersets

The arms of the Duke of Beaufort are an almost exact copy of the Royal Arms used by King Edward III (1312–1377). Quartered, they feature the three lions of the kingdom of England that Edward inherited from his father, and the fleurs-de-lys of the kingdom of France which he thought he should have inherited through his mother Isabella of France. Almost an exact copy, but for an additional feature: a blue and white border surrounding the Royal Arms. In heraldry, it is termed a 'bordure compony', the traditional mark of bastardy.

There was a time when being illegitimate carried a significant social stigma. William the Conqueror himself was widely known as William the Bastard in a derogatory sense before he gained his more glorious epithet at Hastings. But the existence of royal children born of extra-marital affairs was increasingly seen as a simple fact of courtly life. Kings would not only acknowledge illegitimate children as their own but sometimes grant them titles, allowing them to establish their own noble dynasties.

Such was the case with the Somerset family, whose roots go back to the illegitimate offspring of John of Gaunt, Duke of Lancaster and Aquitaine. John was a royal prince, fourth son of Edward III, and a formidable military leader. His legitimate children founded a royal cadet known as the House of Lancaster (the red rose of the

Wars for the Roses). But Gaunt also had several children by his mistress Katherine Swynford.

Confusingly for this story, Gaunt's illegitimate offspring were not initially given the name Somerset and the title of Beaufort, but rather the surname Beaufort and the title of Somerset! The family was known originally as the House of Beaufort and held the very first creation of the dukedom of Somerset (long before the Seymours were heard of). The reason for the eventual reversal of title and surname was a further illegitimacy some decades later, when Henry Beaufort, 3rd Duke of Somerset, himself took a mistress, Joan Hill, and produced a bastard son of his own. That son could not use the Beaufort surname and so was christened 'Charles Somerset' instead, taking his surname from his father's title. Two centuries later, when Charles's Somerset descendants were created dukes, they were given their ancestors' old surname for a title. It's a bewildering story of dynastic conventions masking a simple fact: the House of Somerset is the legacy of John of Gaunt and a woman whose ambition brought her from servant and mistress to Duchess of Lancaster: Katherine Swynford.

Katherine Swynford, mother of the Beauforts

Beaufort Castle no longer exists. It once stood on a hill in Montmorency-Beaufort in north-eastern France and must have been quite a sight in its day, for its name translates as beautiful fortress. In the 1370s it was under the control of the English. The Hundred Years War was raging, with Edward III claiming the throne of France and his children launching military expeditions, capturing vast swathes of land across the Channel. In 1370, when Edward's heir the Black Prince was losing ground in Aquitaine, the king commanded his other sons to go to the aid of their brother. Among them was John, Duke of Lancaster.

Born at Ghent (then known as Gaunt) in 1340, John inherited his father's compulsion to claim foreign thrones. In 1372, he declared himself to be King of Castile by right of his wife, the Spanish Infanta Constance. Constance was Gaunt's second wife, but very soon after marrying her in 1371, he began an affair with Katherine Swynford. The daughter of a German knight, Katherine was governess to Gaunt's children. Not long after delivering news to Gaunt (who was insisting on being addressed as 'My Lord of Spain') that his wife had given birth to a daughter, Katherine herself gave birth to a son. This apparently happened at Beaufort Castle, which had become Gaunt's base. Three more children were born to Gaunt and Swynford, and all were surnamed Beaufort.

One, Henry, was a churchman appointed a cardinal by Pope Martin V. His contribution to the Hundred Years War was to be present for part of the trial of the French heroine (later saint) Joan of Arc. Katherine was not satisfied with the 'tainted' status of her children. This issue was rectified following the death of Constance of Castile in 1394. To general disapproval, Swynford married Gaunt, and though her children were not accepted as members of the Plantagenet House – retaining the Beaufort name – they *were* retrospectively legitimised. Katherine showed great poise in the face of what was stark hostility from members of the royal family. Most were outraged by the match, considering Katherine to be of such inferior birth that her marriage to a royal was probably illegal. Still, Katherine made her first appearance as a duchess at court, alongside Gaunt, at the St George's Day celebrations of 1396, ignoring the whispers and taunts, and then holding out for an official recognition of her marriage by the Pope, which came in September.

It was a strange twist of fate that one of Katherine's Beaufort descendants (Henry Tudor, son of Margaret Beaufort) would one day become the victor of the Wars of the Roses, while Gaunt's legitimate descendants, the House of Lancaster, would be annihilated. In fact, Katherine's grandson, Edmund Beaufort, was instrumental in starting the whole sorry conflict for the throne through his rivalry with a royal cousin, Duke Richard of York. Edmund (the direct ancestor of today's Somerset family) was one of the closest advisors of his Lancastrian cousin Henry VI, and he served as Regent of England during the king's mental breakdown. Richard grew jealous of Beaufort, who dismissed him from court entirely. This led to a revolt by the York family in 1455, marking the start of the Wars of the Roses. Edmund – by now holding the title Duke of Somerset – led the Lancastrian forces, defending his king and the legacy of their common grandfather, John of Gaunt.

At the Battle of St Albans, Edmund Beaufort was killed. The wars also claimed his son, Henry Beaufort, beheaded by the Yorkists after the Battle of Hexham. Leaving no legitimate children, Henry was the last male Beaufort. He did, however, leave a son by his mistress Joan Hill. To this son he gave the surname 'Somerset' after the title held by his himself and his father before him. So it was that the Somerset family was 'born' in the spring of 1460 with a boy named Charles.

The first Somerset: Charles, Earl of Worcester

Like many a late medieval and Tudor portrait, a painting of Charles Somerset (1460–1526) depicts its subject with his coat of arms in the background. The shield of the Beaufort family, already outlined with the 'bordure' of their illegitimacy, is further marked in Charles's case by a line stretching diagonally across it from bottom-left to top-right. Known as a 'baton sinister' this band was also a common mark of bastardy. This shield then, symbolises the two illegitimate births that separated Charles Somerset from John of Gaunt. (Today, the shield of the House of Somerset does not feature the baton sinister; it was discontinued soon after Charles's time.)

The first Somerset was twenty-five years old when Henry VII came to the throne. Henry ensured his kinsman was well looked after, allowing him to marry his wealthy ward, Elizabeth Herbert, and investing him as a Knight of the Garter. Elizabeth was a mighty heiress, with the Welsh lands of her father, the Earl of Pembroke, and Raglan Castle her inheritance (much to the annoyance of her Herbert cousin, who had to build his family an alternative seat.

Henry VIII rated Charles very highly, making him Earl of Worcester in 1514 and charging him with overseeing preparations for the so-called 'Field of the Cloth and Gold' meeting in France. The sixteenth-century international summit was a bilateral between the emerging European powers of Tudor England and Valois France. France hoped to woo its old enemy into an alliance against the expanding empire of Charles Habsburg, the Archduke of Austria who had been elected to the imperial throne of Germany and inherited Spain and the Netherlands from his mother. A lot was at stake, and the Earl of Worcester was entrusted with ensuring that England demonstrated its power on the world stage.

Somerset organised the transportation of 5000 members of England's ruling elite to France. He also oversaw the ceremonials that saw the summit become an extravagant display of English strength. It was a huge undertaking. A massive wooden castle was built at the site to house the English contingent, while gallons of wine and crates of meat had to be shipped in to feed them. Charles Somerset followed the king everywhere he went in France, riding with him to meet Francis I at Calais, and thereafter to all ceremonial events. Somerset marched with the heads of all the great dynasties – Howard, Percy, Stanley and more – in a demonstration of the might of England's noble establishment. There were lower knights of the shires in attendance also (including Sir John Seymour of Wolf Hall, father of the king's future wife.)

Lord Worcester did everything required of him to establish his own dynasty: he served the monarch loyally, he was advanced in the Peerage, and he had a suitable seat in Raglan Castle, the old Herbert home. Through his talents he ingratiated himself so successfully into the ranks of the nobility that the Somersets would remain at the right hand of monarchs right into the twenty-first century. It was no small feat for a man of illegitimate stock. Though the Somersets were not the only dynasty born of scandal.

Bar sinister

It's said that the rules preventing illegitimate children from inheriting their parents' estates and titles dates to the reign of the Saxon king, Offa of Mercia. In 786, emissaries of the Pope visited Offa and decreed that 'he who was not born of a legitimate marriage' could not inherit his throne. From this injunction originated the clauses in peerage law which allow titles of nobility to pass only to heirs 'lawfully begotten'. If it wasn't for such laws, many extinct noble Houses would still exist today. In the case of the Somersets, so too would a royal House. It would not be the only one. There would be several lines of Stuarts descending from Charles II. Though Charles did not have any legitimate offspring to inherit his throne, he had numerous children with his many mistresses. Several of his natural sons he created dukes, and these titles survive in the male line today.

Invented surnames were chosen in place of 'Stuart'. The most regally styled was Henry Fitzroy (his surname literally meaning 'son of the king') the issue of Charles' affair with Barbara Villiers. Created Duke of Grafton, his descendant Henry Fitzroy, 12th Duke, is today a music promoter who once worked with the Rolling Stones, and lives at Euston Hall in Suffolk.

Another ducal line descends from King Charles and his most famous mistress, Nell Gwyn. Nell was one of the first actresses on the English stage and immensely popular for her comedy performances. The king was besotted with her and had Nell pose in the nude for the court painter Peter Lely. The painting (which Charles concealed in his private apartments, to be viewed only by worthy individuals) depicts Nell as the goddess Venus.

It also features her baby son Charles Beauclerk as Cupid. Master Beauclerk was the king's son and became Duke of St Albans. The present duke is Murray de Vere Beauclerk.

In Scotland there is a Duke of Buccleuch who descends from James Scott, better known as the Duke of Monmouth. Scott's rebellion against his uncle James II might actually have put this illegitimate son on the throne. but the Monmouth Rebellion failed and Scott was executed. His widow, however, Anne Scott (from whom he had taken his surname) had been created Duchess of Buccleuch in her own right, and that title passed to their descendants to the present day.

Finally – in terms of Charles' ducal descendants at least – is the Duke of Richmond, who is also styled as Duc d'Aubigny in the Peerage of France. The Duchy of Aubigny was granted by King Louis XIV to Charles Lennox and his mother Louise Kerouaille (Charles II's last mistress). The family now reside at Goodwood House in West Sussex. The present Duke of Richmond founded motorsport's Goodwood Festival of Speed in 1993 and still controls Goodwood Racecourse where the annual Glorious Goodwood meeting takes place.

The horse lords

If anything defined the Somerset family from their arrival in the Renaissance to the turn of the twenty-first century, it has been their mastery of horses. As earls of Worcester, and then later as dukes of Beaufort (which they became in 1682) they produced several Masters of the Horse. This courtly office was an important one in royal households for centuries. The Master was in charge of the royal stables (and, later, kennels) with responsibility for the ceremonial and the practical work of horses and their grooms. Today, the post is entirely ceremonial, with day-to-day work carried out by the Crown Equerry, though the Master of the Horse is still required to ride alongside the Monarch at state occasions.

The 4th Earl of Worcester did so, as did his descendants the 8th and 10th Dukes of Beaufort.

There were of course other matters to attend to. The 3rd Earl of Worcester sat in judgement at the trials of both Edward Seymour and his rival Thomas Howard. The 6th Earl (and 2nd Marquess) of Worcester spent his days inventing and is said to have nearly invented the steam engine long before the days of the Industrial Revolution. The marquess published a book in 1665 entitled *A Century of Inventions*, containing descriptions of 100 contraptions he had developed. Among them was something he called a 'water-commanding engine' which some have theorised to be a prototype steam engine. It was apparently famous in its day. the Duke of Tuscany, Cosimo Medici, is said to have travelled to Lord Worcester's London workshop to see the invention. Worcester himself was very proud of it: 'I call this a Semi Omnipotent Engine, and do intend that a model thereof be buried with me.' 200 years later an attempt was made by a Victorian archaeologist named Woodcroft to locate the grave of the marquess and discover the model engine possibly buried with him. Woodcroft gained permission from the then Duke of Beaufort to open coffins in the family crypt at Raglan. Several were unearthed and searched, but Woodcroft found no sign of the model or the proof he sought of Lord Worcester's futuristic machine.

For all that, horses remained the chief interest of the Somersets in peace and in war. The 4th Earl of Worcester, Master of the Horse to James I, was described as the finest horseman of his generation. The 8th Duke of Beaufort (1824–1899) was the best-known horseman and sporting figure of his day. An expert in hound lore, his hunt meetings sometimes saw as many as 2000 horsemen sweeping over the hills. Many people today will flinch at his boast to have killed 123 foxes in 102 days in 1856, but he was hugely popular in his day. He was cheered by crowds when travelling in his carriage. This was probably due to his reputation for generosity with his money rather than his hunting skills. He would often provide meals for hundreds of guests at a time. The duke was – like most of his family – a committed Tory, and when the Earl of Derby, Edward Stanley, became Prime Minister, he almost inevitably appointed the Duke of Beaufort as Master of the Horse.

This was a position also held by the 10th Duke of Beaufort (1900–1984) who made his house at Badminton, Gloucestershire, synonymous with the sport of showjumping. After the 1948 Summer Olympics in London, the duke was inspired to begin Badminton Horse Trials. Today, along with the Kentucky Three Day Event and Burleigh Horse Trials, it is one of the Grand Slams of eventing.

Badminton House has been the seat of the Somersets since Henry, 1st Duke of Beaufort, made it his permanent base in the late 1600s. Somerset had little choice in truth, given a dramatic turn of events.

Six generations passed between the first Somerset, who became an earl in 1514, and the Somerset who became 1st Duke of Beaufort in 1682. Throughout all that time the family's main powerbase had been in Wales, on the Raglan Castle estate that they had inherited from the Herberts. Henry Somerset was born in Raglan Castle in 1629 and was originally styled as Lord Herbert of Raglan (a title that came with Raglan Castle, and which was held by the Somersets until 1984 when it fell into disuse).

The Somersets were arch-royalists and Henry was forced to flee England during the Civil War. In his absence, Raglan Castle was captured by Cromwell's forces and left a ruin from which it was never to recover. This that meant Lord Worcester, upon returning from exile, was forced to find a new seat. He decided to move to an estate in Gloucestershire that had been purchased back in 1608 by his great-grandfather, the 4th Earl of Worcester.

Family seat: Badminton House

The Badminton estate was bought originally to act as a half-way house between the Somerset's Welsh estates and London. But when it became the principal family seat – and a ducal seat at that, after Henry Somerset became 1st Duke of Beaufort – improvements were immediately begun. Henry added state rooms, built new stables for the precious Somerset horses, kennels for greyhounds and even an aviary. A banqueting house was built in the gardens, which were laid out in the formal baroque style of the period with orchards, kitchen gardens and the obligatory labyrinth. Later, the 3rd Duke commissioned William Kent to transform the exterior of the house. On the north front he added the pediment flanked by twin cupolas, the curved gables, and the long low wings which end in pavilions. Inside, he remodelled the hall to create a setting for the sporting paintings of the duke's protégé John Wootton. Kent also designed the building known as Worcester Lodge as an entrance to Badminton Park. It included a summer dining room on the first floor. The duke also swept away the formal gardens, hiring Capability Brown to create the landscape captured by Canaletto.

The tale that Badminton was the site where the game of badminton was invented is probably apocryphal. True, the entrance hall reflects the dimensions of a modern badminton court, but the idea that British army officers returning from India set up nets in the hall, creating a derivative of the ancient game of shuttlecock, is highly suspect.

After the Restoration, Lord Herbert – as Henry Somerset still was – entertained King Charles II and Queen Catherine at Badminton. Given their origins, the Somersets were staunch supporters of the Crown. King Charles was grateful for Lord Herbert's support for his brother the Duke of York against attempts to exclude him from the succession. Charles granted the dukedom of Beaufort to Henry in 1682. When James II did succeed to the throne, Somerset defended Bristol against the threatened invasion of the Duke of Monmouth. King James visited Badminton in 1686 to thank the duke personally.

Royal visits became regular at Badminton, a residence which, like its owners, is royal in all but name. And it looks it. When the Chief Justice of England visited, he was awestruck by the opulence that surrounded the 1st Duke of Beaufort. Francis North thought that only the crowned heads of Europe lived in such a manner. Even in more recent times, the royals have loved Badminton. During the Second World War, Queen Mary stayed there for the duration. She arrived with a retinue of servants in 1939 and essentially took over the house for six years (graciously allowing the Duke and Duchess of Beaufort to use a few of the rooms). Queen Elizabeth II, a famous lover of horses, was always happy to be at Badminton where she regularly stayed as a guest of her great friend, 'The Master', Henry Somerset, 10th Duke of Beaufort. She followed the Badminton Horse Trials in person from its earliest days.

The forgotten Somersets

Today, Badminton House is overseen by the 12th Duke of Beaufort, Henry Somerset (b. 1952) who is the son of the 11th Duke, Henry Somerset, and his wife, Caroline Thynne of Longleat. It is perhaps inevitable that many members of a line as long as the Somersets should be overlooked in history, particularly when shared names further obscure their identities. But pick out the lesser members of a family tree, look closer, and some fascinating figures emerge.

One forgotten Henry Somerset was a younger son of the 8th Duke. He led a tragic life, his marriage collapsing after his wife revealed that he was homosexual. She was ostracised by society for publicly shaming her husband, and he withdrew to Italy to live out the rest of his life. There, he composed music that was relatively popular in its day, including *A Song of Sleep* (1903) and a successful musical accompaniment to Christina Rossetti s *Echo*

(1900). He was also a poet, publishing a book in 1889 entitled *Songs of Adieu*. Literary scholars consider it an important book of verse by a member of a clandestine circle of *fin de siecle* homosexual poets and writers. Outside of academia, Lord Henry Somerset is now obscure. He died in Florence in 1932 aged eighty-two.

Also now shrouded in the historic mists are several Mary Somersets who were as famous as any of the dukes in their time. The first Duchess of Beaufort, born Mary Beauchamp, was one of the foremost botanists in an age when gardens – including that at Badminton – had rarely been as prominent. Mary was a renowned collector and propagator of plant species, and she was in communication with all the principal botanists. She obtained seeds and plants from all over the world, from the East and West Indies, from the Canary Islands to the Cape, China and the Americas. In so doing, Mary introduced many new varieties into England. Diffident about her abilities, in her letters to the experts she asks to be forgiven for not understanding the Latin names of plants.

Another Mary Somerset was a daughter of the 4th Duke. She was a celebrity of the Georgian Age of fashion and gossip columns. Like many of her contemporaries, her political interests were thwarted by her gender, though it is known she corresponded with Prime Minister Pitt on behalf of others. Also like her contemporaries, she was celebrated more for her beauty than her work. The author Nathaniel Wraxall wrote that Mary Somerset was 'Grace itself formed in limbs' and that 'the Plantagenets could not have been represented by a more faultless sample of female loveliness'.

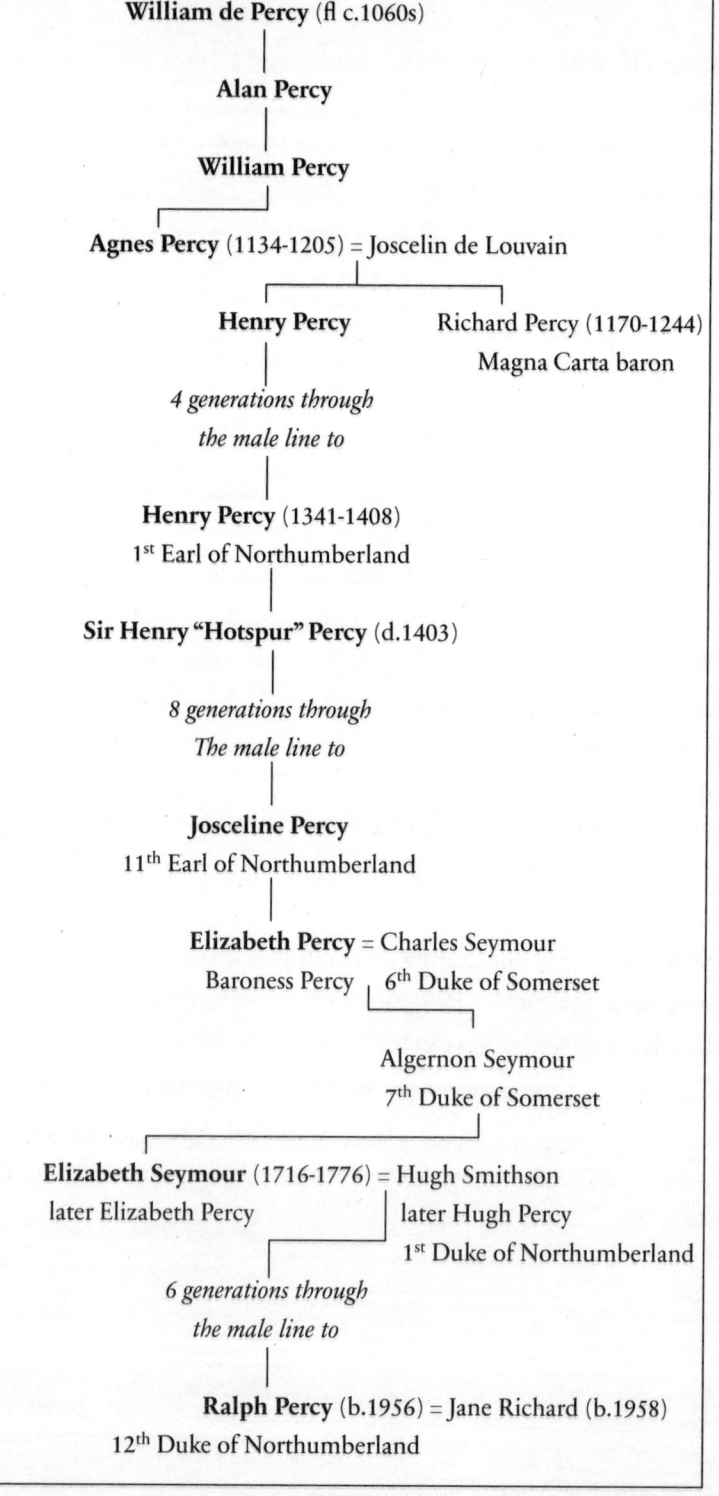

The Percys of Alnwick Castle

Duke of Northumberland

Dukedom created	1766
Monarch	George III
Subsidiary title	Earl Percy

The present Duke of Northumberland descends from a knight named William de Percy (c. 1030–1096), scion of a Norman family whose line stretched back to the 9th-century origins of the Duchy of Normandy itself. He arrived in England in 1067. From then – and for nearly 1,000 years – the Percys have been among the most powerful dynasties of warlords in the North. Their history in the Peerage is second to none: barons since the Conquest, Lords of Alnwick from the turn of the fourteenth century, Earls of Northumberland from the reign of Richard II, Dukes of Northumberland in the Georgian heyday of landed society. By contrast, the name of Percy itself has died out twice in the male line over that time and been subsequently adopted by the sons of an heiress. The estates, centred around the formidable Alnwick Castle in Northumberland, have remained largely intact, even through the inheritance battles and the real battles of so many generations.

The kings in the north

When the Roman Emperor Hadrian built a wall across the north of Britannia in the second century through what is now Cumbria and Northumberland, garrisoning legions along its length, he was answering a threat that would vex English rulers for millennia to come: the danger that came from the north of invasion. After the fall of Rome, the ancestors of the Scots and English fought over the borderlands. Swathes of Northumberland changed hands through battle and counterattack. The medieval kings of England – seated far to the south in London, and unable to move their forces north quickly enough to meet any surprise invasion from Scotland – needed their own legions stationed on the border, just as Hadrian had. The kings also needed loyal generals to command the defence of the realm. Whichever nobles were granted this task were in a privileged position. They knew that the king relied on them militarily, and thus that they held uncommon influence (or leverage) over the monarch. More than this, the nobility of the north were expected to govern their lands with near-sovereign authority. It was simply impossible for the king to administer the entire country from London, so the northern vassals did so on the king's behalf, making 'The North' a virtual principality, and its lords pseudo-monarchs. They were certainly of far more importance to the communities who lived in places like Northumberland than any of the crowned heads in Westminster.

All of this is why the Percys became so powerful. It was this noble House that became the marcher lords of the north of England, charged with keeping watch over the borders. The north – and not just the English north – seems to have been in their blood. The family traced its descent to a Northman, a Viking chieftain named Mainfred, who had given up his voyaging lifestyle to settle in the north of France in 886. This was before even Rollo the Walker, the Norse leader who besieged Paris around the same year, was granted lands by the Frankish king that stretched from the beaches to the River Epte and became the first Duke of Normandy. (The place name stems from Norse – or north.) Thus, Mainfred's family dwelt in close proximity to the family of the Norman dukes, who in time would come to rule England.

Mainfred's descendants were settled in the Caen region of Normandy, in a fief named Perci. From there, they took their name, and from there William de Percy (c. 1030–1097) followed Duke William of Normandy across the Channel and founded the Percy family of England.

William de Percy is referred to in some contemporary documents as '*Als Gernons*', a nickname that literally means 'bewhiskered'. The existence of his whiskers is therefore better recorded than his arrival from Normandy, details of which are sketchy. Percy first appears in English history amongst the warband of Hugh d'Avranches, known as 'the Wolf', for his ferocity in battle (and a member of Grosvenor family. Hugh granted Percy lands in Yorkshire, the county that became the family's first powerbase. They included Topcliffe, of which they became feudal barons, and Whitby on the north Yorkshire coast. It was appropriate that a dynasty whose fame would arise from a demi-royal status in the north, and from their loyalty to Roman Catholicism, should have made their first home in Whitby. This was an ancient seat of northern power, founded by the Saxon kings of Northumbria. It was also the site of the 7th-century Church Synod of Whitby, which helped unite English Christians with Rome in their customs and practices. St Hilda (niece of the first pagan king of Northumbria to convert to Christianity, King Oswy) had founded an abbey at Whitby which had fallen into disuse; William de Percy reestablished it and appointed his brother as its abbot. The ruins of the Benedictine monastery still stand atop the cliffs overlooking the North Sea, and although most of the Percy abbey was replaced by later buildings, the heart of William de Percy still lies there – apparently literally. Percy left England sometime after 1096, joining the First Crusade with William the Conqueror's son, Robert Curthose, and marching to the Holy Land. Percy was, by all accounts, in sight of Jerusalem when he died of causes unknown. He never took part in the Siege of Antioch but was buried there soon after. Some accounts tell of how his heart was removed from his body and returned to Yorkshire where it was interred somewhere in Whitby Abbey. Whether or not this is true, Percy's heart – metaphorically if not in fact – certainly resided in Whitby.

Lords of Alnwick

William de Percy's direct male line was to last only three generations after his death. In the mid-1100s, his great-granddaughter, Agnes Percy, was his sole heiress. She married very grandly as befitted her position to a brother-in-law of Henry I named Jocelin of Louvain. Their sons took their mother's name of Percy (as Agnes's husband had at their marriage) and continued the family's illustrious traditions. The elder son Henry (d.1198) is the ancestor of today's Percy family. But the younger son, Richard (d. 1244) achieved greater immortality as one of the twenty-five landed magnates appointed to oversee the provisions of the Magna Carta in 1215. From this, their first famous rebellion against royal power, the Percys would go on to play arguably the longest continuous role in challenging the monarch's authority. If it was a truism that the greatest threat to kings came not from foreign invaders but from the noble dynasties of England, then the Percys were perhaps the most powerful enemies the Crown ever had.

Nevertheless, the Crown needed them, and if the Percys were happy with their monarch, they served the realm dutifully. Henry Percy (1273–1314) was Keeper of Northern Marches for Edward I, and he battled the Scots with relish. He was not so much a guard against Scotland as its scourge. As part of King Edward's wars with Scotland – which saw the English king claim the Scots throne – Percy managed to extend his border northward, gaining several Scottish baronies.

It was also this Henry who acquired the estate of Alnwick in Northumberland, which remains the family seat today. He purchased the castle and barony from the Bishop of Durham, establishing the Percys as Northumberland's premier warring dynasty; the deeds to the property, signed and sealed in 1309, can still be viewed at Alnwick. It was on the seal of this 1st Baron Percy of Alnwick, that the 'modern' coat of arms of Percy was first recorded. Until then the Percy shield had displayed golden diamonds (or *fusils*) on a blue field. Henry discarded those 'ancient' arms in favour of a blue lion rampant on a golden field. It is thought that the design was a nod to Henry's great-great-grandfather Jocelin of Louvain, who had hailed from Brabant in the Netherlands, and whose arms had been a golden lion on a black field before he had adopted his wife's. Henry Percy thus blended the lion symbol with the traditional colours of Percy to create a new shield combining the arms of his male line (Louvain) with those of his family name (Percy).

Henry's son, the 2nd Baron of Alnwick (1314–1352), shifted the family seat away from Yorkshire to the new estate in Northumberland, where he was closer to the Scottish marches. From Alnwick, he spent a lifetime guarding the borderlands.

Family seat: Alnwick Castle
The second largest inhabited castle in England (after Windsor), the mighty Alnwick Castle is recognisable to millions of children today after doubling as Hogwarts School of Witchcraft and Wizardry in the film version of *Harry Potter and the Philosopher's Stone*. If you visit the castle, you'll likely be invited to try out broomstick 'flying' in the grassed courtyard where Harry and his friends had

their lessons. Beloved as a film and TV location long before Potter due to its forbidding medieval appearance, Alnwick is certainly the real thing. It was begun around 1096 by Ivo de Vesci, a Norman baron tasked with guarding the strategic location in the former Saxon earldom of Northumbria. The castle was a notable fortress by the 1100s, besieged by successive kings of Scotland, including William the Lion, who was actually captured during the Battle of Alnwick in 1174.

A quintessential motte and bailey in design, and an important powerbase, Alnwick has been attacked from within the kingdom as well as from without. It changed hands numerous times during the Wars of the Roses, and after so many sieges by the 1700s the castle was lying near derelict. Its revival was the work of the dukes of Northumberland, descendants of Henry Percy who acquired the castle in 1309. The 1st Duke employed architects including James Paine and Robert Adam to repair Alnwick in the gothic style.

The most dramatic transformation was of the interiors, overseen by the 4th Duke, Algernon Percy (1792–1865). He employed the Italian architect Luigi Canina, whom he had met in Rome in 1853, to restore and design the interior apartments. Their design follows those of Renaissance Roman palaces, the duke choosing Italian artists and craftsmen to furnish a fitting ducal residence. The most striking features of the State Rooms are the carved, painted and gilded ceilings. But the lasting impression visitors take from Alnwick is the sheer contrast between its outer appearance and its inner: an impregnable and darkly medieval fortress, with a brightly sumptuous Italianate palace hiding within.

The Earls of Northumberland

When the 3rd Baron of Alnwick became the 1st Earl of Northumberland in 1377, it marked the beginning of an extraordinary period in the Percy story. The earls were exceptionally powerful magnates who were instrumental in deposing monarchs and attempting to depose many more. The 1st Earl started this tradition. Henry Percy (1342–1408) had been a great friend of King Richard II, who gave him his title. But when the king failed to show enough favour and financial reward to Percy and his son for their work fighting the Scots, Percy switched his allegiance to Henry Bolingbroke (son of John of Gaunt) and conspired with Bolingbroke to overthrow Richard. Percy helped capture the king, force his abdication, and present him to Bolingbroke. The new King Henry IV rewarded Percy with the sovereign lordship of the Isle of Man.

Percy's son and heir, who was also key to bringing Henry IV to the throne, was the most renowned of all the Percy warlords in history. Sir Henry Percy (1364–1403) was nicknamed 'Hotspur' by his enemy the Scots. He never succeeded his father, for he died five years before the earl, but his name reverberates through history more clearly than any of the Northumberlands. Hotspur fought France on land and at sea. He fought the Scots in the borders. The chronicler Froissart relates the rivalry between Hotspur and his Scottish counterpart, the Earl of Douglas, whose border wars were frequent and bloody. Their last confrontation ended in failure for both. At the so-called 'Midnight Battle', fought in the moonlight at Otterburn in 1388, Douglas was killed by Hotspur's English forces, while Hotspur was captured by the Scots and taken as a prisoner of war. It was said that he showed enormous courage during his captivity. He was released after payment of a substantial ransom. Hotspur became a romantic figure in folk history; Shakespeare subtitled his Henry IV Part One, 'The Life and Death of Henry surnamed Hotspur'.

The death of Hotspur which Shakespeare relates resulted from his – and his father's – apparent addiction to overthrowing kings. They turned on Henry IV just as they had Richard II. The new king had not proven any more eager to reward the House of Percy for its service against the Scots, nor given it the preeminent place at court which the earl and his son felt it deserved. Perhaps a little intoxicated by their own reputation (Hotspur's squire reportedly warned the king that the Percys 'Held the hearts of the people by North and ever had') they rebelled against Henry IV. This time, however, the Crown held firm. Hotspur was killed in 1403 at the Battle of Shrewsbury. His father the Earl of Northumberland fought on until, five years later at Bramham Moor in Yorkshire, he, too, was killed, bringing a definitive end to the Percy Rebellion. The lordship of Man had been taken from the family and passed to the Stanleys. The family had lost everything.

There was, however, a Percy heir yet surviving, Hotspur's son and the grandson of the 1st Earl. Ironically, young Henry Percy was forced to flee into exile in Scotland. In the long run, his father and grandfather were proven right about the Percys' exalted position in the north, and indeed the Crown could not do without them for long: Henry V restored Percy to his family lands, and he became the 2nd Earl of Northumberland in 1414. He resumed his dynasty's duties on the correct side of the border. Much of his time was spent fighting the Scots until the looming crisis within England began to encroach, and a personal rivalry between the Percys and that other northern powerhouse, the Nevilles, was subsumed into the Wars of the Roses.

At the first battle, the Earl of Northumberland was a Lancastrian, fighting under Edward Beaufort, Duke of Somerset. The pair of them were killed. His son was also a victim of the wars, killed on the defeated Lancastrian side at the Battle of Towton in 1461. Given the record, the Percys unsurprisingly switched sides. The 4th Earl was – along with John Howard, Duke of Norfolk – a key supporter of Richard III. Maybe Percy support was simply bad luck during in the fifteenth century, for Richard was unsuccessful at the Battle of Bosworth. Although his failure was partly due to the inaction of the 4th Earl of Northumberland, leader of the Yorkists reserve, who never committed his troops to the fight. Like

Thomas Stanley, who is considered to have betrayed Richard III at the pivotal moment, Henry Percy played a controversial role at Bosworth. He may have defected to Henry Tudor, or he may simply have run out of time to get involved in the battle before Richard was killed. Tudor certainly did not trust Percy; the earl was imprisoned alongside Thomas Howard. Percy was, however, released much faster than Howard, after only seven months, retaining his earldom and estates, so was perhaps trusted more than his nominal incarceration would suggest.

Catholic rebels

The Percys entered the dangerous Tudor age in opulent style; the 5th Earl was known as 'Henry the Magnificent' because he rivalled the king in the lavishness of his lifestyle. But the accession of Henry VIII marked a new phase in the struggles of the House, as the Reformation put the Percys and the Crown on a collision course. Upon Henry's break with Rome in 1536, the Catholic north erupted in rebellion. Traditionalist nobles like Sir Thomas Percy (brother of the 6th Earl and father of the 7th and 8th Earls of Northumberland) became involved in the unrest. When this 'Pilgrimage of Grace' – the most serious Catholic uprising during the reforms – ultimately failed, Thomas Percy was among the magnates executed.

The Northumberland title reverted to the Crown after the death of the 6th Earl, with the traitor Sir Thomas Percy's sons deprived of their lands. The title was almost lost to the family for good when King Edward VI handed the earldom to one John Dudley, the man who led the palace coup against the regent, Edward Seymour. Having seized power, Dudley was elevated further as Duke of Northumberland. The Percys must have seethed from the shadows. The brothers were plucked from the precipice, however, by the succession of the Catholic Queen Mary I, who executed the usurper Dudley and gave the earldom of Northumberland back to the Percys. The son of the rebellious Sir Thomas became the 7th Earl.

This turbulent period of alternate Catholic and Protestant successions saw the Percys, like the Howards, thrust from the corridors of power into the cells of the Tower, and *vice versa*, depending on the religion of a new monarch. When Queen Mary died and the Protestant Elizabeth I came to power, the 7th Earl embarked on his own pilgrimage of grace, the Northern Rising of 1569. With the Duke of Norfolk, he marched to restore Catholicism, remove the hated Protestant, William Cecil, and place Mary Stuart on the throne. This Percy fared no better than his father. He was captured and beheaded in York in 1572 (the same year the 4th Duke of Norfolk lost his head).

Even this did not end the Percys' quest to bring England back to the Catholic fold. The 9th Earl spent sixteen years in the Tower of London for complicity in the Gunpowder Plot to kill James I. He was, it appears, wrongly accused, having had no personal part in the plot. The case against him was never proven anyway, but he was still imprisoned as a precaution. The earl's cousin, Thomas Percy, was however one of Guy Fawkes s Catholic co-conspirators.

The 10th Earl, Algernon (a name which recalls the family founder's facial hair) shocked his family by marrying a Cecil. His father's anger at an alliance between a Percy and the arch Protestant family was palpable: 'The blood of Percy would not mix with the blood of Cecil if you poured it on a dish,' he is reported to have said. The marriage did not produce a son, which was an existential crisis for the House of Percy whose line was nearly spent. Algernon married again, this time to the daughter of an appropriate Catholic family, Lady Elizabeth Howard, from whom all later Percys descend through her son, the 11th Earl of Northumberland. Elizabeth brought to the Percys the great London residence henceforth known as Northumberland House, overlooking what is now Trafalgar Square.

The Percys of Alnwick Castle

The heir crisis intensified again when the 11th Earl's only son died in infancy, leaving Josceline Percy as the last remaining male Percy. His daughter Lady Elizabeth Percy was just four years old when her father died, leaving her as heiress to Alnwick. The earldom of Northumberland became extinct as did the ancient name of Percy. Or so it seemed, for that name was not to submit to oblivion so easily. For the second time in history, the name Percy would be adopted. The second revival was a more protracted and messier affair than the first, a story beginning with the lonely figure of the child Elizabeth Percy

Nicknamed Carrots due to her red hair, Elizabeth was the richest heiress in the land and as a result was married three times before she reached her sixteenth birthday. Her first husband was Henry Cavendish, who died just six months after the wedding. Her second marriage was to Thomas Thynne. He also died, in more infamous fashion. Finally, in 1682, Elizabeth married Charles Seymour, the 'Proud' Duke of Somerset. The couple had a son and a daughter. The son was Algernon Seymour, heir to both the dukedom of Somerset and the Percy estates. Algernon's own son and heir, however, died aged only nineteen, and while the dukedom of Somerset would pass to a cousin, the only person alive with a right by blood to the Percy fortune was now Elizabeth Percy's granddaughter, Elizabeth Seymour.

In time, the Alnwick estates were passed to Elizabeth Seymour. It was then that the name of Percy reemerged, in an act that stretched dynastic tradition to say the least. Lady Elizabeth Seymour was the granddaughter of the last Percy, and the great-granddaughter of the last Earl of Northumberland, who had died in 1670. Eighty years later, in 1750, Elizabeth Seymour changed her name to Percy. Her husband Hugh Smithson also adopted the name and arms of Percy, and the couple became Earl and Countess in a new creation. Just like that, the Percy earls of Northumberland were reborn at Alnwick Castle.

The Dukes of Northumberland

The Percys of today should then, by the usual conventions, be named Smithson. Sir Hugh Smithson could never have imagined that he would one day transmute into Percy, earl of Northumberland, and later 1st Duke of Northumberland. He was of an old, though far from grand, family of Yorkshire gentry. He was also deeply unpopular with every section of society, from the nobility – who balked at his vanity and his unentitled rank – to the crowds in London who once dragged him from his carriage and robbed him. Unperturbed, Hugh sought further advancement. Not enough to be an earl – the title held by generations of the great House of Percy – he believed himself worthy of a dukedom. Though it sat less than happily with the king, the former Hugh Smithson was elevated to ducal rank in 1766.

It was Hugh Percy, as he now was, who began to turn Alnwick Castle into the comfortable palace it became. He took his new position very seriously and wanted to create a residence that fit the aesthetic tastes of a Georgian duke, not a Dark Age warlord. He employed Robert Adam to redesign Alnwick and the London house at Syon. He also deployed Capability Brown to landscape the park around Alnwick.

Despite that legacy, the 1st Duke of Northumberland is a fairly obscure figure today. Ironically, it was an illegitimate son (to whom he gave the old family name of Smithson) who acquired more lasting fame, though in the United States rather than in England. James Smithson, born in secret in Paris in 1766, left his fortune to the US government, stipulating in his will that it be used to found an educational organisation under the name of the 'Smithsonian Institute'. To this day the Smithsonian Museums in Washington DC are among the most visited anywhere in the world.

Hugh's legitimate son, who became the 2nd Duke, also had history with the US, having fought against its formation. A month after the Declaration of Independence was signed in 1776, he commanded a division at the Battle of Long Island, New York, in the opening stages of the Revolutionary War.

In fact, the 2nd Duke was secretly sympathetic to the colonists. The dukes of Northumberland in general have had a reputation as modern, enlightened men. The 3rd Duke introduced a bill to abolish slavery in 1808, though it did not pass. Indeed, political success always eluded the dukes. Their iteration of the Percy dynasty never had the influence of the medieval earls. The duke did take an interest in the goings-on in Northumberland during his tenure. When Grace Darling, a twenty-two-year-old lighthouse keeper's daughter, helped rescue the crew of the shipwrecked *Forsashire* by rowing out in stormy seas from her home on the Farne Islands off Bamburgh, the duke was awestruck. He helped make Grace's story famous, and he sent her family gifts (including waterproof clothing recently invented by Charles Macintosh). The dukes of Northumberland have been associated with the Royal National Lifeboat Institution ever since.

Also known for his kindness was the 4th Duke, dubbed 'Algernon the Good'. He was a naval officer during the Napoleonic Wars before devoting his life to exploration and archaeology. He went on various expeditions in Egypt to study the pharaohs' tombs. Some of his finds were donated to the British Museum where they are still on display.

Few of the Smithson Percys have achieved great fame despite being interesting characters. The 8th Duke of Northumberland was a talented writer of ghost stories, which are all forgotten today. The 9th Duke, born in 1912, was killed in action during the retreat to Dunkirk in 1940.

The current duke, the 12th, Ralph Percy, has done much to uncover his family history, writing several books on the Percys. He learnt how to run a landed estate by working for several years in the Arundel Castle estate office of the Duke of Norfolk. His wife, Duchess Jane, is responsible for the biggest development seen on the Alnwick Castle estate for centuries. She masterminded the creation of the Alnwick Garden, the most ambitious new garden seen in England for decades, a project not attempted on a landed estate since the days of Capability Brown and Joseph Paxton. The cost was enormous, rising to the tens of millions, and caused controversy with planning authorities. Yet it proved a massive success upon first opening in 2001. Its grand cascade is reminiscent of that installed in the baroque era at Chatsworth, but decidedly more twenty-first century in design, and the entire 42-acre garden is a remarkable revival of aristocratic tradition in the modern age.

Not satisfied with merely emulating the past, the Duchess of Northumberland sought something new and intriguing for her garden. In 2005 she came up with the concept of adding a 'Poison Garden' to the site. Here is grown everything from foxgloves to belladonna, or deadly nightshade. Fenced off with black gates featuring skulls and crossbones, the garden is now the most popular attraction on the ancient Alnwick estates.

The Grosvenors of Eaton Hall

Duke of Westminster

Dukedom created	1874
Monarch	Victoria
Subsidiary title	Earl Grosvenor; Viscount Belgrave

Few surnames exude such an aristocratic aura as Grosvenor. From Grosvenor Square in exclusive Mayfair to the luxury Grosvenor House Hotel on the site of their former London mansion, the family of the dukes of Westminster have long been associated with wealth far exceeding even the usual patrician standards.

The name derives from the dynasty's founder, Gilbert le Gros Veneur, Chief Huntsman to William the Conqueror, who arrived with the Norman leader in 1066. The Grosvenors are therefore among the oldest surviving noble lines in the country. Yet paradoxically, they did not begin to climb the Peerage ladder until much more recently in their history. The title of 'Westminster' itself is the youngest dukedom in England, created by Queen Victoria in 1874.

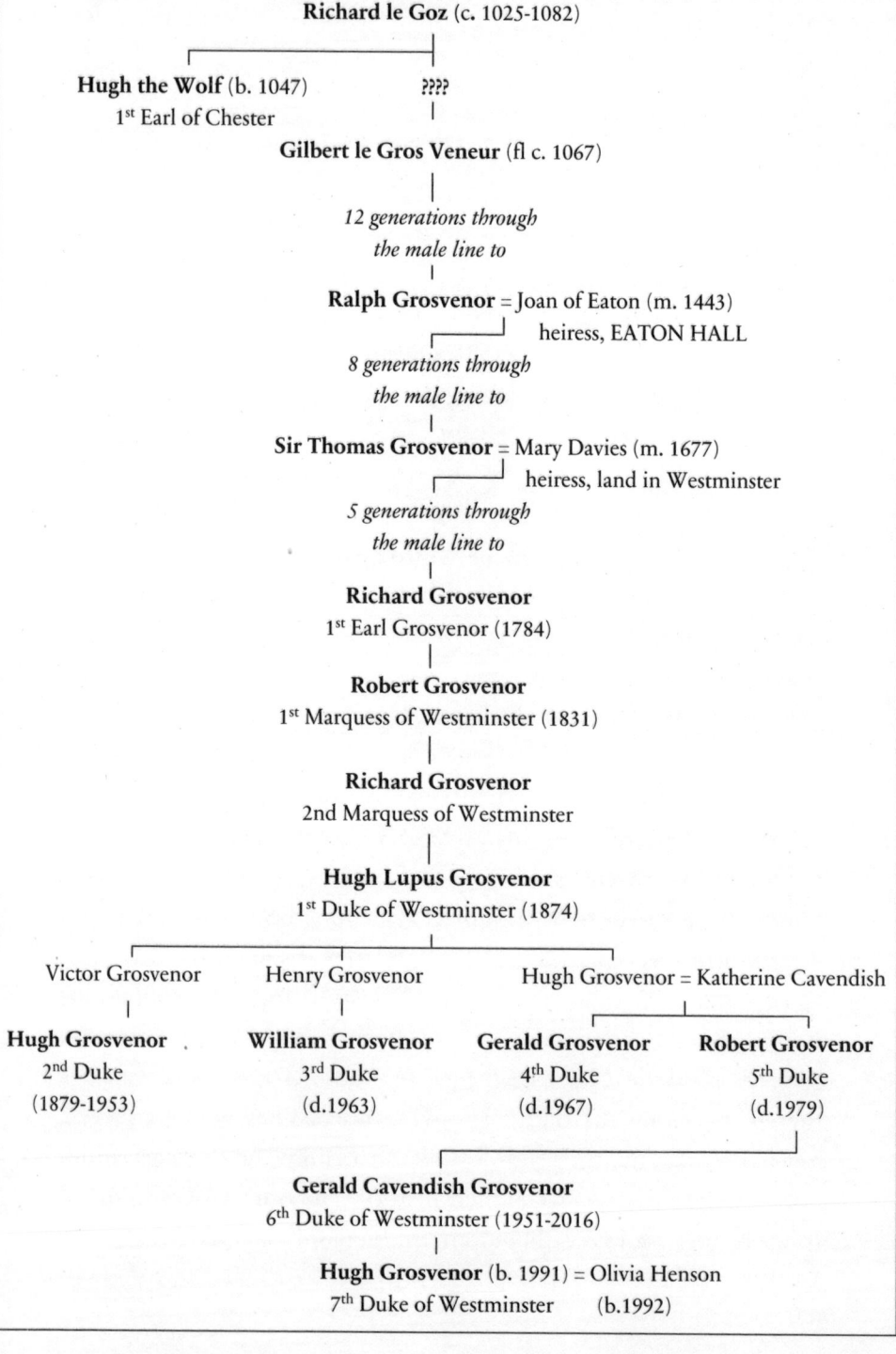

The Huntsman and the Wolf

Little is known about the Gros Veneur, the 'great huntsman' who arrived in England with William of Normandy. It is thought that he might have been a relation of William, though how close is impossible to say. Gilbert le Gros Veneur certainly did have other relations with him on arrival, most notably his uncle Hugh d'Avranches. A statue of Hugh – nicknamed Lupus, or the Wolf – now stands in the grounds of Eaton Hall in Cheshire, the Grosvenor seat. The family have been in Cheshire almost from the start; in 1071 the Conqueror made Hugh Lupus the 1st Earl of Chester. Hugh was responsible for building Chester Castle. Hugh's branch of the family maintained the earldom for several generations. His son Richard died on the White Ship alongside Henry I's heir William Adelin, so the earldom passed to his cousin. It is on the seal of Ranulf, 6th Earl of Chester (1172–1232), that the sheaf of wheat, which became a symbol of Cheshire, and appears on the Grosvenor family arms, was first seen.

It was just before that time, in 1160, that the then earl of Chester granted some lands in Cheshire to his relation Robert Grosvenor, a descendant not of the Wolf uncle, but the Huntsman nephew. These are the Grosvenors who have survived in an unbroken male line from the Conquest to the present day. The head of the House of Grosvenor is today a billionaire and, as Duke of Westminster, is generally regarded as the richest of all the peers of the realm. Cheshire was the source of their power, and Westminster would later become the source of their immense wealth. They did have other lands, too (their early fortune was made by exploiting mineral deposits under their Welsh estates). But it was the expansion of their lands in Cheshire and acquisition of lands in Westminster that turned them into the super-rich dynasty they became. And both these country and town estates were added by the most aristocratic of methods: marriage to heiresses.

Joan of Eaton and the Palatinate

Despite great wealth and an enviable lineage, for more than five centuries after the Conquest, the status of the Grosvenors was no more than that of landed gentry. It wasn't until 1622 that they received some form of hereditary title (even then a non-peerage title, baronet) and not until 1784 that they finally became nobility (as Earl Grosvenor). But they did derive significant local status as a family synonymous with the Cheshire.

In 1450, Raufe Grosvenor married the heiress Joan of Eaton, and thereby came into possession of Eaton Hall, just south of the city of Chester. The estate included the village of Belgrave, which later would lend its name to the family's London estate, Belgravia. Though not yet nobility, their Cheshire lands gave the Grosvenors a certain aristocratic burnish. Their relations had been earls of special status, for Cheshire was a 'county palatine', which gave it an unusual degree of independence from national government, operating like a miniature kingdom. Chester had its own parliament of barons rather than being represented in the English Parliament, and it retained certain special privileges as late as the nineteenth century.

Palatinates were a special form of county that emerged in Norman England. A palatinate was created when the king granted 'palatine' powers (or powers 'from the palace') to a nobleman to act in the manner of a king within their estates. This was usually because the nobleman in question was based near a border with a potential enemy and required the power to organise defences and muster armies quickly, without having to wait for a say-so from London. Palatinates were therefore closely linked to marcher lordships. The earldom of Chester was one of the earliest created by William the Conqueror to guard the border with Wales, the earls of Chester obtaining palatinate status, including powers to levy taxes and build defensive castles. The descendants of Gilbert the Great Huntsman were never earls of Chester themselves, but they were very much bound up with the identity of their Wolfish cousins who had. They even took the arms of the earls of Chester as their own. That adoption was in fact forced upon them in a controversial episode from heraldic history that ended up in court.

Scrope v Grosvenor

In 1385, King Richard II led an army north in a campaign against the Scots. He summoned noblemen and knights from across England to aid the expedition. One of the knights who answered the summons was Sir Robert Grosvenor of Cheshire. Along the way he met with a baron from Lancashire named Richard Scrope. To the pair's consternation, they found that they were bearing the same arms on their shields. The design was blazoned as *Azure, a bend Or*, a blue shield with a golden band. The two families had never come into contact before, so did not know their arms were duplicated. This was before the formation of the College of Arms which kept detailed records of grants. Yet heraldic law still prohibited the use of the same arms by separate families. An argument then ensued as to who was entitled to keep the arms.

The year after, Scrope brought a lawsuit against Grosvenor which was heard before the Court of Chivalry, presided over at that time by the Constable of England, Thomas of Woodstock. The importance of the case can be gauged by the witnesses called to attest. The court heard evidence from the king's uncle, John of Gaunt, and from Gaunt's friend, the poet Geoffrey Chaucer. Unfortunately for the Grosvenors, these distinguished witnesses spoke on behalf of Scrope. The court found in Scrope's favour and directed that Robert Grosvenor should difference his shield in some way. Unhappy with the verdict, Richard II himself was called to give his personal opinion on the matter. The king decided that Grosvenor could not bear the *Azure, a bend Or* undifferenced.

Thus, in 1390, Robert Grosvenor adopted the ancient arms of his cousins, the earls of Chester: *Azure a Garb Or* (a blue field with golden wheatsheaf). *Scrope v. Grosvenor* was a landmark dispute in heraldic law and among the most famed cases ever heard by the Court of Chivalry.

Moving south: Westminster

By the 1600s the Grosvenors were a highly significant family of baronets, but still not peers. One thing holding them back was the lack of a London base. This was to be rectified in spectacular style after Sir Thomas Grosvenor married a young girl named Mary Davies, known to posterity as the Maid of Ebury.

In truth, the marriage was not considered particularly lucrative by the Grosvenors at the time, nor for two centuries afterwards. The lands which the twelve-year-old Mary brought to the family were far from desirable. True, the manor of Ebury was close to London, but it was then little more than swamp land, a rural estate with some pasture suitable for grazing sheep. The whole area had once belonged to Westminster Abbey but had been taken by Henry VIII during the Dissolution of the Monasteries. He kept some of it himself, fencing it off to create a deer park (now Hyde Park). The rest was good for nothing, being regularly flooded. By the early 1800s, it was still a rural spot known as the Five Fields, a dangerous place for travellers, the notorious haunt of highwaymen and footpads.

Then, in 1825, a former ducal residence nearby – Buckingham House – was rebuilt as a royal palace. The following year Robert Grosvenor obtained an Act of Parliament allowing him to drain the land at Five Fields and remove the topsoil of clay. Grosvenor had sensed an opportunity, and his plans would make his family one of the wealthiest in the country – surpassing the fortune of the royal family – and change the face of the capital city: today, the area formerly known as Five Fields is a Westminster estate of unparalleled worth, the districts of Belgravia and Mayfair.

Robert Grosvenor and his son Richard were responsible for this extraordinary property development. They were now peers of the second degree – the 1st and 2nd Marquess of Westminster in succession. It was William Pitt the Younger who had finally raised the family to the Peerage, first as Earl Grosvenor. The Marquessate of Westminster was granted in 1831, recognising the family's extravagant developments beginning to take shape in London. They employed Thomas Cubitt to create their Belgravia as a fashionable residential area with grand terraces, easily recognisable by their white stucco houses. At the corner of two such terraces today stands a statue of the 1st Marquess of Westminster unveiled in 1998. It features a quote from John Ruskin: 'When we build, let us think we build forever.' Belgravia is a stunning architectural achievement, beautifying Westminster. The statue of its developer also includes the new quartered arms he took, incorporating the arms of Grosvenor and those of the City of Westminster (the portcullis with a Tudor Rose and the emblem of Edward the Confessor, founder of Westminster Abbey). The Grosvenor Estate still extends over huge swathes of Westminster. The family retains control over structural alterations to buildings, and Belgravia's terraces must be repainted in the correct colour every three years.

The Dukes of Westminster

In 1874, the Prime Minister William Gladstone wrote to the 3rd Marquess, Hugh Lupus Grosvenor: 'My dear Westminster, I have received authority from the Queen to place a Dukedom at your disposal and I hope you may accept it, for both you and Lady Westminster will wear it right nobly, with my dying breath, Yours sincerely, W. E Gladstone.'

Hugh Lupus Grosvenor replied that he would humbly accept but asked that if his family 'have any option in the matter we should like to retain the title of Westminster and that of Earl Grosvenor for the eldest son at present'.

By now the areas that his father and grandfather had built were London's most fashionable districts. His grandson the 2nd Duke increased the family fortunes further, turning Grosvenor Estates into an international business. Nicknamed Bendor after the Grosvenor's lost armorials, the 2nd Duke was among the most infamous figures of his age. A notorious Nazi sympathiser in the run-up to the Second World War, he openly supported any number of extreme right-wing and anti-Semitic groups. His racist speeches in the House of Lords, defending Nazi Germany, caused shock and anger. He was a heartless man, vicious in his opposition to homosexuality. He gathered evidence to expose his brother-in-law, Lord Beauchamp, as homosexual, forcing him to resign political office and move into exile on the Continent in 1931. The duke sent a letter after him that read, 'Dear Bugger-in-law, you got what you deserved. Yours, Westminster.'

Apart from his extreme conservatism, Bendor Grosvenor was known for a ten-year affair with one of the icons of the twentieth-century fashion world. In 1923, while in Monte Carlo, he was introduced to Coco Chanel. He was fairly obviously smitten with the French designer. He gave her a house in Mayfair and land on the French Riviera where the villa, La Pausa, was built by Chanel. The affair brought Chanel into the heart of London high society. Chanel was vastly wealthy in her own right, with a successful fashion business established thirteen years before meeting Grosvenor, and a massively popular perfume, Chanel No. 5, launched in 1921. She would find further inspiration on her visits to Scotland, where she accompanied the Duke of Westminster on his fishing expeditions at his Reay Forest estate in Sutherland. Chanel began sourcing fabrics from Linton Tweeds, close to the Scottish Borders. She also found ideas in Cheshire. During her stays at Eaton Hall, she was inspired by the uniforms of the Grosvenor footmen. The resulting designs were dubbed 'Le Style Anglais'. Chanel apparently took to country house life with ease. At shooting parties in Cheshire she would ride with the hounds and act as hostess to the eminent guests, including Winston Churchill. The future Prime Minister wrote to his wife:

> The famous Coco turned up & I took a gt fancy to her – A most capable and agreeable woman – much the strongest personality [Bendor] has yet been up against. She hunted vigorously all day ... & is today engaged in passing & improving dresses on endless streams of mannequins... She does it with her own fingers, pinning, cutting, looping, etc. [She is] really a [great] & strong being fit to rule a man or an Empire. [Bendor is] I think extremely happy to be mated with an equal – her ability balancing his power.

Although the duke married four times, Coco Chanel never became Duchess of Westminster. Her friendship with the duke continued after his marriage, however, and the lasting impact of the relationship on Chanel can be seen in the British textiles that became a key part of her designs.

When the 2nd Duke died in 1953, one commenter wrote:

> So Bend Or the great Duke of Westminster is dead at last; magnificent, courteous, a mixture of Henry VIII and Lorenzo il Magnifico, he lived for pleasure – and women – for seventy-four years. His wealth was incalculable; his charm overwhelming; but he was restless, spoilt, irritable, and rather splendid in a very English way. He was fair, handsome, lavish; yet his life was an empty failure; he did few kindnesses, leaves no monument.

Family seat: Eaton Hall

Unlike the other present-day seats explored in this book, Eaton Hall did not survive the widespread destruction of English country houses in the twentieth century. Most of what had been a gigantic mansion was demolished in the 1960s, leaving only the chapel and a number of outbuildings intact. A new, much smaller residence was built in the grounds, and completed in a French chateau style in 1991.

The scale of the architectural loss is all too clear when we look at photos of the lost hall. It had been the culmination of centuries of design and redesign. Little is known of the first house the Grosvenors inherited through Joan of Eaton in the 1400s, though it was likely a small semi-fortified manor house. The first large house was built near the site of the old hall for the Grosvenor baronets in the late 1600s and surrounded by formal gardens. In the early 1800s, the 1st Marquess of Westminster hired architect William Porden to reimagine the hall as a flamboyant neo-gothic fantasy. Paintings of this version of Eaton show its ecclesiastical character, like a bishop's palace or an Oxford college chapel. It was described by contemporaries as 'magnificent and opulent' and also 'gaudy... a monument to wealth, ignorance and bad taste'.

From 1870 to 1882, the house was remodelled and expanded by the 1st Duke of Westminster, creating a sprawling complex with a chapel and clocktower 175 feet tall (which survives today). Spectacular in scale, with 150 bedrooms, the house does seem to have had an oddly civic, rather than domestic, appearance, that wouldn't look out of place in a city centre. This is not surprising given its architect was Alfred Waterhouse, designer of Manchester Town Hall, the archetypical Victorian gothic municipal building of the type that stands in northern cities like Sheffield and Bradford.

By the early 1960s, the fabric of this massive house was in a poor state, with dry rot setting in. The 4th duke decided to

The coronets of peers. (*Chambers's Encyclopaedia*, 1889)

Achievement of Arms of the Duke of Beaufort. A ducal coronet lies above the Somerset shield (the Plantagenet arms with bordure for difference). A portcullis crest sits atop the helm with mantling. A spotted panther and a wyvern stand as supporters. (University of Delaware Library)

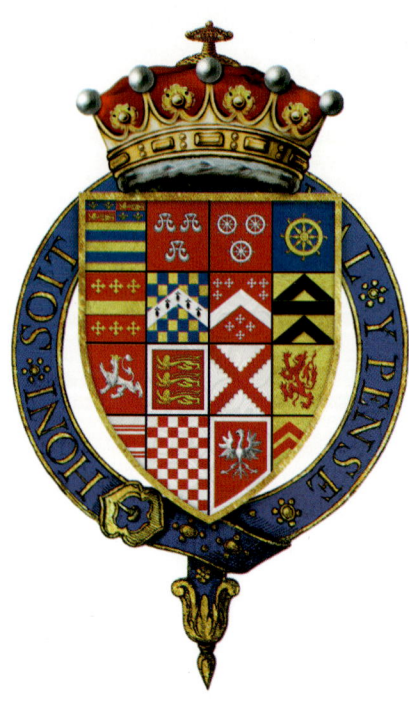

Left: Quartered shield of the 1st Earl of Rutland featuring the Manners arms in the first quarter, with matrilineal ancestry represented alongside, including de Ros and de Todeni. (Rs-nourse, Creative Commons Attribution-ShareAlike 3.0)

Below left: Quartered shield of John Howard, 1st Duke of Norfolk. The Howard arms appear in the first and fourth quarters. The arms of his mother's family (Mowbray) appear in the third quarter, while the royal arms of Thomas of Brotherton are in the second. Today's version includes the Fitzalan arms and the augmentation of the 2nd Duke. (Rs-nourse, Creative Commons Attribution-ShareAlike 3.0)

Below: Augmentation granted to the 2nd Duke of Norfolk after the Battle of Flodden. (Ipankonin, Creative Commons Attribution-ShareAlike 3.0)

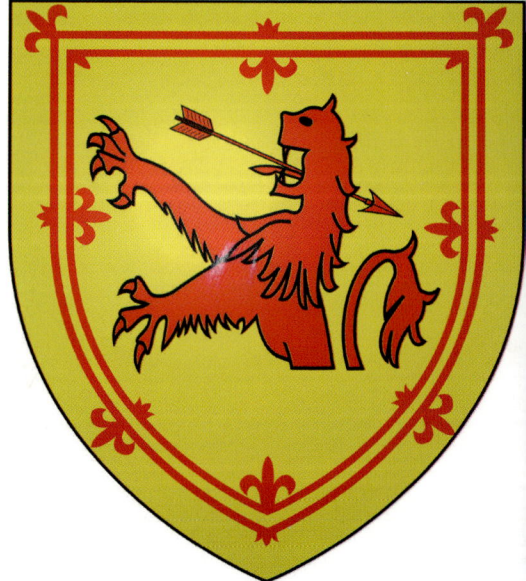

The House of Lords, London. For centuries the heads of noble dynasties ruled from its benches. Some hereditary peers remain members, though no longer as an automatic right. (© House of Lords / photography by Roger Harris, Attribution 3.0 Unported (CC BY 3.0))

Castle Howard as depicted by Robert Sayer, 1758. (Rijksmuseum)

Burleigh House, seat of the Marquess of Exeter, built by the founder, William Cecil. Painting by John Buckler, 1817. (Yale Center for British Art)

Hardwick Hall, Derbyshire. Builder, Bess, placed her monogram atop each tower. Painting by John Buckler, 1813. (Yale Center for British Art)

Above: Chatsworth. Painting by John Buckler, 1812. (Yale Center for British Art)
Below: Highclere Castle in its surrounds. (Gormakuma, Adobe Stock 666621184)

Eaton Hall as it once was, designed by William Porden. The present house is much smaller. (Yale Center for British Art)

Badminton House, home of the horse trials (and the Somersets). (Morris, *The County Seats of the Noblemen and Gentlemen of Great Britain and Ireland*)

Belvoir Castle. (Neale, *Views of the Seats of Noblemen and Gentlemen in England, Wales, Scotland and Ireland*)

Marcia Pitt and her brother George Pitt, later 2nd Baron Rivers, with Stratfield Saye in the background. The Pitts were the original builders of the house. Painted by Thomas Gooch, 1782. (Yale Center for British Art)

Top: Blenheim Palace in a print by Paul Foudriner, eighteenth century. (Yale Center for British Art)

Above: Alnwick Castle as drawn by Samuel Buck, 1728. (Yale Center for British Art)

Left: Henry, Lord Percy of Alnwick. His seal shows the 'modern' Percy arms upon his shield. (De Walden, *Some Feudal Lords and Their Seals*)

demolish most of it and build a new modern house in its place. This was begun in 1971, with later alterations from 1989.

In 2016, the 6th Duke of Westminster, Gerald Cavendish Grosvenor, died unexpectedly leaving his twenty-five-year-old son as England's youngest and richest duke. Gerald had not taken his seat in the House of Lords, though he was entitled to before 1999. He was a committed democrat and glad to see the removal of hereditary peers from the chamber. His son, Hugh, inherited – as the only person left in remainder to the dukedom – an estimated £9 billion fortune.

Hugh was born in 1991, and King Charles III is his godfather. While still Earl Grosvenor, he went to Newcastle University to study Countryside Management. In marked contrast to his ancestor Bendor, the duke – and his sister, Lady Edwina Grosvenor – are generous and philanthropic. The duke's charitable foundation focuses on helping vulnerable young people and fighting inequality of opportunity. During the Covid-19 pandemic, the duke donated £12.5 million to the national Covid relief effort and to support the NHS, and £1 million to fund research projects on mental health.

The 7th Duke was married in June 2024 at Chester Cathedral, after several years of being dubbed the nation's most eligible bachelor by gossip columnists. In a mark of the British aristocracy's continued ability to make headlines around the world, the *New York Times* billed the wedding as 'England's Social Event of the Year'. The duke's close friend Prince William served as an usher. Crowds gathered in the city which his family has called home for near on a millennium, just as they had in decades and centuries past, to witness a Grosvenor wedding. The bride, Olivia Henson, worked in the sustainable food sector before becoming Duchess of Westminster.

The duke's sister, Lady Edwina, is a criminologist and prison reformer who made her own high-profile marriage to the historian and television presenter Dan Snow in 2010. Edwina became interested in prison reform and rehabilitation of offenders from a young age, volunteering in prisons abroad and at home while a student. She founded the charity The Clink to help train prisoners for work and break the cycle of repeat offending.

In April 2025, the duke and his wife, who are rather publicity-shy, visited the University of Chester to tour a suite of new facilities. The visit was the duchess's first public appearance since the announcement of her pregnancy in March. The baby, born in July 2025, is the 36th generation of her family in line of descent from Gilbert le Gros Veneur.

The Cecils of Burleigh and Hatfield

Marquess of Exeter
Marquess of Salisbury

Marquessates created	1789 (Salisbury); 1801 (Exeter)
Monarch	George III
Subsidiary titles	Earl of Exeter; Earl of Salisbury; Viscount Cranborne; Baron Cecil

No English dynasty can claim to have held such high office over so long a period as the Cecils. The founder of the House, William Cecil (1520–1598) was, as Lord Privy Seal, the chief minister to Queen Elizabeth I. Four hundred years – and fourteen generations – later, his descendent, Robert Cecil (b. 1946) was Lord Privy Seal to Queen Elizabeth II and Leader of the House of Lords. In between these two, was another Robert Cecil, Prime Minister to Queen Victoria. These later Cecil politicos were of the Salisbury branch of the family seated at Hatfield House. It is the junior line of Cecils, but the more famed, its members becoming Earls and then Marquesses of Salisbury. The senior branch, based at Burleigh

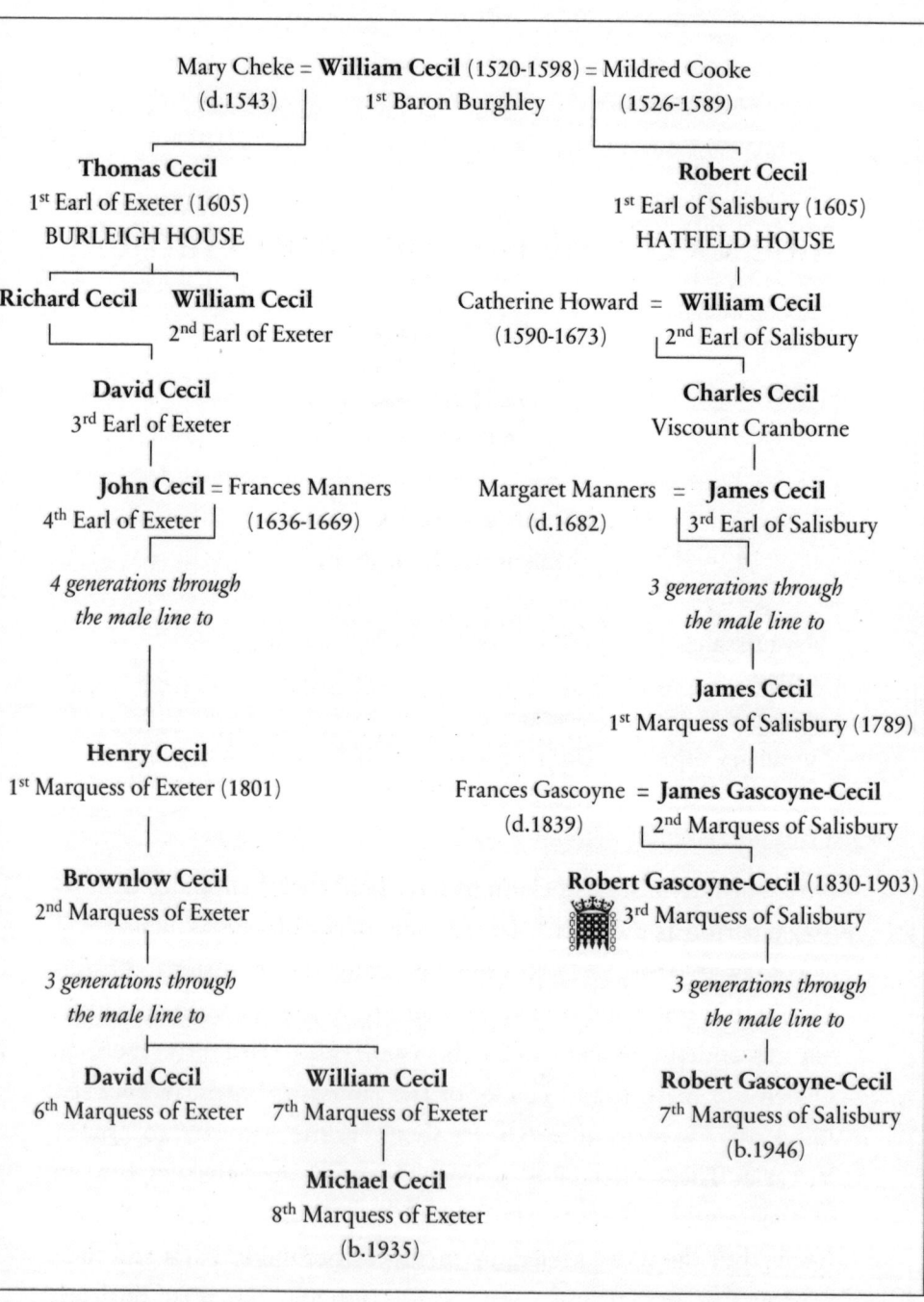

House, also became Earls and Marquesses (of Exeter in their case) but despite many serving as MPs and in the Lords, they never scaled the political heights of their Hatfield cousins. The Exeters did nevertheless inherit their founding fathers great Prodigy House at Burleigh in Lincolnshire, and produced scholars, writers and the organiser of the 1948 London Olympics.

Cecil 'the Spirit'

The common ancestor of today's Lord Salisbury and Lord Exeter is a courtier whose name became a byword for political ruthlessness: Sir William Cecil. The man Elizabeth I called her Spirit was far from alone in his Machiavellian doings in the Tudor age, but as a minister, diplomat, and spymaster, he was the prime practitioner of low cunning; an artful, apparently all-knowing court shadow, whose supreme position within Elizabeth's regime was unquestioned in his time.

Born during the reign of Henry VIII, William Cecil was a member of a family that had not left any great mark in history up to that point. His grandfather David was – like the Tudors – of Welsh stock, being the three-times great-grandson of Adam Ap Seisyll (*fl. c.* 1270). David was the first of the family to be recorded as holding public office, rising to be High Sheriff of Northamptonshire. His son Richard was a royal page to King Henry VIII at the Field of the Cloth of Gold in France. His son was a different character: William Cecil had far grander ambitions than to be a local squire and royal hanger-on. He also had the intelligence to achieve them. Before the age of fifteen, he was studying Greek at St John's College, Cambridge. During this time he fell in love with his tutor's sister, Mary Cheke. Cecil's father was unhappy with the potential match, which would do nothing to enrich the family or to raise its profile. In a romantic turn not generally associated with Cecil, he defied his father. When he was removed from Cambridge and sent to Gray's Inn to train as a lawyer, he organised to marry Mary

Cheke in secret. She was his only real love, and he was devastated when she died in 1544. He did remarry, to Mildred Cooke, an intellectual who very much suited his temperament, but it was said that he never got over Mary.

In common with Sir John Thynne, William Cecil began his court career in the service of the Protestant Reformer Edward Seymour. He was with Seymour and Thynne during their campaign against the Scots and was apparently nearly killed at the Battle of Pinkie. Cecil was still with Seymour when things began to turn sour for the Duke of Somerset. His master was tacitly supporting the popular rebellions against the enclosure of common land by landowners, depriving ordinary people of the right to graze their animals, something that had been the norm in England from time immemorial. The Duke of Somerset was sympathetic to uprisings like Robert Ket's in Norfolk. This rebellion was brutally put down by John Dudley, who had Ket executed. Dudley and his faction then moved against Seymour. When the duke was arrested, Cecil was in some danger. Like Thynne, he, too, was detained and imprisoned in the Tower. It could conceivably have been the end for Cecil. But likely because of his abilities – which were widely recognised by the new ruling cabal – Cecil was released after just two months in captivity.

As with Thynne, certain provisos were put in place regarding his release, but it was generally believed that Cecil was not a threat to the new order. On the contrary, he was soon rewarded for his loyalty: he became a Privy Councillor and was knighted, even before Seymour had been taken for execution in 1552. Loyalty to the established sovereign, or their regent, became Cecil's creed. Dudley (briefly Duke of Northumberland) attempted to usurp the right of Mary Tudor to the Crown and place his daughter-in-law Jane Grey on the throne, William Cecil refused to endorse the plan or put his signature to it. When the plot failed and Dudley and Queen Jane were beheaded by Mary's forces, Cecil was able to survive the transition. He was saved by his shrewd loyalty to whoever was on-the-up, even when it meant a change in his religion.

Sir William was also wise enough to keep a low profile during the reign of Mary I. His father had left him significant estates as well as funds, so he retreated to his seat at Burleigh where he began what would – over the following three decades – become the magnificent Burleigh House. At the same time, Cecil ingratiated himself with the heir to the throne Princess Elizabeth, whom he obviously admired as a potential great in the gallery of English monarchs (his judgement proving very sound). He had already become Elizabeth's chief courtier when she succeeded her sister as queen in 1558. She was to trust Cecil implicitly throughout her long reign, believing him to be a man of intellect, ability, and, above all, loyalty; Elizabeth once said to William Cecil: 'This judgement I have of you, that you will not be corrupted with any manner of gifts and that you will be faithful to the state.' (Her judgement also proved very sound.)

Family seat: Burleigh House

Few family seats reflect their founder's personal tastes in quite the way that Burleigh House does, for it was designed almost entirely by William Cecil himself. Unmistakably Elizabethan in style, it nonetheless features several idiosyncratic elements, such as the towering obelisk clocktower, which makes Burleigh appear from the distance like a village surrounding its church spire.

The house took thirty-two years to build using limestone from a nearby Northamptonshire quarry. Alterations were made to the interior in the late 1600s by Cecil's descendant the 5th Earl of Exeter, who wished it to reflect the emerging baroque fashion. He hired the Italian artist Antonio Verrio to paint the ceilings, creating the so-called Heaven Room and Hell Staircase. The 'heaven' depicted is the Olympian heaven of the Ancient Greeks: the gods and goddesses consort with satyrs, cyclops and other figures of classical mythology (and even a self-portrait of Verrio himself if you know where to look). The hell above the stone staircase next door is like a scene from Dante's Inferno: a hooded, skeletal Grim Reaper soars high with his sickle in hand, presiding over tormented souls. The walls were painted later by Thomas Stothard (1755–1834).

In the mid-1700s, the 9th Earl of Exeter, Brownlow Cecil, made some alterations to the grounds around Burleigh. Like the 5th Earl, he was a man who admired contemporary fashion, and so he hired Capability Brown to create a landscape park in keeping with the neoclassical vogue. He did not, however, remove any of the baroque decoration inside the house, or attempt to radically alter the Elizabethan facades. Brown was permitted to raise the roofline on the south front to create a more harmonious skyline. But Burleigh House remains today a prime example of the Prodigy House, even when – like the mansion of William Cecil's colleague John Thynne – it reflects the changing tastes of its occupants down the generations.

In the early part of Elizabeth's reign, William Cecil repealed much of the anti-Protestant legislation passed under Queen Mary. In so doing, he made enemies among the old Catholic nobility who recoiled at this arriviste wielding such power in the realm. Among Cecil's greatest adversaries were the Howards. Just as they had despised the upstart Edward Seymour, so they balked at his former secretary Cecil acting as chief minister to the Crown. The Duke of Norfolk was among the faction seeking Cecil's removal from power. The duke's ally, Thomas Percy, Earl of Northumberland, went one stage further by attempting to remove Queen Elizabeth herself along with her minister. When the rising of the Catholic north ensued in 1569, Cecil implored Queen Elizabeth to show no mercy and to crush the rebellion without hesitation. That is exactly what she did. 800 rebels including Thomas Percy were executed. The Duke of Norfolk was already languishing in the Tower. William Cecil's strategic instincts were proven to Elizabeth. The 'new man' was victorious over 'yesterday's' feudal aristocrats.

Cecil's entire tenure as Elizabeth's right-hand man was dominated by the struggle to keep Mary Stuart – deposed Queen of Scots – off the English throne, and guard Elizabeth against countless Catholic plots to replace her with her cousin. It was Cecil who persuaded Elizabeth to keep Mary in 'protective' custody. He was in no doubt as to the danger his queen was in, or that he himself faced. Cecil was widely regarded by traditionalists as the greatest obstacle to the restoration of Catholicism in England. He became the focus of several assassination attempts. In response, Cecil and his ally, Sir Francis Walsingham, set up a notorious spy network. Sometimes described as the start of the British Secret Service, this counterintelligence web, with Cecil as the spider at its centre, gives him a claim to be the country's first true spymaster. His agents could be brutal, indulging in torture to extract information. Walsingham's men uncovered the Ridolfi Plot, among many others.

Cecil could be merciless in all his judgements. It was he who finally convinced Queen Elizabeth to sign the death warrant of Mary Stuart, putting an end to any possibility of a Catholic takeover in her name. After Mary was executed in 1587, Elizabeth had a sudden crisis of conscience, giving Cecil a rare taste of royal disapproval. Elizabeth projected her guilt for Mary's death onto Cecil: he it was who had persuaded her to put her own cousin – and sister queen no less – to death, to commit regicide. Elizabeth banished Cecil from her court, casting him as the true villain in the Tragedy of Mary, Queen of Scots. His exile did not last long, however. Elizabeth needed him too much. The following year saw the launch of the Spanish Armada, a very real threat to Protestant England from Catholic Europe. Cecil the Spirit was once again at Elizabeth's side as Spain's invasion faltered in the stormy seas, along with the hopes of England's

Roman Catholics. Cecil would now stay by Elizabeth's side for the rest of his life. When he died in 1598, his loss was keenly felt. Lord Essex reportedly told the queen that Willam Cecil had after all, been 'the greatest, gravest, and most esteemed Councillor that Your Majesty ever had'.

The 'second Cecil', Robert, 1st Earl of Salisbury

William Cecil was survived by his two sons, Thomas and Robert. Both founded their own line of Cecils, and both were created earls by King James I in 1605. Their father had died having secured a place in the Peerage; in 1571 Elizabeth had granted him the title of 1st Baron Burghley. His elder son Thomas inherited the barony along with Burleigh House and was later made Earl of Exeter. But it was his younger son, Robert, who was the more politically successful of the two siblings.

In 1598, it was Robert Cecil who took up his father's position as chief minister to Queen Elizabeth I. He continued to serve as chief minister after King James I (son of the executed Mary Stuart) finally succeeded to the English throne in 1603. The younger Cecil was then created Viscount Cranborne and Earl of Salisbury, establishing a branch of the family that would keep the pages of Britain's political history turning for centuries to come.

The smooth transition from the Tudor to the Stuart monarchy was largely down to Robert Cecil. His father had never persuaded Queen Elizabeth to marry, and without children her heirs had remained her Scots cousins. Robert Cecil had been well prepared for the big moment. He had secretly been in contact with King James of Scotland for some time before Elizabeth's death, carefully preparing the ground for what was to come. When the last Tudor died, it was Robert Cecil who wrote a Proclamation of Accession, declaring that James VI of Scotland was now James I of England. He then addressed the assembled Privy Councillors in London, presenting the succession as a *fait accompli*. A few days later, James left Edinburgh for London. Robert Cecil went north, meeting James at York to begin planning the coronation. James was crowned at Westminster Abbey in July, and he remained forever grateful to Cecil for ensuring a speedy and largely uncontested succession. The king made his minister a Knight of the Garter, alongside his elevation as Earl of Salisbury.

King James had a reputation for elevating new favourites at quite a rate. As a result, it was difficult for any figure to maintain their position for long. The 'Second Cecil' fell from royal favour along with many other former favourites. Yet Lord Salisbury had ensured that his heirs would have a suitable seat from which to plot their future return to power. As the younger son, Robert had not been in line for Burleigh House. Instead, he had been bequeathed an old family home in Hertfordshire. This was the house at Theobalds, where Cecil had once welcomed King James, his queen, Anne of Denmark, and his brother-in-law the King of Denmark, Christian IV. (This had been in the days of his favour. The masque which was performed for the royal visit had cost Cecil a fortune in sugar treats and sets built by Inigo Jones. Worse, it was all reportedly a shambles because royals were far too drunk to take in the entertainment.) James must have enjoyed his visit, for he later took Theobalds for himself, compensating Cecil by handing him an old royal estate at nearby Hatfield. Here, Robert built himself a house to rival his brothers at Burleigh, a Jacobean palace fit for Salisbury Cecils.

Family seat: Hatfield House

The seat of the Salisburys was built by Robert Cecil, 1st Earl of Salisbury, between 1607 and 1612. The site had been home to a minor royal palace where Elizabeth I had spent a happy part of her childhood. A portion of the medieval residence still stands in the grounds today, but Cecil tore down most of the structure to build his new Hatfield House.

A masterpiece of Jacobean architecture, Hatfield looks like a fusion of two separate houses. Its south front shows a central section of pale stone, ornately carved, and with a clocktower (inscribed 1611) similar to Burleigh's Renaissance style. To either side of it are contrasting redbrick wings with unmistakable Jacobean corner towers crowned with their curving cap roofs.

Hatfield is extremely popular with film crews and public visitors today. Housing an excellent collection of objects related to Elizabeth I, it has hosted Elizabethan costume dramas including *Elizabeth: The Golden Age*.

'Bob's your uncle': the Prime Minister, Lord Salisbury

There were seven successive earls of Salisbury until James Cecil was promoted to Marquess of Salisbury in 1789. The Salisbury branch of the Cecils (since 1821, known as the 'Gascoyne-Cecils', after the 2nd Marquess adopted the additional surname of his wife Mary Gascoyne) have been among the most influential of political dynasties. In the world of Victorian high politics, the name Lord Salisbury refers to one exceptional figure: Robert Gascoyne-Cecil, 3rd Marquess of Salisbury (1830–1903).

Salisbury was the product of the typical ruling class education and political apprenticeship: Eton, Christ Church College, Oxford, then entering parliament as MP for Stamford in 1853. He retained the seat until 1868, when his father died and he entered the House of Lords as the new marquess. A high Tory, he served in Lord Derby's government and was opposed to parliamentary reform. He resigned from government over Disraeli's reform bill, which he thought expanded the voting franchise too far. When Disraeli died in 1881, Lord Salisbury led the Conservatives, forming three separate administrations between 1885 and 1902. He was the last Prime Minister to lead his governments from the House of Lords rather than the Commons.

Salisbury's premierships coincided with the high point of imperialism. It was a time of jingoistic nationalism across Europe, with empires vying for control of resources around the globe, exacerbating tensions that would eventually boil over. One of the precursors to the Great War, overseen by Salisbury, was the Boer War in southern Africa, as Britain sought access to gold and diamond deposits discovered in two independent states. Britain already had colonies in the area (including Cape Colony, run by Cecil Rhodes) but now wanted control of the riches in the 'Boer Republics' of Transvaal and the Orange Free State. The Boers were descendants of Dutch settlers and repelled various British attempts to seize control of their lands. Angered by the Boers and by the gloating of the German Empire who supported them, Britain prepared a large military campaign that broke into all-out war in 1899. By 1900, Britain had annexed the Boer Republics. Lord Salisbury decided to capitalise on this success by calling a general election (the 'khaki election', so-called for the colour of army uniforms). Patriotic sentiment ensured that Salisbury won. Celebrations proved premature, however. The Boers launched a guerilla resistance. British forces under Kitchener responded with a scorched earth policy, burning Boer farms and setting up concentration camps, leading to international outcry. Salisbury struggled on until a treaty was signed in 1902 giving Britain control of the territories.

Even so, Britain's preeminent position as the world superpower was starting to wane as Germany and the United States grew economically and militarily. Salisbury's foreign policy was reactionary, though domestically his governments did oversee some notable reforms. Salisbury introduced County Councils in 1888. This may sound like a small, rather dull achievement, but it was a genuinely democratising move, changing how localities across Britain were run. Since the Middle Ages it had been local Justices of the Peace (magistrates) who, as well as dispensing justice, had overseen government in the counties. Though initially tasked in the 1300s with keeping law and order by directing parish constables and watchmen, they soon became the natural managers of other local officials like the overseers of the poor law (welfare). The whole machinery of local government in the countryside thus grew under the auspices of appointees, who had, in effect, been an oligarchy, and an extension of the great dynasties' grip on the provinces. The setting-up of elected County Councils was therefore a significant moment of reform.

Towards the end of his time in office, Salisbury grew ill. He couldn't retire because of the death of Queen Victoria and the subsequent coronation of Edward VII. He died the year after his resignation in 1903. His name today is not widely known except by political history buffs. Though many people will have referred to him without knowing it thanks to a popular saying, coined to describe Arthur Balfour, a minister in Salisbury's government, who succeeded as Prime Minister. Balfour was generally considered to have been promoted far beyond his abilities. The reason: Robert 'Bob' Cecil was his uncle.

The Salisbury Convention and the fall of hereditary peers

In a turn of events that would have shocked their predecessors, the later Marquesses of Salisbury became leading advocates for democracy and were key figures in dismantling the power of the great dynasties from within. The 5th Marquess, 'Bobbity', gave his name to a parliamentary rule known as the Salisbury Convention, which severely curbed the power of the House of Lords, the main institution through which the Great Families had always exercised their right to rule. While leading the Tory opposition in the Lords during the Labour government of Clement Atlee from 1945-50, Bobbity Cecil argued that the socialist reforms Labour was introducing should not be restricted by the House of Lords, even if most peers were against them on principle. In Salisbury's view, if a government had been elected on a policy manifesto, then they had a democratic mandate to implement it. The unelected Lords should not block the policies no matter how much they may personally object to them. To do so would make them no better than if King George VI overruled Prime Minister Atlee. The Salisbury Convention thus established the complete supremacy of the House of Commons in lawmaking. In the twentieth century, the Lords was to be a chamber for revising legislation and advising the Commons, and nothing more.

Later, the 7th Marquess played a notable role in the reform that brought to a close a near-millennium of hereditary peers having an automatic right to sit in Parliament. This Robert Gascoyne-Cecil (b. 1946) was elected an MP in 1979 when Margaret Thatcher became Prime Minister. Cecil then entered the House of Lords in 1992, unusually, while his father the 6th Marquess was still alive. This was sanctioned by the then Prime Minister John Major, who summoned Cecil through a writ of summons 'of acceleration' to sit in the Lords as Baron Cecil (though Cecil continued to use his courtesy title, Viscount Cranborne). In May 1997, Labour won its famous landslide victory under Tony Blair, and Cecil became leader of the opposition in the Lords. Blair had been elected on a promise to reform the Lords, and under the Salisbury Convention he had the right to pursue it. Cecil negotiated with Blair, agreeing in principle that the majority of hereditary peers should now be removed from the House. This did not suit the Conservative Party leader, William Hague, who reacted angrily by sacking Cecil. Despite this, Blair got his way, and this profound constitutional change was enacted in autumn 1999.

Titles: Exeter and Salisbury
In the feudal era, noble titles were linked to their owners' landholdings; you could be quite sure that a baron of Lincolnshire, for example, held estates in Lincolnshire. Later on, extinct titles

would be revived for grantees who were related in some way to previous holders but who may not own lands in the territory. By James I's reign, all protocol concerning territorial titles went out the window. James was unconcerned about such trivial matters. He sold more than a few earldoms, and he created the baronetage (hereditary knighthoods) as a way of raising money. The earldoms he gave to the Cecil brothers in 1605 had long histories of their own in other families, and there does not seem to be any significant kinship with the Cecils in either case.

There were several Exeter earldoms and dukedoms created in the Middle Ages. On 29 September 1397, John Holand, Earl of Huntingdon, was created Duke of Exeter by Richard II, on the same day that the king created four other dukes, including making Thomas Mowbray Duke of Norfolk. Like Mowbray, Holand was related to the Plantagenets, though in Holand's case the relationship was closer. He was the king's half-brother through their mother Joan, the 'Fair Maid' of Kent. John did not survive the overthrow of Richard II. He was executed and the Exeter dukedom expired. It was created anew for other royal relations but never lasted very long.

In the case of Salisbury, there was an even longer history, beginning in the 1140s when the Empress Matilda granted the earldom to Patrick of Salisbury. Several more creations were made, with the earldom allowed to pass through the female line. In this way it was shared by two famous dynasties, the Montagus and the Nevilles. The second Montagu earl was a loyal commander for Edward III in the early stages of the Hundred Years War. He was also a founder member of the Order of the Garter. The following century, Alice Montague became Countess of Salisbury and married a Neville. Their son was the 'Kingmaker', Richard Neville Earl of Warwick and Earl of Salisbury through his mother.

The last Salisbury before the Cecils was Margaret Pole (1473–1541), a Countess in her own right. Born Margaret Plantagenet, she was lucky to survive the Wars of the Roses. She did not survive Henry VIII's Reformation, however, and was executed at the Tower, later declared a Catholic martyr by Pope Leo XIII. Her son Reginald Pole was the last ever Catholic Archbishop of Canterbury.

The Cecils of Burleigh

It is time to go back and consider the contributions of the other branch of Cecils, those that descend from William Cecil's elder son, Thomas, who became 1st Earl of Exeter in 1605. None of the earls or marquesses (they were promoted in 1801) of Exeter had a political career to rival their Salisbury kin, but several won fame in other ways.

The 5th Earl of Exeter was inspired by his wife, Anne Cavendish of Chatsworth, to a life of travel, crisscrossing Europe. Anne had an adventurous spirit and a passion for ancient cultures. She and John became some of the earliest 'Grand Tourists', collecting sculptures, paintings and tapestries in an era before the fashion for touring – more associated with the Georgians – took off. Much of their collection can still be seen at Burleigh House along with treasures bequeathed to Anne by her mother Elizabeth Cavendish, given for 'her peculiar use ... with which the Earl of Exeter should not intermeddle'. Clearly some tension existed with the in-laws. The earl and countess also met artists on their travels, many of whom they employed and brought back to Burleigh. These included Antonio Verrio who painted the Heaven and Hell murals, the u.s.p. of Burleigh's state rooms.

The 10th Earl, who became 1st Marquess of Exeter, Henry Cecil (1754–1804) is remembered for a romantic love affair with the 'beautiful peasant girl' Sarah Hoggins. He married Sarah, the 'The Cottage Countess' and had three children with her, before she died in 1797. Later, Alfred, Lord Tennyson, wrote a ballad called 'The Lord of Burleigh', celebrating the love story. In Tennyson's version, young Sarah marries not realising that her husband is master of Burleigh House until, after the wedding, he brings her to her new home:

> ... When beneath his roof they come.
> Thus her heart rejoices greatly,
> Till a gateway she discerns
> With armorial bearings stately,
> And beneath the gate she turns;
> Sees a mansion more majestic
> Than all those she saw before:
> ... Leading on from hall to hall.
> And, while now she wonders blindly,
> Nor the meaning can divine,
> Proudly turns he round and kindly,
> 'All of this is mine and thine.'
> Here he lives in state and bounty,
> Lord of Burleigh, fair and free,
> Not a lord in all the county
> Is so great a lord as he.

The 6th Marquess, David Cecil (1905–1981), was a champion hurdler between 1924 and 1933. In 1927, during his final year at Cambridge University, Cecil made himself famous by sprinting around the Great Court of Trinity College at midnight, in the time it took for the college clock to toll twelve. This event was dramatised in the 1981 film *Chariots of Fire*. Cecil was portrayed by Nigel Havers in the Oscar-winning film about young athletes at the 1924 Paris Olympics. The character's name was changed to 'Lord Andrew Lindsay' because Cecil would not allow the use of his own, the film being considered historically inaccurate. David Cecil did, however, make his Olympic debut in 1924, and went on to win gold in the 400m hurdles in Amsterdam in 1928. He also won relay silver in Los Angeles in 1932. His gold medallist running shoes are now on display at Burleigh House.

The current marquess of Exeter does not live at Burleigh. He is an expat in the United States. He visits the estate often, while members of his extended family run the house and the renowned Burleigh Horse Trials, which were founded by their Olympian forebear in 1961.

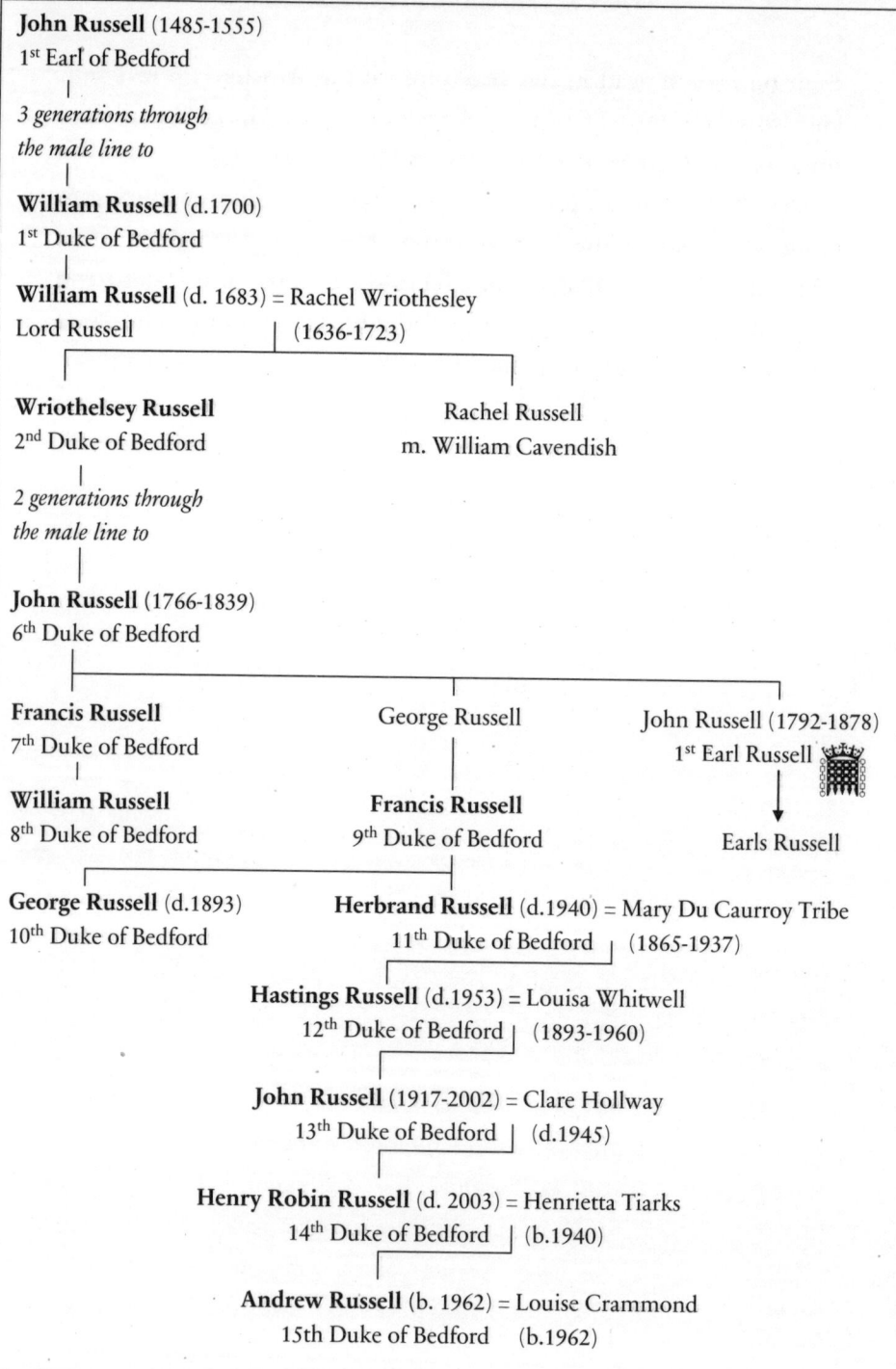

The Russells of Woburn Abbey

Duke of Bedford

Dukedom created	1694
Monarchs	William III & Mary II
Subsidiary titles	Marquess of Tavistock; Baron Howland
Cadet branch	Russells of Pembroke Lodge (Earl Russell)

Woburn Abbey was once a flourishing Cistercian monastery, established in the mid-twelfth century in Bedfordshire. After Henry VIII dissolved it in 1538, he passed the abbey's lands to his trusted minister John Russell (1485–1555), and it has been in the Russell family ever since. Lord Russell (Henry made him a baron in 1539) had once worked as a wine merchant in Weymouth, but through a combination of luck, talent, and charisma, ended his days as Earl of Bedford and founder of a dynasty that stayed at the heart of national events for ever after.

In the late 1600s, the Russells became founding members of the Whig party that conspired to dethrone the Catholic Monarch James II. One of their number – William, Lord Russell – was executed for involvement in a plot to assassinate James. Lord Russell's cousin, Edward, then put his signature to the letter inviting William of Orange to invade England. The family remained committed Whigs after being made dukes of Bedford by the grateful King William in 1694. They provided a highly consequential Prime Minister in Lord John Russell (1792–1878). Privately, the lives of the Russells have often been touched by tragedy. The present duke succeeded in 2003, just seven months after his own father's succession.

The founder: John, Earl of Bedford

The Russells hailed from Weymouth on the Dorset coast. Apart from that fact, not much is known of their early history. The great-great-grandfather of the first Russell peer was a Stephen Russell, who served as Bailiff of Weymouth in the 1380s and, around the year 1400, made a sound marriage to Alice de Blynchesfield, which brought him into possession of several manors. Of no noble lineage, the Russells were very much beneficiaries of the Tudor Crown's 'promotion scheme' for able and ambitious new men who would come to prominence on their own merit, so long as they took advantage of whatever chances came their way.

Such a chance presented itself to John Russell in 1506. The Archduke Philip Habsburg was about to visit Henry VII at Windsor. As luck would have it, Philip landed in Weymouth, where John was living. As further luck would have it, a man named Sir Thomas Trenchard was despatched to greet the Archduke. Trenchard happened to know Russell personally, knew of the merchant's gift for foreign languages, and asked for Russell's help as an interpreter. Russell obliged and accompanied Philip to Windsor Castle where he met the king. Henry recognised Russell's talent, liked his character, and so employed him as a gentleman of the Privy Chamber.

John Russell's rise was meteoric. He advanced politically, as a counsellor to the king and foreign diplomat, socially, as a member of the highest court circles, and financially. He was given vast lands by Henry VIII and Edward VI. Though it was Henry who gave John his first peerage, creating him Baron Russell in 1539, it was under Edward that he laid out the estates upon which his dynastic future was founded. Two of these estates became immensely famous, lands taken from the Monasteries at the Dissolution. One was Woburn Abbey, which became the Russell seat. The other was land that once belonged to Westminster Abbey, known as the Convent Garden – later Covent Garden – in London, which remained Russell property for the next 400 years. As a final gift, King Edward elevated John Russell as 1st Earl of Bedford in 1552.

Title: Earl and Duke of Bedford
It's surprisingly rare for dukes in England to have their family seat in the county that their title refers to, but the Russell dukes of Bedford do actually live in Bedfordshire. John Russell was granted both the Bedford title – originally as an earldom – and also the Woburn estate. When the title was upgraded to a dukedom in the seventeenth century, it was the sixth time that the title had been created. On every other occasion, the title was never passed on, but became extinct with the death of its holder, or through attainder. The first creation was for a son of Henry IV. He was granted the dukedom twice with different remainders for inheritance, not that it made any difference as he died without having any children. The third creation was for a Neville in 1440. George Neville was the nephew of Warwick the Kingmaker. Like many members of that family, he lost his titles through attainder, in this case simply for not being wealthy enough to support the 'dignity' of a dukedom. The title was granted a fourth time to a child of Edward IV, who died at the age of two. The final creation before the Russells was made in 1485 when Henry VII made his uncle Jasper Tudor a duke. He died without legitimate heirs.

It was a mark of the esteem in which John Russell was held that the title of Bedford, which last belonged to a Tudor, was given to him by the Tudor boy-king.

William, Lord Russell, and the Whigs

The Russell dukedom of Bedford is peculiar in that it was not really created for the man who became the 1st Duke in 1694. It was created to honour his son who had predeceased him, having died eleven years earlier in 1683. Had William, Lord Russell, lived, it would likely have been he who was created the 1st Duke. In his absence, it was his father who was issued with the Patent of Creation, a bizarre document which praised him for having fathered such a remarkable son ('from his loins issued the ornament of our age,' it read).

William, Lord Russell, may have been celebrated as the ornament of his age in the 1690s, but a decade earlier he had been considered a traitor, placed on trial, and led to his execution. What happened in between to change perceptions of him was the Glorious Revolution of 1688. Having been opposed to the succession of the Catholic James II, he was vindicated by the succession of William of Orange and Mary II. As a leading Protestant, Lord Russell had led the opposition to the then Duke of York in Parliament. In so doing he was the first of his family since John, 1st Earl, to play a central role in political events.

There were five earls of Bedford in the Russell line between the creation of the earldom in 1552 and the creation of the dukedom in 1694. The earls were courtiers and soldiers, but none were political heavyweights. The 4th Earl (1587–1641) is best remembered for building Covent Garden Piazza with St Paul's Church, employing Inigo Jones as architect.

The 5th Earl, who became the 1st Duke, was an indecisive combatant in the Civil War. He started out as a Parliamentarian, became a Royalist, then returned to the Parliamentarians. As a result, he was trusted by neither Charles I nor Oliver Cromwell, and he spent the Commonwealth years quietly at Woburn. At the Restoration in 1660, the earl was welcomed back into the court and given a role in the coronation. His relationship with Charles II was generally cordial. His son and heir Lord Russell, on the other hand, grew to dislike the king immensely, though whether he was involved in treasonous designs remains doubtful. He certainly opposed Charles in Parliament and sought to prevent the king's brother inheriting the Crown. But did he seek to kill the royal brothers?

Lord Russell and his wife, Rachel, had grown uncomfortable with the king's increasingly absolutist tendencies and the Duke of York's open Catholicism. The couple hosted political meetings at Bedford House in London where the early Whig movement was formed. Encouraged by Rachel, who was if anything more of an anti-papist than her husband, William proposed that an Act be passed to prevent any Catholic from succeeding to the throne. He then fought passionately for the Exclusion Bill, which would have barred the Duke of York from succeeding. Unsurprisingly, all this put him at odds with the Stuart court. Yet his methods were wholly constitutional, his arguments advanced through Parliament.

Unfortunately for Lord Russell, some of his acquaintances, had more direct action in mind, and hatched a plot to kill the king and his brother as they travelled by coach to Westminster. The chosen site for the assassination was the Rye House, after which the plot was named. Though it seems that Russell did not know anything about the plans, his name was brought up during the investigation following the discovery of the plot. He was arrested in June 1683 and tried at the Old Bailey later that summer. Russell pleaded not guilty of treason but added that it was the rightful duty of subjects to resist tyrannical monarchs, setting himself up as heir of the Magna Carta barons of generations past.

Russell was found guilty, nevertheless. The death sentence caused untold grief among Russell's family and friends. His father, the earl, offered £100,000 to the Crown simply to spare his son's life. Russell's friend and fellow Whig, William Cavendish, Earl of Devonshire, was said to have offered to help Russell escape by swapping clothes with him in his cell. Almost certainly an apocryphal story, it nonetheless illustrates just how desperate the attempts were to halt the execution. It was all to no avail. William, Lord Russell was executed at Lincolns Inn Fields on 21 July 1683. Henceforth, he was to be known as a martyr of English liberty.

Russell's widow, Rachel, was not just the subject of sympathy after the execution, she became a symbol of the Whig resistance to royal autocracy. In the age of William and Mary, she was among the most revered public figures in the country. Born Rachel Wriothesley, heiress to Bloomsbury manor north of Covent Garden, she brought extensive new London estates to her son by Lord Russell. This son was Wriothesley Russell (1680–1711) who eventually succeeded his grandfather, becoming 2nd Duke of Bedford. The Bedford dukedom was one of several granted by William and Mary after the overthrow of James II in 1688.

The Glorious Revolution
The Russell dukedom was ostensibly granted in recognition of William, Lord Russell, slain in 1683. But King William III and Queen Mary II were grateful to the Russells for more than their past heroism. The 1st Duke's nephew, Edward Russell, had been one of the 'Immortal Seven' who sent the letter of invitation to William of Orange, asking the Dutch stadholder to depose King James II through military intervention. The letter, carried to William in The Hague by secret code, was signed by six other leading Protestants including Charles Talbot and William Cavendish, all furious at James's sidelining of the Protestant establishment and his disregard for Parliament. When the king and queen produced a

Catholic heir in 1688, it had been the last straw for the great Whig dynasties. Even when James panicked and recalled Parliament, they were in no mood to back down. A full-scale military coup was planned.

When William of Orange landed in Torbay in November 1688 with 500 ships in his retinue, he led the first successful invasion of England since the Norman Conquest. Following James II's abandonment of the throne and the installation of William and Mary, legislation was passed to create a constitutional monarchy to guard against royal absolutism, ensuring the supremacy of Parliament, and therefore of the Protestant Whig dynasties. Often mythologised as a popular revolution promoting liberty for all, the Glorious Revolution was in reality a coup by a cousinhood of noble families, though a cousinhood that held to principles that were liberal for their time.

Having been born in the Exclusion Crisis of 1678–1681, with a failed attempt to prevent James Stuart becoming king, the Whig movement went on to achieve immense and long-lasting power by conspiring to remove him. Motivated by a fear of absolute monarchy, they ended up laying the groundwork for our modern parliamentary democracy. Families like the Russells believed strongly in individual rights and liberties, that Parliament – representing the people – should have authority over the king. Catholicism was viewed as incompatible with those principles, clinging as it did to notions of the Divine Right of kings and decidedly against religious freedom.

After 1688, the Whigs were in power almost continuously for nearly a century – a period often known as the 'Whig oligarchy' – and that was before the period of Great Reform they spearheaded in the 1830s. No Whig family was more involved through all this than the Russells, who were there at the start and provided key leadership even after the party became the Liberal Party around 1859. The Whig dynasties were still a distinct group within the

Liberal Party, yet as time went on, they found themselves ever more at odds with their political home. The Russells who had helped organise a Glorious 'Revolution', were not really that revolutionary at all; they had always argued that the overthrow of James II was a reaffirmation of England's ancient constitution represented by Magna Carta. If anyone had been a revolutionary, the Whigs claimed, it was King James in attempting to overthrow the Parliamentary establishment. The Whigs had merely safeguarded England from James's despotism. Any reforms they then undertook in government, which may have appeared quite radical, had also been done to ensure that calm, ordered progress took place without the need for revolutions such as that witnessed in France from 1789: change in order to conserve. All this sounded very like the modern conservatism which future Prime Minister, Edward Stanley, Earl of Derby, had espoused in the 1830s. In the 1880s the great Whig dynasties split from the Liberals, eventually to merge with the Conservatives.

Yet the Whigs were defined by more than a political creed. They may have been founded on commitments to political principles of liberty over despotic rule and parliamentary (and aristocratic) supremacy. But Whiggism meant more than politics. Part of it was economics. These particular landed magnates surfed, rather than sank, on the incoming tides of the Industrial Revolution, adding railway shares, mineral mines and other enterprises to their traditional agricultural portfolios. As a result, they became very rich. Their wealth then allowed them the leisure for other pursuits. They were the epitome of glamour and grandeur.

In the Georgian era, the Whig dynasties became the cultural leaders of their day, far more so than the Monarchs who gave their name to that period. The Whigs imagined themselves as modern versions of the senators of Ancient Rome, guardians of civilisation and patrons of culture. As part of their classical education, they went on Grand Tours around Europe and brought back crates of antiquities. As art connoisseurs they were arbiters of beauty and good taste. Palladianism was the architectural language of Whiggism. Those who did not rebuild their family seats in Palladian style as the Russells did, often built or obtained other houses in the style. The Cavendishes had Chiswick in London. The Spencers also built themselves a mansion in Westminster. To the Whigs, family was the true qualification; they were related to each other many times over down the generations. The Russell family tree stands in a garden alongside, and intricately intertwined with, those of Cavendish, Spencer, Grosvenor and others. The garden is obviously landscaped, in the grounds of a neoclassical house.

Family seat: Woburn Abbey
Described as one of the principal 'Temples of Whiggism', the house at Woburn was constructed in its present form in the mid-eighteenth century. One of its leading architects was Henry Flitcroft, the Palladian designer who had been draughtsman to the 'Architect Earl' of Burlington. Flitcroft was responsible for updating many a country house to Georgian tastes. As mentioned in the introduction, the sweeping east front of Wentworth Woodhouse in South Yorkshire (at over 600 feet, the longest private house facade in Britain) was Flitcroft's design. What he found at Woburn was a house built in the reign of James I, following the rectangular courtyarded layout of the old abbey cloister. Flitcroft was employed by the 4th Duke of Bedford to turn Woburn into a more suitable setting for Whiggish gatherings. He retained the basic shape of the house but completely rebuilt the west front with perfect Palladian symmetry and characteristic terminating pavilions. Afterwards, the park and gardens were redesigned by Humphrey Repton, last of the great Georgian landscapers, who had succeeded Capability Brown as the aristocracy's go-to for producing pleasure grounds.

The east wing of the house was demolished in the 1950s due to dry rot, but Woburn Abbey remains a substantial example of

Palladian architecture. In the mid-2020s, the house was closed for a major renovation programme, ensuring that the Woburn remains so for years to come.

Lord John Russell and the Earls Russell

In 1861, the third son of the 6th Duke of Bedford was granted his own peerage as the 1st Earl Russell. Before his peerage, he had been known by his courtesy title of the younger son of a duke, Lord John Russell. It was under that name that he first became Prime Minister in 1846. Russell had entered Parliament in 1816 as a Whig (naturally). He was the most influential Russell in politics since the family helped establish the Whigs over a century before. Lord John was responsible for leading the efforts to pass the Great Reform Act in 1832 on behalf of then Prime Minister Earl Grey. As Home Secretary, Russell was also a modernising force, overseeing reforms that were socially liberal for their time. He reduced the number of offences that were punishable by death. He also supported the funding of state education. As Prime Minister, he reduced the legal length of the working day in factories and established a Board of Public Health.

Russell's legacy was far from unblemished, however. There were serious failures. His government's disastrous response to the Irish Famine in the late 1840s left a stain not only on government but on the British State as a whole. A quarter of Ireland's population was lost to starvation or emigration. In Russell's brief second term (which he led from the House of Lords as Earl Russell) he attempted another Reform Act but was unable to keep his party united behind it. It was said that his two premierships were in fact the ruin of the Whig Party and might have stunted the emergence of the Liberal Party that succeeded it.

Despite the earldom, this Prime Minister is still usually referred to as Lord John Russell in the history books. And he is not the only Earl Russell to be better known by his full name. The most notable holder since John was the 3rd Earl, more familiar as Bertrand Russell (1872–1970). Bertrand was among the most influential of British philosophers. Having studied mathematics at Cambridge, he produced works on logic, but became famous as a public intellectual, writing on social issues as well as history and politics. An active social and political campaigner, Russell was imprisoned for his opposition to Britain's involvement in the First World War. He remained a committed advocate for peace and, later, for nuclear disarmament. In 1958, Russell became the first president of the Campaign for Nuclear Disarmament. By this time, the polymath was already a Nobel Laureate in Literature, recognised for his 'varied and significant writings in which he [championed] humanitarian ideals and freedom of thought'.

The seat of the Earls Russell (no longer in family hands) was Pembroke Lodge in Richmond, London. It was given to the 1st Earl by Queen Victoria, and frequented by the greatest names of the age, from Liberal grandees like Palmerston and Gladstone, to the literary immortals Thackeray, Tennyson and Charles Dickens (who dedicated *A Tale of Two Cities* to John Russell).

The Earls Russell have remained politically active liberals. Even after the removal of hereditary peers from the House of Lords, the 7th Earl Russell became a member in 2023, having been elected to the chamber by a vote of the whole House. He now sits as a Liberal Democrat.

What will be will be

Few members of Woburn's Russell family had a happy time in the nineteenth and twentieth centuries. Successive dukes of Bedford led strangely reclusive lives. Some were cold-hearted in their isolation. Some encountered tragedy. In terms of dynastic reach, the Russells, like other notable families, gave up on their extraneous estates. They sold off Covent Garden in 1913. By that time the area had become a slum, and not a good advert for its landlords.

The area had been infamous as a red-light district for a long time (so much so that in the late 1700s, an 'essential guide' to the area's prostitutes was published annually: *Harris's List of Covent Garden Ladies* was the directory for 'any serious gentleman of pleasure'). Covent Garden was ignored by the Russells for so long that in the end it was better passed to investors.

The Bedfords' strange withdrawal from society had certainly begun by the time of the 8th Duke, William (1809–1872). A misanthrope who went to bizarre lengths to avoid contact with the outside world, he would travel – when he had to – in a shuttered carriage so nobody would see him.

Equally reclusive was his cousin the 9th Duke, Hastings (1819–1891). His issues included hypochondria, which seemed to run in the family. Known as the 'Iceberg' for his hatred of people, he was described by Prime Minister Disraeli as 'a strange character [who] enjoys his power and prosperity, and yet seems to hold a lower opinion of human nature than any man'. Suffering from deep depression, the duke committed suicide, shooting himself, the inquest stated, while temporarily insane.

When Brian Masters interviewed many of the then dukes of the realm in the 1970s, it was clear that the Bedfords of living memory had inherited their forebears' peculiarities. The 11th Duke, Herbrand (1858–1940) was an intensely cold-hearted man. His son, the 12th Duke, Hastings (1888–1953) inherited the hypochondriac 'gene' which led to Woburn Abbey apparently smelling like a hospital from the use of disinfectant. Nancy Mitford claimed the duke had a pet spider to which he fed roast beef! He was an avowed pacifist and conscientious objector, which put an end to whatever relationship he might have had with his father. Herbrand thought his son a disgrace, bringing shame on the House of Russell. His pacifism was founded on Christian grounds. He spoke up on behalf of conscientious objectors during speeches in the House of Lords. His argument that Britain's treatment of pacifists revealed that its people were just as capable of victimisation and 'man-hunting' as were the Nazis caused uproar, and the Lords passed resolutions declaring that 'the Duke of Bedford be no longer heard'. MI5 suspected him of collaboration with the Germans. He funded fascist movements in Britian, as well as socialist parties. One of the most complex and controversial peers of mid-twentieth century, he died of an accidental gunshot wound, though it was strongly suspected that suicide had again ended a Duke of Bedford's life.

His son 'Ian' John Russell, 13th Duke (1917-2002) was one of the best-known peers of the later twentieth century. He founded Woburn Safari Park in 1970 and successfully turned Woburn Abbey into a major visitor attraction. He was also a writer and an actor, appearing in a variety of feature films and even Coronation Street! His son 'Henry' Robin Russell, 14th Duke (1940-2003) was also a media personality, having appeared in the BBC reality show *Country House*. Sadly, he died just over seven months after his father and was the shortest serving Duke of Bedford. He had achieved much during his life as Marquess of Tavistock, particularly in the world of conservation. A statue of him stands in Beijing's Nan Haizi Garden, erected by the Chinese government to commemorate Russell's part in preventing the extinction of Père David's deer, a species native to the river valleys of southern China. Lord Tavistock had acquired the remaining deer from zoos across Europe, bred them in Woburn Park and reintroduced them in China. The duke's loss at the age of sixty-three was yet another shock for the family. It left his son Andrew (b. 1962) as the 15th Duke and 19th Earl of Bedford. The motto of the Russells, 'what will be will be', seems won by experience.

The Flying Duchess

Largely forgotten today – oddly, considering that her life would make an extraordinary docudrama – is the woman nicknamed the 'Flying Duchess of Bedford', Mary Russell (1865–1947). At the age of sixty-three, she became interested in aviation and learnt how to fly. This was no mere passing fancy or diverting personal hobby. She didn't just fly her planes from Woburn Park to her house at Wispers in Sussex (where she had constructed a hanger); she was a pioneering and record-breaking aviator. In 1929 she headed off on a 10,000-mile flight from Kent to Karachi in present-day Pakistan. The year after, she broke records again by flying from Kent to Cape Town, South Africa, in 'The Spider', her G-EDTS *Princess Xenia*. She financed these flights herself and was at the time a media sensation. She achieved her solo pilot licence at the age of sixty-six.

Her life before taking to the skies was remarkable enough. Born Mary Tribe, she had married the 'Iceberg' 11th Duke of Bedford in 1888. Her achievements during the First World War were the subject of much publicity for which she was honoured in later life. She had turned Woburn Abbey into a military hospital and been highly influential as a nurse and was honoured with the Royal Red Cross. The duchess had also been instrumental in helping to bring about women's suffrage. She was a member of the Women's Tax Resistance that protested against the taxation and disenfranchisement of women.

Meanwhile, her pastimes were as unexpected as they were diverse. She was one of the first Western women to practice jujutsu, the Japanese martial art, even appearing in an instruction book on the subject in 1905. She was an expert on birds and bird migration, keeping her *Bird-Watcher's Diary* (published posthumously in 1938).

Through all this, she dealt with near-constant tinnitus and later total deafness. Her love of flying was partly encouraged by the relief she got from her from her hearing problems while in the air. She continued to make staggeringly ambitious flights for the rest of her life, including into the Sahara Desert. Her life was to end on such an expedition. In March 1937, she set off on a solo trip from

Woburn Abbey. Her plane crashed in the North Sea, her body never recovered. The duchess was seventy-one years old.

The present holder of Mary's title, Louise, Duchess of Bedford, is a driving force behind the business of keeping the Woburn Estates going in the twenty-first century. In so doing, she is part of a long tradition of duchesses who have ensured the survival of their respective Houses.

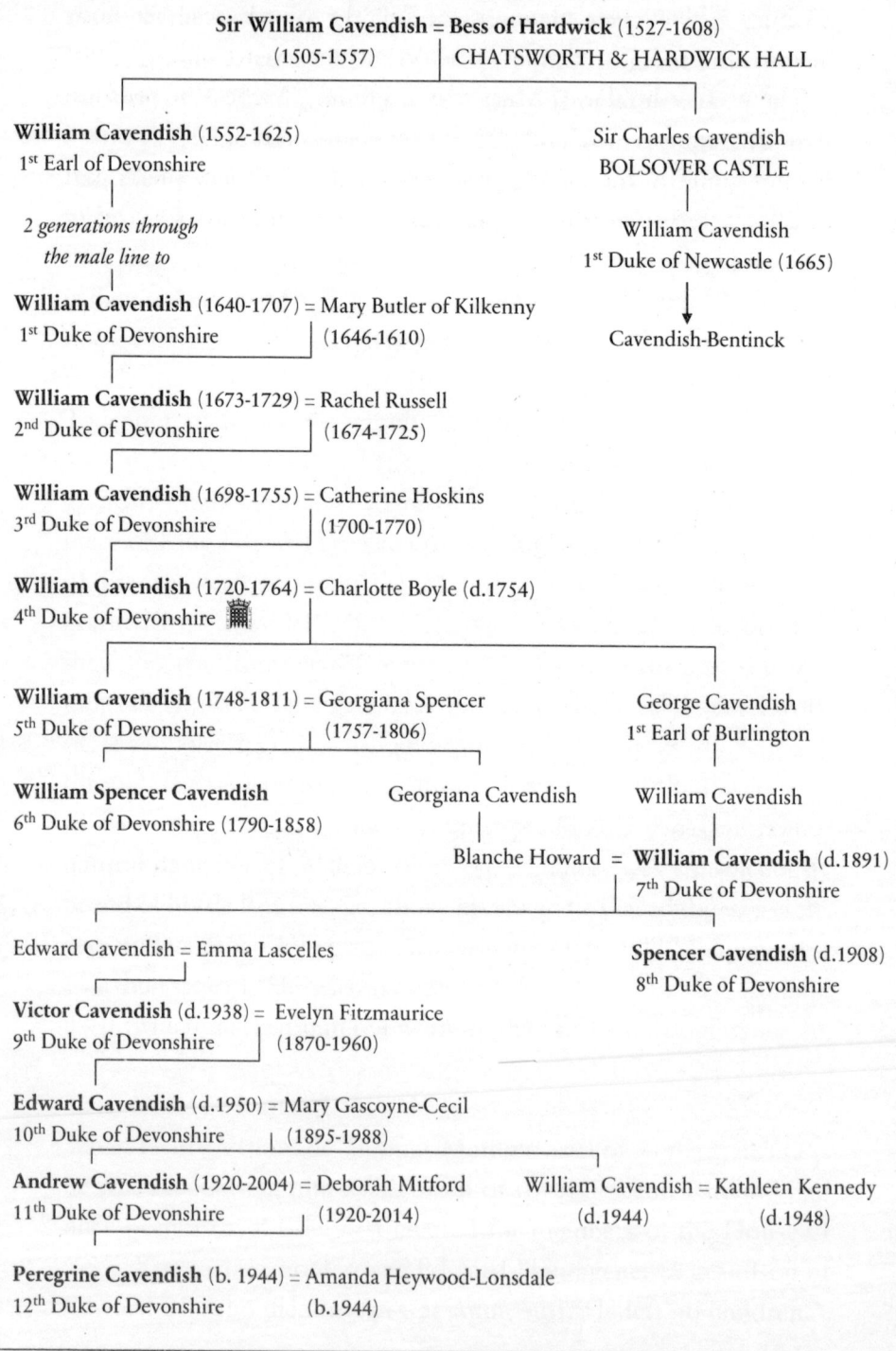

The Cavendishes of Chatsworth

Duke of Devonshire

Dukedom created	1694
Monarchs	William III & Mary II
Subsidiary titles	Marquess of Hartington; Earl of Burlington; Baron Cavendish

The Cavendish family is one of a number of ambitious dynasties that rose to prominence under the Tudors. Sir William Cavendish (1505–1557) was not as eminent a political figure as Williams Cecil or Russell, he was a civil servant of decidedly middling rank. But the remarkable success his family enjoyed over the following centuries was not down to Sir William anyway, but to his remarkable wife Elizabeth Hardwick (1527–1608). 'Bess of Hardwick', as she is better known, established the Cavendishes in her own native Derbyshire, built the great palaces of Chatsworth and Hardwick Hall there, and amassed a fortune that would see her family ride out more than one economic storm. Bess's descendant, the 1st Duke of Devonshire, was one of the first Whig grandees, inviting William of Orange to England. The Cavendish family remained one of the greatest Whig, and then Liberal, families into the twentieth century. Even as the fortunes of the aristocracy waned, they remained central figures in high society, making glamorous matches to a Mitford and to a member of the American political dynasty, the Kennedys. At Chatsworth, they also helped pioneer stately home tourism, saving that iconic house from destruction.

'Building Bess' of Hardwick

The foundations of the mighty House of Cavendish were laid down by a young girl born with very few prospects in the wilds of Derbyshire sometime around 1527. This girl's ambition for herself, and later for her children, led her to diligently – even ruthlessly – build an inheritance that would make her the richest woman in England after Queen Elizabeth I. Her grandchildren included the ancestors of the dukes of Newcastle, Portland and Devonshire, and a woman seriously considered as a possible successor to the Queen. Without Bess of Hardwick, few today would know the name of Cavendish. As Roy Hattersley observed in his 2013 history of the Devonshire branch, this great dynasty 'did not have a founding father. It had a founding mother [even if] the name was bequeathed to her descendants by her second husband, William Cavendish.'

The Cavendish family of Cavendish in Suffolk – where they lived before Bess brought them north – was not of any great not in the fifteenth century. Their lineage was also uncertain. They are likely of the family of John de Cavendish, a lawyer killed during the Peasants Revolt in 1381, who used the heraldic device of three silver stags' heads on a black field, the arms used by William Cavendish when he married Bess of Hardwick. (The entwined serpent crest was Bess's addition to the arms, aptly symbolising cunning and caution.) William himself started out his career in the retinue of the chief ministers Cardinal Wolsey and then Thomas Cromwell. He deftly survived the fall of Wolsey by becoming a

Protestant rather swiftly, and acting as Cromwell's strong man, enforcing the Dissolution of the Monasteries. He would equally quickly revert to Catholicism when Mary I became Queen. William was a treasurer in the Exchequer when he took Bess of Hardwick as his third wife. Elizabeth Hardwick was married four times in her life, but only had children with William Cavendish, the one husband for whom she seems to have had genuine affection. Thus, the enormous wealth and property empire Bess accumulated in her lifetime went solely on aggrandising the House of Cavendish.

Bess's early life was far from opulent. She was the daughter of a farmer-squire who had fallen on particularly hard times. John Hardwick died soon after Bess was born, leaving her mother, elder brother, two sisters and Bess at the mercy of the Tudor Court of Wards. Because Bess's eldest brother was only eight years old, the Exchequer took control of his lands, administering it for profit until he turned twenty-one. Little is known about how the family survived; Bess's mother remarried to an even poorer man, Ralph Leche, of a small estate nearby called Chatsworth. It was certainly not wealth or social standing that set Bess upon the road to greatness. If anything at all helped her, it was a very distant familial relationship to an old feudal family named Zouche, with whom Bess managed to procure a position. She was essentially a servant, but the role gave Bess a taste for the more refined lifestyle, as she travelled to the Zouche's London home.

At the age of fifteen Bess was married off by her family to a Derbyshire neighbour, Robert Barlow. This might have put an end to any ambitions she then had for advancement, except that her first husband, being sickly from a young age, died soon after the marriage. Bess then returned to London and used the connections she had made there to gain another place as a Lady in Waiting in the household of the Greys. Here she mixed with true nobility, even royalty, meeting a young Princess Elizabeth with whom she formed a friendship. It was also among the friends and hangers-on of the Greys that she met the twice-widowed accountant William Cavendish. The pair were married at Greys manor house in Leicestershire on 20 August 1547. Sir William (he was knighted for services to the Crown) had been given land from the monasteries he had helped to dissolve (he had literally overseen the roofs being taken off buildings to prevent them ever re-opening). Bess persuaded her new husband to sell these lands in favour of purchasing an estate in her native county. She remembered her stepfather's manor at Chatsworth, which the Leches had recently sold to their relations, the Agards. Sir William made an offer of £600 in 1549, and Chatsworth became the seat of the Cavendishes.

Bess and William were ambitious kindred spirits, even, it seems, sharing a disregard for financial legality. Bess spent a fortune building at Chatsworth; in place of a manor, there rose a huge Tudor house for the Cavendish heirs. William, a royal accountant, was eventually summoned to court to answer for irregularities appearing in his records. Bess hurried down to London to be with her partner-in-crime when he was ordered to pay back £5000 to the Royal Chamber, the equivalent of nearly £1.25 million today. William wrote to Queen Mary, begging her to have mercy, if not on him, then on his 'poor wife and miserable and innocent children', signing off, 'Your very humble, meek, and poor sick man, William Cavendish'. It wasn't all a play for sympathy. He must have been sick because he died soon after, plunging Bess into grief. She entered in her diary: 'Sir William Cavendish, knight, my most dear and well beloved Husband departed this present Life ... on whose soul I most humbly beseech the Lord to have Mercy and rid me and his poor children out of our great misery.' His death, followed soon by the death of Queen Mary, did put an end to the financial issues, with Bess's old friend Elizabeth coming to the throne. Two marriages then followed: William St Loe died in 1565; Bess then married George Talbot in 1567. Talbot, 6th Earl of Shrewsbury, was by far the grandest of her husbands, head of an ancient House that made her a countess, nobility at last. For the rest of her life, she was known as 'Elizabeth Shrewsbury'.

Talbot was a man of immense import in the realm, who would be appointed Earl Marshal by Elizabeth after the execution of the 4th Duke of Norfolk. He was as aware of his lineage and dignity as any Howard, and as good as a monarch to the people of the Midlands. He married Bess believing that he could take advantage of the vast estates she had put together. Talbot's principal seat was Sheffield Castle, which was very near to Bess's lands in Derbyshire, and some of his own estates at Bolsover and Glossop. Talbot's plan was to join these estates into a mini-kingdom.

His plan did not succeed. Bess had no intention of allowing Chatsworth to pass to the Talbots, she was determined her fortune should go to her children, the children of her 'well-beloved' husband, William Cavendish. Her chance to ensure it came about when Talbot found himself in financial difficulty owing to the expense that came with being the personal jailor of Mary, Queen of Scots. Elizabeth I had charged Talbot with keeping an eye on her cousin-queen. He provided secure accommodation for Mary at Sheffield and at Chatsworth, but the cost was telling. Bess offered to help out, on the proviso that Talbot should sign a guarantee allowing Chatsworth to pass to her son. He did so but was not at all happy with the situation. When one of his stepsons – the second of many more William Cavendishes to come – took control of Chatsworth, Talbot marched with a private militia from Sheffield to take it back. Cavendish barred the gates, and the queen ordered Talbot's forces to retreat.

Bess's favourite son was always William. She fell out with her eldest, Henry, who by law of primogeniture nevertheless inherited Chatsworth. For that reason, Bess set about building another great house to be handed down to William. This was Hardwick Hall, the Elizabethan Prodigy masterpiece designed by

Robert Smythson. She built it on her birth family's old lands at Hardwick, which she had shrewdly purchased from her penurious brother. Later, William also bought Chatsworth from his outcast brother Henry. And thus, all Bess's plans for a great Derbyshire dynasty came to fruition in William. He was advanced to the Peerage as Baron Cavendish just before Bess's death in 1608. Ten years later, James I would grant him the title of earl of Devonshire in return for a small fee. (Derbyshire might have been preferable, but confusion would have arisen with similar titles like the earldom of Derby, and James never did care much about peerage custom anyway.)

The brief blossoming of the Newcastle branch

The Devonshire branch persists at Chatsworth to this day. Of ducal status since 1694, it is in fact the younger of two ducal lines established by Bess's descendants. An older dukedom burnt brightly but did not survive more than two generation before flickering out. This was the dukedom of Newcastle, based at Bolsover Castle (purchased by them from the Talbots). The 1st Duke was a famous horseman and Civil War cavalier. His wife, Duchess Margaret, was a fascinating figure who defied her times to become an author of fiction, poetry and philosophy, publishing under her own name in an age when women were usually excluded from such pursuits. Her novel, *The Blazing World* (1666), is often cited not just as the only utopian novel written by a woman in the seventeenth century, but as the first ever work of science fiction, predating Mary Shelley's *Frankenstein* by a century and a half. In the novel – which, like Shelley's, is set partly in the Arctic – an abducted woman is set free by the wrath of the gods and discovers a portal to another dimension near the North Pole. In the parallel world she finds a society of animal-human hybrids and becomes their empress. It's an extraordinary forerunner to so many 'other world' fantasies, yet virtually unknown today. The book began with a sonnet written by Margaret's husband the duke, which praises her extraordinary imaginative abilities. She was groundbreaking in other ways, becoming the first woman to attend a meeting of the Royal Society in 1667, where she engaged in passionate scientific debate with Robert Boyle among others.

The line of dukes of Newcastle ended with the 2nd Duke, Henry Cavendish (d. 1691). Bolsover Castle passed through his daughter into the Bentinck family, dukes of Portland. A later duke cemented the Cavendish inheritance by marrying a daughter of one of the dukes of Devonshire and changing his family name to Cavendish-Bentinck. The dukes of Portland lived at Bolsover, and at their old seat of Welbeck Abbey in Nottinghamshire, until that dukedom's extinction in 1990.

Related family: the Talbots

Next to Arundel, Shrewsbury is the most ancient and storied earldom in the English Peerage. It was granted to John, 7th Baron Talbot, a soldier of the Hundred Years War, in 1442. Even then, the family's lineage was legendary. They traced their descent from Richard Talbot (*fl. c.* 1086). The 1st Baron's grandmother had been the Welsh heiress Gwenlian, daughter of a prince of the family of Rhys ap Gruffydd of southern Wales.

The Talbots are popularly associated with the hunting dog which appears as their heraldic badge. It's thought the Talbot breed (now extinct) was only fully developed by the 1600s, and its name may derive from the fact that 'Talbot' was often a name given to individual hunting dogs in medieval times. The exact relationship between the family, their badge, and the dog breed remains mysterious.

Over the centuries, the Shrewsbury title passed to some very distant cousins of previous holders, and their huge collection of houses has been broken up. The 12th Earl was a signatory to the Glorious Revolution and was created Marquess of Alton and 1st Duke of Shrewsbury in 1694 (just as the Cavendish signatory became 1st Duke of Devonshire). He was also the last, however, for he had no son, and the dukedom became extinct on his death. The ancient earldom passed to his cousin. That earldom managed to endure through various other failures of the direct line. In 1860, the House of Lords was asked to determine a male-line successor following the death of the 17th Earl. The Lords declared that Henry Chetwynd-Talbot, a very distant cousin, should become the 18th Earl. It was a gigantic jump genealogically, with Henry descending only from the 1st and 2nd Earls. The current earl, the 22nd, is also a Chetwynd-Talbot. If the family has often threatened to follow the Talbot hounds to extinction, their houses have largely succumbed. Sheffield Castle in no more, and they sold their last ancestral seat of Alton Towers in 1924. It is now surrounded by one of the nation's most popular theme parks.

'The architect of England's liberty': William Cavendish, 1st Duke of Devonshire

Bess of Hardwick's descendants at Chatsworth survived the Civil War and Commonwealth years by generally staying out of state affairs. After the Restoration, there was nothing to suggest that Bess's great-great-grandson, the 4th Earl of Devonshire, would be any more political, still less be remembered as a founding father of England's modern constitution. In his youth William Cavendish (1640–1707) was a notorious brawler and libertine, who had numerous affairs and a bad habit of challenging any man he disliked to a duel. Lord Cavendish (as he was known until his succession as earl in 1684) was imprisoned twice, once for arrogance, once for violence. The former came while he was MP for Derbyshire, and he insulted a gentleman. Parliament rebuked Cavendish, and he pinned a note to the gates of Whitehall Palace, doubling down on his insult, by declaring the gentleman in question to be 'a rogue, a rascal, and a coward'. Parliament sent the member for Derbyshire to the Tower to think about how he conducted himself in future. The second imprisonment was for what first appears the relatively harmless, not to say comical, charge of 'tweaking the nose of a certain Colonel Culpeper'. In fact, the charge masked what was a violent assault on a man with whom Cavendish had fought over land in Derbyshire. While Culpeper had been violent towards Cavendish in the past, this incident involved an unprovoked attack which ended with Cavendish giving Culpeper 'some despising blow with the head of his cane'. It had all happened in the drawing room of Whitehall Palace, to the anger of the king, James II. Lord Devonshire was ushered to King's Bench Prison and given a huge fine of £30,000.

The arrogance displayed by Cavendish throughout his life was on show soon after when he informed his jailor that, actually, he didn't really have the time to sit in prison, paid a fee to keep his cell open for him should he require it again, and simply left for Chatsworth. No one at King's Bench dared to contradict him. When King James found out, he was furious and issued a warrant for Cavendish's arrest. The High Sheriff of Derbyshire was tasked with apprehending the earl. A few sources say that the sheriff was too afraid of Cavendish to enforce the warrant, others that he attempted an arrest at Chatsworth but that he and his men were instead arrested by the Chatsworth staff and ejected from the estate. Either way, it was impossible for the royal authorities to touch Cavendish while in Chatsworth; despite his arrogance, he enjoyed the loyalty of the Derbyshire people.

While in exile from London, the earl devoted his energies to improving his ancestor Bess of Hardwick's house at Chatsworth. At first, he did not seek to undertake a major renovation. He began by taking down the south front of the house and replacing it with a more fashionable classical facade. Once he started, however, he was unable to stop, and for a further two decades, he transformed Chatsworth into England's first baroque house.

Family seat: Chatsworth House
The term 'Palace of the Peaks', according to art historian James Miller, perfectly encapsulates Chatsworth. It is 'a palace: a huge, magnificent house, embowered in its own lushness', ultra grand, like nothing else in the Peak District, and one of the most famous stately homes in Britain.

There was probably a house at Chatsworth when Bess of Hardwick bought the old Leche family lands in 1549, though no trace of it has ever been found. Bess built an enormous new house with a gate tower that gave the appearance of a forbidding Tudor prison, far removed from the Renaissance style she later adopted at Hardwick. Nothing now remains of Bess's house, though the Hunting Tower she built in the 1580s does still stand on the hill overlooking Chatsworth, and does bear striking similarities to Hardwick Hall's architecture.

The house as it now appears was the work of the 1st Duke of Devonshire, building between 1686 and 1707. Because it was created bit-by-bit on the footprint of Bess's house, with no initial overall plan, the new Chatsworth was like its predecessor in shape: a square block around a central courtyard. Had it been built from scratch, it would probably have had the meandering look of later baroque houses like Castle Howard and Blenheim. The interior also followed the structures of Bess's house. The Elizabethan Great Hall was replaced by a baroque Painted Hall by Louis Laguerre, scenes from the life of Julius Caesar across the ceiling. The old long gallery became the interconnected State Apartment rooms. Outside, George

London and Henry Wise created a grand formal garden. Leonard Knyff recorded the changes made before the West Front was finally rebuilt, and a canal pond dug in 1702.

In the eighteenth century, the 4th Duke created a new park with Capability Brown. In the early 1800s, the 6th Duke employed architect Jeffry Wyatville to build a 400-foot-long North Wing on the house, with the huge Belvedere Tower at its end. The wing was designed for entertainment and pleasure: it housed (and still does) the duke's sculpture collection in a purpose-built gallery, a theatre, great dining room, and orangery.

William Cavendish and James II were on bad personal terms to say the least, then. And they were increasingly at political odds, too. An early biographer of Cavendish suggests that the earl's time in hiding at Chatsworth saw his political views refine toward rebellious Whiggism. While reading the Roman historian Tacitus, Cavendish began to mull on similarities between James II and the despotic emperor, Diocletian. When news came that King James' wife had given birth to an heir, foreshadowing an absolutist succession, Cavendish realised that although 'a prince governing by law deserved his allegiance, yet he could never digest the notion of passive obedience to tyrants'. As a member of the Protestant aristocracy, being so much disregarded by James, Cavendish now took a leading role in the effort to dethrone him.

Cavendish met in secret with his co-conspirators one night in a small inn near Chesterfield to begin planning the Glorious Revolution. (The inn still stands, incidentally, as the Revolution House Museum.) Lord Devonshire agreed that if required, he would personally secure the Midlands for William of Orange, capture Nottingham and march south against King James. In the event, a military intervention was not needed, for James II fled.

The following year, Cavendish married Rachel Russell, daughter of his friend, the executed Whig martyr William, Lord Russell.

The pair returned to Chatsworth to continue turning it into a dazzling symbol of the power of the great Whig aristocracy over the despotism of Monarchs. Cavendish had already made his voice heard on the matter of the status of the Prince of Orange. Some peers believed that the prince's wife Mary should alone be Monarch; as James II's daughter, she was the rightful hereditary heir to the 'abdicated' throne. Her husband was most unhappy at the prospect of being a mere prince consort, however, and Cavendish was key to convincing the House of Lords to crown William and Mary as joint sovereigns. In return, King William III made sure that Cavendish's status was also elevated, dubbing him Duke of Devonshire in 1694.

Politics and prestige

Bess would have been proud of the dynasty she had established. The dukes of Devonshire remained at the heart of national events from decade to decade, century to century. The first seven dukes were all named William Cavendish. The 4th served briefly as Prime Minister, but the House of Cavendish preferred to shape political events from behind the scenes rather than in the limelight. The 5th Duke was a Whig leader whose London mansion, Devonshire House, was virtually Whig headquarters where he would influence the likes of Charles James Fox over dinner. He made a sound – though unhappy – Whig marriage to Lady Georgiana Spencer, herself a radical campaigner for the party. The other towering Whig was the 8th Duke, Spencer Cavendish (1833–1908), who, as Marquess of Hartington, had been leader of the dynastic retinue in the Liberal Party, and was largely responsible for the decamping of those families to the Conservative Party.

Many dynasties have been known more for their political power than their glamour and cultural impact, or vice versa. The dukes of Devonshire have been famous for both, and at the highest levels. They seemed to inherit (partly via the 4th Duke's wife, Charlotte

Boyle, daughter of the 'Architect Earl' of Burlington) a taste for the arts and architecture, which led to extraordinary contributions to national culture. Duchess Georgiana's son, William Spencer Cavendish, known as the Bachelor Duke for never marrying, was a patron of the architect and horticulturist Joseph Paxton. Together they transformed the garden at Chatsworth into one of the most celebrated anywhere on Earth (and where they cultivated the Cavendish Banana). They built an incredible fairytale castle in Lismore in southern Ireland, an estate inherited from the Boyles. The duke did much more for his tenants there during the Great Famine than Lord John Russell's government did on a national level. Indeed, the Devonshires had so many estates far beyond Chatsworth that their legacy can still be found dotted across England and Ireland.

Walk down Picadilly in the bustling heart of London and you will find a set of ornate iron gates leading into Green Park. They bear the coat of arms of the Cavendish family, the three stags' heads and the entwined serpent. Until the 1920s, these gates led into Devonshire House. Built by the 3rd Duke between 1734 and 1740 to designs by William Kent, it was not only a Whig powerhouse under the 5th Duke, it was the social centre for the 'It' crowd, reaching a zenith under the 8th Duke and his duchess, Louise, in the *fin de siècle* 1890s. Duchess Louise was the widow of the Duke of Manchester when she married Spencer Compton Cavendish in 1892 (hence her epithet, the 'Double Duchess'). Every season, they threw lavish parties at Devonshire House. The most renowned of these occurred to mark Queen Victoria's Diamond Jubilee in 1897. Described as the 'Ball of the Century', guests were ordered to wear fancy dress: 'allegorical or historical costume before 1815'. A troop of characters thus processed through the gates of Devonshire House: Duchess Louise attended as Zenobia, Queen of Palmyra; the duke came as Emperor Charles V; Lady Ormonde dressed as Guinevere attended by Knights of the Round

Table; Lady Warwick was Marie Antoinette; Lady Wolverton was Britannia, complete with Union Jack shield; Lord Rowton was Archbishop Cranmer. There were also Norse Valkyrie and Greek Furies flouncing about. The Duke and Duchess of Marlborough went all the way to Paris to have their costumes created, those of the French Ambassador and his wife at the Court of Catherine the Great of Russia.

The great stage actor Henry Irving (said to have inspired the character of Dracula in Bram Stoker's novel published the same year) came as a cardinal, annoying Lord Dunraven who had himself come as Cardinal Mazarin. It was a spectacle unlike any seen before, Devonshire House decked out in flowers brought all the way from the conservatories at Chatsworth. It could not have been lost on many of the participants that – with the exception of the mythological characters – their ancestors may have met many of the actual historical figures they had dressed up as.

The historic photos of Devonshire House bring home, in the words of one historian, the 'tragedy of this urban loss'. It was demolished soon after the Devonshires sold it off. But other of their houses survived. A raft of them were acquired through the Boyle marriage. These included Lismore, and yet another mansion on Picadilly, Burlington House. Owning two mansions next door to each other seemed too vulgar even for the 5th Duke, who gave it to his younger brother. George Cavendish was then presented with a revived earldom of Burlington to begin his own cadet line. But Burlington House was not so easily cast aside. George's grandson, the 2nd Earl, ended up succeeding as 7th Duke of Devonshire, due to his cousin being a bachelor. The Bachelor Duke's favourite London residence had been Chiswick House, the Palladian villa built by his great-grandfather, the Architect Earl. (It was in Chiswick Gardens that he had first met Joseph Paxton.)

Bolton Abbey in Yorkshire was a Boyle legacy, while the Devonshires also inherited Compton Place in Eastbourne through marriage to heiress Elizabeth Compton. Many of these houses are now in use by various organisations (Compton Place as a school, Burlington House as the Royal Academy of Arts). But Bolton and Lismore remain, like Chatsworth, family homes. That these were saved was due to the sheer determination and managerial genius of the 11th Duke, Andrew Cavendish, and his duchess, the former Deborah Mitford.

Tax and revival

In 1950, the 10th Duke of Devonshire died unexpectedly at the age of fifty-five. Edward Cavendish had seen a fair amount of tragedy. He and his wife Mary Cecil (of Hatfield) had lost their eldest son William in 1944, killed fighting in the Netherlands. William's widow Kathleen Kennedy (sister of the future US President) was killed in a plane crash four years later, she was brought back to Chatsworth and buried in the family plot in Edensor, a mile from the House. In the post-war climate of staggering death duties payable on great estates, the loss of the 10th Duke left his younger son and heir, Andrew, owing 80 per cent on everything he now owned.

 He surrendered objets d'arts from the Chatsworth collection to the Treasury. As he was travelling to London one day he decided to take drastic action: 'It was then and there that I realised that Hardwick Hall would have to go. I made my mind up while the train was waiting at the platform, and although it was horrible to think of getting rid of Bess of Hardwick's house, it proved the best decision of my life.' Hardwick Hall, in the family for fifteen generations, was given to the nation and is now administered by the National Trust. That loss meant that Chatsworth could be saved as the family seat. The tax bill still took until 1967 to pay off, but by that time, the tide was turning in favour of the country house, and the public were starting to fear the idea of somewhere like Chatsworth being lost.

When they succeeded, Andrew and Deborah (known as Debo) were living in Edensor House in one of the estate villages. They moved into Chatsworth in 1959. Together, they not only saved the house but turned it into a flourishing business and world-class landmark visitor attraction. They also led a remarkable revival of aristocratic culture thought to have disappeared in the social earthquake of two World Wars. They achieved this by a combination of entrepreneurial skill and an ability to adapt the old aristocratic way of life for the modern world.

Debo's business instincts became almost legendary. She used to serve in the house giftshop and opened a farm shop in Pilsley, another estate village. The Great Stables built by the 4th Duke became a mini shopping centre with restaurants. When an outbreak of foot and mouth disease in cattle closed the house for a year in 2001, she and her husband decided to open to visitors at Christmas (then unheard of for stately homes) to recoup some of the financial loss. It was so successful that Chatsworth – and every other major house – has decorated for Christmas visitors every year since.

At the same time, Chatsworth became a social and cultural centre of a type that the old aristocracy would have recognised. They could not live in the manner of their ancestors with regiments of domestic servants, but these two children of the 1920s tried their best to remain true to the old ways (sometimes eccentrically so; the pair dressed for dinner – black tie – every evening even when dining alone). They managed to live in the sprawling palace of the peaks by creating a smaller house within the house. They installed a new kitchen below the suite of rooms they chose as their private home, with a lift to bring food up. With only a corner of the house lived-in, they could manage with one butler, footman, housekeeper, plus two cooks, maids, and two chauffeurs, a small staff by comparison with the legions that came before. The rest of the house would now be run by the curators and visitor services staff of the heritage industry.

With Chatsworth no longer under threat, once again the duke began collecting and commissioning art from the likes of Lucien Freud. Social gatherings included Evelyn Waugh, John Betjemen, and the family's Kennedy relations. They and their servants travelled with the seasons in the old nomadic-noble style, to Bolton Abbey for August shooting and Lismore for salmon fishing in the spring. The duchess was at the centre of these gatherings; famously witty, a prolific writer, she was not as keen on some of the art now being collected: 'Contemporary art is another subject altogether. The creators of these strange daubs have given up and *Untitled* is often as far as they will go – a wise decision.'

The 11th Duke died in 2004, Duchess Deborah in 2014. Their deaths marked the end of an era, but their funerals were very much in keeping with their traditionalist principles. *The Guardian* covered the duke's funeral by asking, 'Can this be England in 2004? The pictures of the Duke of Devonshire's funeral ... appear to show there exists in trim, green private parkland a world of fealty, aristocratic paternalism and domestic excess thought to have vanished on the battlefields of World War I. There they are ... head bowed before the departing Duke ... cooks in their big hats, maids in their white aprons, gardeners in green.' But as the article explains, all was not as it seemed. The 'maids' were really waitresses from the visitor cafeteria, dressed in uniforms designed to evoke the bygone age of country house idylls.

The Duchess's funeral ten years later saw similar scenes, attended by the then Prince Charles who walked behind the coffin as it was taken from Chatsworth to Edensor. Members of the Mitford family were also there, as the music of Elvis Presley played over loudspeakers in tribute to his aristocratic fan, Duchess Deborah.

Dynasties: The Noble Families of England

> ### Related family: the Mitfords
>
> Deborah, Duchess of Devonshire, was the youngest of the famed Mitford sisters who fascinated and scandalised high society with their political views in the 1930s. Their family originated at Mitford, Northumberland, where they had raided the Scottish borders in the Middle Ages. A junior line of these 'reivers' was elevated to the Peerage as Baron Redesdale in 1902. The Mitford Sisters were the daughters of the 2nd Baron.
>
> Nancy was a novelist, author of *Love in a Cold Climate* and *The Pursuit of Love*. Diana married first Bryan Guinness, of the Irish brewing family, and then Oswald Mosley, leader of the British Union of Fascists. The couple were imprisoned during the Second World War as they were thought so dangerous. Unity Mitford was a friend and admirer of Hitler. She shot herself when war was declared but survived for nine years with brain damage. Jessica Mitford leant to the other political extreme, being a communist, and fighting the fascists in the Spanish Civil War.
>
> Their only brother, Tom, was killed in action in 1945. The barony of Redesdale is now held by their cousin, once removed, Rupert Mitford.

'House Style'

In 2017 an extraordinary exhibition was held at Chatsworth. 'House Style: Five Centuries of Fashion at Chatsworth' was curated by Hamish Bowles, Editor-at-Large of American *Vogue* and Laura Cavendish, the current Countess of Burlington. The pair wrote a book to accompany the extravagant show that which aimed to showcase 'the story-telling power of clothes and the potency of these objects that can tell us so much about the wearer, the times they lived in, and the spaces they inhabited'. On show was everything from the ducal robes and cornets to Debo's 1953 Carmel Gown by Christian Dior, the current Duchess, Amanda's, wedding dress made for her in 1967 by Hubert de Givenchy, and Lady Burlington's own pieces by Erdem and Alexander McQueen. The exhibition celebrated the Cavendish family as drivers of fashion (in the broadest sense) as well as noting the power projected by the ermine robes and tiaras. It was also a mark of the Chatsworth's status today as an art and design museum of world renown.

The 12th Duke has had the exterior of the house cleaned and regilded, to preserve it for years to come. His son, the Earl of Burlington recently moved into Chatsworth himself with his family, including his own son and heir, James, Lord Cavendish, the eighteenth generation of his family to live there.

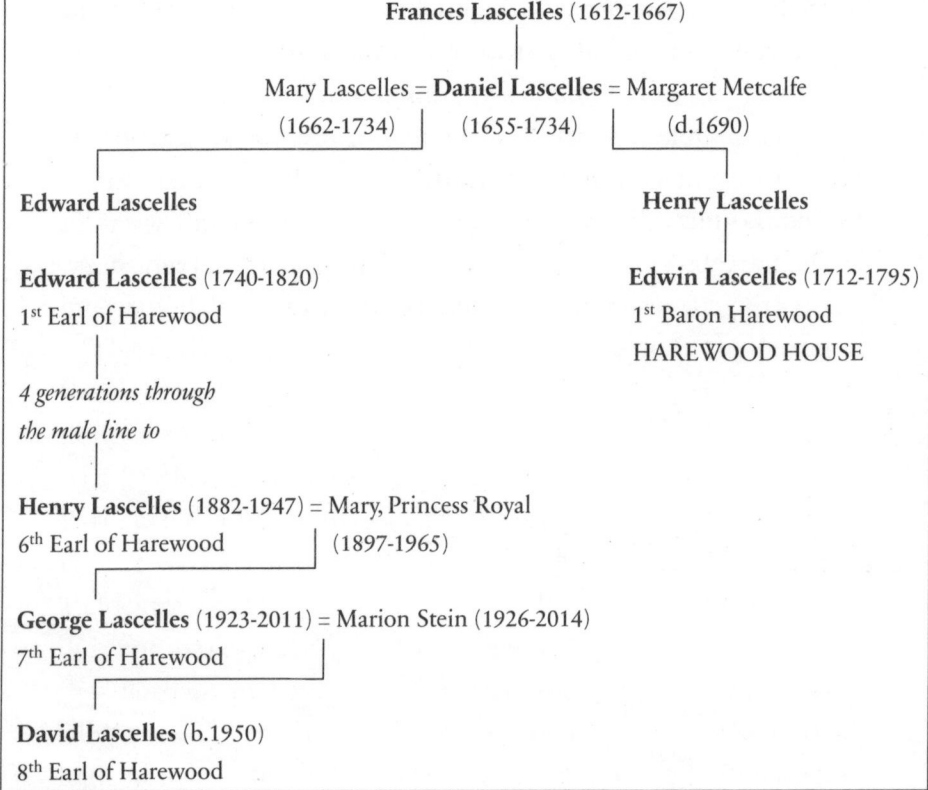

The Lascelles of Harewood House

Earl of Harewood

Earldom created	1812
Monarch	George III
Subsidiary titles	Viscount Lascelles; Baron Harewood

In recent times, the Lascelles have tried to uncover, and reckon with, a difficult history. The family fortune was founded upon the transatlantic slave trade, which saw captive Africans shipped in their millions to the Americas to work for white colonists in brutal conditions. Though that hateful practice enriched many an English dynasty, in the case of the Lascelles it was the driving force behind the rise to riches. The family founded its prosperity on several estates in the West Indies in the eighteenth century, which they personally oversaw; the builder of the family seat – Harewood House in Yorkshire – was himself born on a Barbados plantation in 1712.

Before that time, the Lascelles had been squire-farmers in Yorkshire, minor gentry seemingly descended from a Norman,

Picotus Lacelle, who fought at Hastings. They came nowhere near the Peerage until they purchased the Harewood estate, from where their title derives.

The barons of the Caribbean

'Harewood is a place of dazzlement,' wrote Simon Jenkins, former Chair of the National Trust, 'a St Petersburg palace on a Yorkshire ridge.' Harewood is a distinctive architectural achievement. It was built on land acquired by Henry Lascelles, a Director of the East India Company, in 1738. As a member of a prominent landed gentry family in Yorkshire, Lascelles (1690–1753) had a degree of status but not great wealth before the time he came to Harewood. His grandfather Francis (1612–1667) had been a prominent Roundhead general during the Civil War who had been at the trial of Charles I. The Lascelles clearly had a county position, but Henry Lascelles was eager to follow any new opportunity for enrichment. In the early eighteenth century, large fortunes were being made through the trade of enslaved Africans, who were packed onto ships in unspeakable conditions to be taken to the Caribbean. There, they were put to work on plantations that produced luxury goods for Europe: sugar, cotton, rum and tobacco among them. This repugnant business was legal at the time, and money made from it went to line the coffers of many British institutions. Henry Lascelles sailed to Barbados in 1711 at the age of twenty-one.

Henry set his sights on monopolising the sugar trade and managed to gain the exclusive contract to supply the Royal Navy whenever their ships were docked in Barbados. He bought shares in several slave ships to ensure the continuing arrival of slave labour for his plantations. Soon, Henry Lascelles was exactly what he had wanted to be: one of the wealthiest men in England.

English he may have been, but his son Edwin (1712–1795) was born in Barbados, a subject of the British Empire. Henry wanted to ensure that his son became a proper English gentleman, perhaps even a potential nobleman. So, Edwin was sent over to England, to Cambridge, to receive a classical education before heading off on a Grand Tour of Europe. In 1738, Henry and his heir Edwin made their dynastic ambitions plain by purchasing the Harewood estate in Yorkshire.

Harewood was then a site knitted together from older estates, on which had stood a fourteenth-century castle (the ruins of which still stand) and a small manor house. Edwin inherited the estate in 1753, by which time he was wealthy enough to begin planning the construction of a suitable family seat. Edwin owned around twenty-four Caribbean sugar plantations with over 3,000 slaves who were considered his property, stripped of their human rights. It is shocking to think that a place as beautiful as Harewood should have been built on the spoils of such an ugly business.

Family seat: Harewood House
Edwin Lascelles began building Harewood House in 1759. He was a miserly man who instructed his managers not to 'exceed the limits of expense' he had set down. Yet he also wanted to compete with the very best mansions then appearing in England. He thus hired the finest architects and designers (Robert Adam and John Carr), landscape gardener (Capability Brown) and furniture maker (Thomas Chippendale) to create his house.

Carr designed the exterior of Harewood, Adam the interior. Chippendale supplied sofas, chairs, tables, mirrors and beds, all in his highly sophisticated designs, the best that England had so far produced. Lascelles was not an easy man to work for (surely he disliked paying) and arguments over costs led to delays. The house was completed by 1765.

Not until the 1840s were any alterations made, when Sir Charles Barry was employed to add a second storey to the wings at either end of the house. This was at the bidding of the 3rd Earl and

Countess, who had thirteen children and required more bedrooms. Barry also added the parterres in the garden.

In common with many country houses, Harewood became a convalescent hospital for injured servicemen during both World Wars. In more recent times it has been a media centre. The present earl is a TV producer. Harewood has been seen in the first *Downton Abbey* film, while the village of Emmerdale (the set built for the ITV soap) is located on the Harewood estate.

In 1790, Edwin Lascelles achieved his ultimate ambition and was created the 1st Baron Harewood. Five years later he died childless, and his barony became extinct. His fortune and his house at Harewood passed to his cousin Edward Lascelles (1740–1820). Within a year, in 1796, Edward was created the 1st Baron Harewood in a new creation. In 1812, he was promoted as 1st Earl of Harewood.

A royal match

Edward Lascelles was still a baron when the Act for the Abolition of the Slave Trade was passed in 1807. This prohibited the trade in enslaved people and banned British ships from transporting Africans across the Atlantic. It was the beginning of the end of legal slave labour, as Britain attempted to atone for its past crimes, sending the Royal Navy to intercept slave ships and pressuring other nations to follow. Edward's son, the 2nd Earl (1739–1820), then witnessed the passing of the Slavery Abolition Act of 1833, which finally made slavery an illegal practice throughout the British Empire. It meant many of the Lascelles' family lands in the Caribbean had to be sold off (though by 1906, they still owned four estates in Barbados). The business model based on the exploitation of African peoples was, nevertheless, dismantled, and a shameful period for Britain was coming to a close.

The Lascelles of Harewood House

Henceforth, the House of Lascelles increased their status and wealth through the usual aristocratic method of marriage. The 3rd Earl married Louisa Thynne of Longleat. The 4th Earl married Elizabeth de Burgh, sister of the fabulously wealthy Lord Clanricarde. This strange man left everything he had to his great-nephew the 6th Earl of Harewood. It was apparently because young Harry Lascelles – then Viscount Lascelles – had asked Clanricarde to join him for dinner one evening at his London club, while the boy was on convalescent leave during the First World War. If that seems small reason to leave Lord Lascelles all his worldly goods, but it was only because none of his other relations ever spoke to Clanricarde. He was such a cold-hearted and vicious miser that he repelled any company whatsoever. As he grew older, he grew lonely. He had been amazed (and clearly delighted) when his great-nephew showed him a small act of kindness, and he made Lascelles his heir. Lord Lascelles used the money to purchase works by Renaissance masters, the only such collection acquired in the twentieth century by an English country house.

Before succeeding to the earldom, Harry Lascelles made his own spectacular marriage to a member of the royal family: Princess Mary, daughter of King George V and Queen Mary. As the wedding of a princess, it took place in Westminster Abbey, with cheering crowds thronging the processional route back to Buckingham Palace. This was the moment that the mass media truly became interested in selling royal weddings; the Windsor-Lascelles nuptials became the first to be featured in *Vogue*. Harewood House then became a royal residence, and when Lascelles succeeded as 6th Earl of Harewood in 1929, Mary was known as 'Princess Mary, Countess of Harewood'. She is better remembered by the title given to her by her father in 1932, that of 'Princess Royal', the traditional form for the eldest daughter of a Monarch.

The couple had two sons, one of whom, George Lascelles, 7th Earl of Harewood (1923–1911), as a grandson of George V, was also in line of succession to the throne. During the Second World War, Lord Lascelles was captured by the Nazis and became a prisoner of war at Colditz. As the nephew of the then king, George VI, he was considered an important bargaining chip in any negotiations with Britain. In 1945, when Hitler realised the war was lost, he signed Lascelles' death warrant. But the commander of the POW camp also knew that Germany was defeated and instead released Lascelles into the care of the Swiss. He succeeded to the earldom in 1947 and was faced by crippling death duties. In common with many peers of the time, he sold off items from the family collections to pay the debt. The earl also oversaw the opening of Harewood House to the public. His mother the Princess Royal was still alive and living with her son and his family when the first visitor guidebook was produced in 1959. From the 1960s, further attractions were opened in the grounds, including an adventure playground.

A reckoning with history

2007 marked the bicentenary of the abolition of the slave trade. As the current Harewood House guidebook states: 'This was not something we at Harewood could simply let pass by, to contribute by omission to what has been called a collective national amnesia about this terrible episode of British history.' Harewood has not been timid in addressing its past, but has played a leading role in efforts to uncover, study and highlight the role that slavery had in enriching British institutions, including its noble dynasties.

The present Earl of Harewood, David Lascelles (b. 1950) wrote, 'We had decided some years previously that we had to try to discover more about the exact nature of the Lascelles family's involvement with the sugar trade and the slave trade.' Harewood worked with the University of York to research the early history of the family's Barbados plantations, using grants from the Heritage Lottery Fund to digitise and share the Lascelles archives with the

West Indies and Barbados Museum. Harewood also works with schools and community groups to help educate people about slavery and its legacy.

Harewood House itself has been reassessed by curators. In 2022, a project entitled 'Missing Portraits' was launched to address the fact that, of all the hundreds of paintings and photographs on show in Harewood, there was not a single black face among them. The family began commissioning portraits of men and women of colour with a contemporary connection to Harewood, in an attempt to redress the balance. The first portrait to be unveiled was of Arthur France, a community leader in Leeds. The second was of the actor David Harewood, whose own ancestors had been slaves of the earls of Harewood in Barbados.

Sir Robert Manners (d.1495) = Eleanor de Ros (d.1487)
heiress BELVOIR CASTLE

Sir George Manners (d.1513) = Anne St Leger (1476-1526)
11th Baron Ros | niece of King Edward IV

Thomas Manners (1488-1543)
1st Earl of Rutland

Sir John Manners = Dorothy Vernon
heiress HADDON HALL

Henry Manners
2nd Earl of Rutland
↓
3rd-7th Earls

2 generations through the make line to

John Manners (1638-1711) = Catherine Wriothesley Noel
1st Duke of Rutland | (d.1733)

John Manners (d.1721) = Catherine Russell
2nd Duke of Rutland

John Manners (d.1779) = Bridget Sutton
3rd Duke of Rutland

John Manners (1721-1770) = Frances Seymour
Marquess of Granby | (1728-1761)

Charles Manners (1754-1783) = Mary Somerset
4th Duke of Rutland | (1756-1831)

John Manners (1778-1857) = Elizabeth Howard
5th Duke of Rutland | (1780-1825)

3 generations through the male line to

Charles Manners (1919-1999) = Frances Sweeney
10th Duke of Rutland | (1937-2024)

David Manners (b.1959) = Emma Watkins
11th Duke of Rutland | (b.1963)

The Manners of Belvoir Castle

Duke of Rutland

Dukedom created	1703
Monarch	Anne
Subsidiary titles	Marquess of Granby; Baron Manners

The Manners family were late bloomers. They arrived on the political scene under King Henry VIII, who granted them the earldom of Rutland in 1525. But unlike other Tudor protégés, who seemed to come from nowhere to sudden prominence, Thomas Manners belonged to a very old landowning family. Their sudden rise resulted from two outstanding marriages. Sir Robert Manners (d. 1495) married the heiress to Belvoir Castle, Eleanor Ros. Their son, George Manners, married Anne St Leger, niece of the Yorkist king, Edward IV. Their son Thomas – and all Manners after him – thus had a strain of Plantagenet blood, which drew him to court at a perilous time; the earl was to sit in judgement at the trial of Anne Boleyn. Thereafter, the family reverted to their favoured habit of keeping a low profile, concentrating on their beautiful houses at

Belvoir and Haddon Hall. Their elevation to dukes came in 1703, and against the wishes of the 1st Duke, who just wanted to be left alone! Only in more recent times, in the age of social media, have the family come out of their shell again: the 11th Duke's three daughters became socialites, models and online personalities, dubbed by the tabloids as 'the *real* Crawley sisters'.

Marrying up

The House of Manners can be traced with certainty to around 1232 when they lived in Etal, Northumberland, and were having squabbles with their neighbours over land boundaries. Some records suggest that they were involved in more dangerous disputes of a military kind against the Scots, which would make sense given their border location. It is likely that the family came from Normandy and that their name derives from Mesnières near Rouen. In England, from the thirteenth to the sixteenth centuries, the historical line of Manners produced a steady succession of Roberts, Johns and Georges.

It was a Robert Manners (d. 1495), knighted in 1485, who hurried his family into noble circles. In the summer of 1469 he married Eleanor de Ros, daughter of the 9th Baron de Ros of Helmsley. That powerful magnate was descended from a Magna Carta baron, with enormous wealth and no male heir to carry his line forward. His daughter's marriage to Sir Robert produced a son, George Manners, who was permitted to inherit his mother's family possessions, including the ruined de Ros fortress at Belvoir in Leicestershire. With it came the title of Baron de Ros, catapulting George Manners into the cousinhood of titled nobility. Through marriage the Manners had gained their noble status, as well as a perfect new home.

Family seat: Belvoir Castle

Constructed in 1067 by the Hastings knight Robert de Todeni and named in Norman French as 'Belvoir' after the 'beautiful view' it afforded, this storied castle has been razed and rebuilt at least four times in its history. Pronounced 'beaver', Todenis castle was a motte and bailey, built to defend the Norman progress north. Three times, the castle was passed down through the female line: from Adeliza de Todeni to the Bigods; from Cecily Bigod to the Aubignys; and from Isabel Aubigny to the de Ros family. The castle did not survive the Wars of Roses. The de Ros were Lancastrians, their home falling victim to Yorkist plundering in the 1460s.

What remained of the castle was passed once more through an heiress into the Manners family in 1508. Thomas Manners, 1st Earl of Rutland, rebuilt it in the early Tudor style. His building lasted until the Civil War, when it was captured by Parliamentary forces and demolished. A third castle was constructed around 1668. It was overseen by Frances, Lady Rutland, wife of the 8th Earl. She had it designed as a lavish – but plain rectangular – country palace, nothing like a castle.

The fourth and present castle at Belvoir was the creation of Elizabeth Manners (née Howard) Duchess of Rutland, during the Georgian regency. Elizabeth hired the Gothic romantic architect James Wyatt (who had worked on improving Windsor Castle) to build her a fantastic monument to the Age of Chivalry. Before completion, the new castle was almost destroyed by a fire on 26 October 1816. Artworks by Titian, Rubens, Van Dyck and Reynolds were all lost in the blaze. The builders ploughed on, and the new castle was completed by 1832. Today, Belvoir is a sumptuous, yet somehow very homely and friendly seat.

Thomas Manners and his coat of many colours

George's son Thomas Manners (1488–1543), succeeded as the 12th Baron de Ros in 1513. It was in this capacity that he was summoned to attend King Henry VIII at the Field of the Cloth of Gold. Clearly doing well, he was chosen to be present when Henry met the Habsburg emperor, Charles V. Soon, Manners was made a Knight of the Garter and entrusted with Henry's most vital state and personal matters (the signature of Thomas Manners actually appears on a letter to Pope Clement VII, urging the pontiff to grant a divorce to the king of England from his wife Catherine of Aragon).

In 1525, King Henry elevated Lord de Ros to an earldom. Thomas had then revealed a pride in his pedigree worthy of any Howard when, as 1st Earl of Rutland, he displayed an achievement of arms that was less a coat, more a patchwork quilt, so many charges did it flaunt. The shield was quartered to draw attention to the sundry noble Houses from which Thomas Manners descended through his female ancestors. They included the arms of the Norman knight Todeni, founder of the family seat, and of the Aubignys. They also included the de Ros arms of his grandmother and – still more grandly – the Plantagenet Arms of his own mother, Anne St Leger, niece of King Edward IV. The lions of England and the fleurs-de-lys of France were set upon the Manners coat as an augmentation granted by Henry VIII. To this day, the Manners shield declares their descent from the Plantagenet kings and from the Capetian kings of France, all the way back to Hugh. The dazzling patchwork of royal ancestry also includes the medieval kings of Scotland through the de Ros line. William de Ros (d. 1316) had even tried to claim the Scottish throne, his great-grandmother having been a natural daughter of William the Lion. Manners was conspicuously proud of his de Ros lineage; above his shield he placed the Ros crest, very aptly a peacock in pride, dispensing with the old Manners crest of a bull's head. He was also delighted with the title of Rutland itself, which marked him out as more than ordinary nobility.

Title: Duke of Rutland

When Henry VIII made Thomas Manners earl of Rutland in 1525, he was recognising him as a cousin of royal descent. Rutland had once been a royal title, first created for members of the House of York. The earliest holder was Edward Plantagenet (a grandson of Edward III) who died in 1415 at Agincourt. He left no children.

The Manners of Belvoir Castle

The next holder was Edmund of York, younger brother to Edward IV. He was created earl of Rutland at the age of eleven but died six years later, a victim of the Wars of the Roses. The exact circumstances of his death are mysterious. By some accounts he was captured and executed by the Lancastrians. But Shakespeare has it that Edmund was murdered in cold blood by Lord Clifford of Skipton. Clifford certainly did have a reputation for such behaviour; his nickname was Bloody Clifford the Butcher. The slain Edmund's sister, Anne of York, was the maternal grandmother of Thomas Manners, who received the third creation of the Rutland earldom. The dukedom of Rutland granted nearly two centuries later was the first such creation.

The witches of Belvoir

Between 1525 and the creation of the dukedom in 1703, there were nine earls of Rutland. None were quite as politically important as the 1st Earl, but they were involved in some dramatic, romantic, and even some supposedly supernatural events.

The tomb of the 6th Earl of Rutland (1578–1632) in Bottesford's Church of St Mary the Virgin, bears a curious inscription about him: 'In 1608 he married ye lady Cecila Hungerford, daughter to ye Honorable Knight Sir John Tufton, by whom he had two sons, both of which died in their infancy by wicked practises and sorcerye.'

The 'sorcerye' mentioned involved a local woman named Joan Flower. The earl and countess had employed Joan and her two daughters as servants at Belvoir Castle, when they had needed extra staff to attend to a visit by James I. The other servants at Belvoir did not like Joan, considering her a witch. Her eyes, it was said, were 'fiery and hollow, her speech fell and envious, her demeanour strange and exotic'. She and her daughters had been known in the area as 'herbal healers', so it was only a short leap of imagination during the witch-hunting craze of the 1600s to define the Flower family as sorceresses.

When one of the girls began an affair with a local boy, Thomas Simpson, rumours began to circulate of dark magic. Thomas claimed he was so besotted with his lover that he was unable to leave her. Enchantment was suspected, bewitchment. Soon, Joan and her daughters were dismissed by the earl. But not before Joan had placed a vengeful curse on the House of Manners. Almost immediately the earl and countess fell violently ill. So, too, did their two young sons, both of whom died.

King James himself had written a book on demonology. Belief in everything from demonic possession to pacts with the devil was widespread in Britain and across Europe. The Rutlands were convinced their children were the victims of witchcraft, and Joan Flower and her daughters were arrested and committed for trial. During proceedings, the usual details associated with cases of sorcery emerged. Joan's familiar spirit was apparently a cat named Rutterkin. The girls admitted that they had stolen a glove belonging to the Rutland heir, young Lord de Ros, and given it to their mother, who had stroked it along the cat's back. Evidence like this was more than enough to convict. The witches of Belvoir were executed at Lincoln Castle on 11 March 1619.

The legend of John Manners and Dorothy Vernon

The death of the young Rutland heirs meant that the earldom passed to the 6th Earl's brother. He also died without direct heirs, so the 8th Earl was his second cousin, John Manners (1604–1679), head of what had up until then been a junior branch of the family, the Manners of Haddon Hall. A stunning castellated manor in the Peak District, Haddon was just a stone's throw from Chatsworth House on the River Derwent. The Manners of Haddon had been based there since 1565 and were by now closely entwined with most of the Derbyshire nobility (John himself was a great-grandson through his mother of Bess of Hardwick).

Haddon had come to this branch of the family through another fortuitous marriage. Its founder, John Manners, was a younger son of the 1st Earl of Rutland, who married the Haddon heiress Dorothy Vernon (1544–1584). The marriage itself, which took place in 1563, is part of historical record. But a romantic story grew up around the wedding that is almost certainly the stuff of legend. The tale went that Dorothy had fallen in love with John Manners to the great disapproval of her father Sir George Vernon. He expressly forbade Dorothy to see Manners and ended up locking his daughter in a tower at Haddon to keep the couple apart. Manners disguised himself a forester to visit Dorothy, and they planned a daring escape. On the night of her sister's wedding, as her father was hosting the ball, Dorothy fled down the stone steps to the little bridge over the River Wye, where her suitor was waiting for her. They leapt upon a noble steed and galloped all night long until they were sure of freedom.

The main argument against the story has been the simple question of why George Vernon would have been opposed to his daughter marrying a son of the earl of Rutland. True, John Manners was a younger son, and not likely to inherit the earldom, but he was still of a great and ancient family. Not that it mattered to dramatists. The legend of Dorothy Vernon has inspired everything from a light opera in 1892, a 1903 Broadway play, and a 1924 film.

Whatever the true circumstance of their marriage, John and Dorothy's grandson was the man who succeeded as 8th Earl of Rutland in 1641.

Haddon Hall and the Vernons

Haddon Hall was described by Nicholas Pevsner thus:

> The English castle par excellence, not the forbidding fortress on an unassailable crag, but the large, rambling, safe, grey lovable home of knights and their ladies, the unreasonable

dream-castle of those who think of the Middle Ages as a time of chivalry and valour and noble feelings.

In the wilderness that was the Peak District of the sixteenth century, one name was synonymous with lavish living, the master of Haddon Hall, known far and wide as the 'King of the Peak', Sir George Vernon (1514–1565). His house was ancient even then. Originally held by a favourite of William the Conqueror, the knight William Peveril, it ended up with his tenants, the Avenalls. In 1190, the Vernons arrived from Vernon in Normandy. One of them married the Haddon heiress Avice Avenall and they stayed there, becoming one of Derbyshire's greatest gentry families.

Haddon Hall remains today very much as it was in the medieval age, one of the best-preserved manor houses in the country. For that reason, it features prominently as a set piece for historical dramas. Cult fantasy *The Princess Bride* (1987) was shot at Haddon. So, too, was *Elizabeth* (1998), while Natalie Portman and Scarlet Johanson filmed *The Other Boleyn Girl* (2008) there. Today, the Hall is overseen by the present Duke of Rutland's brother, Lord Edward Manners.

The ducal Manners

The 9th Earl of Rutland (1638–1711) was not particularly interested in becoming a duke. He became one largely because his son had married into a great ducal family – the Russells – whose matriarch had grand ambitions for her Manners in-laws. Rutland's son had wed Catherine Russell, daughter of the executed Whig martyr William, Lord Russell. Catherine's mother Rachel – widow of the slain lord – had grown intensely vain in the years of sympathy over her husband's death. Swollen-headed with status, she wished her daughter to be a future Duchess, not a mere Countess. Accordingly, Lady Russell wrote to William III asking for the Earl of Rutland to be promoted to a dukedom.

The Manners of Belvoir Castle

Unfortunately for Lady Russell, the king died before he could act, and she was obliged to go to his successor, Queen Anne. The queen was more interested in making John Churchill Duke of Marlborough at the time, but eventually, in March 1703, produced Letters Patent making John Manners Marquess of Granby and 1st Duke of Rutland.

The Rutland dukes were never politically ambitious. Probably the most famous Manners since 1703 never actually became duke at all. As Marquess of Granby, the son of the 3rd Duke became a national hero during the Seven Years War. He won fame at the Battle of Warburg in 1760, where he led a cavalry charge against the French, losing his hat and wig along the way. His name today is better known, however, because of the number of pubs named the 'Marquess of Granby'. It is said that more are named for him than any other historical figure (perhaps because he used to set up a lot of his old soldiers as publicans after they retired).

The dukes and duchesses were generally more interested in their properties, in building and beautifying their houses and estates, than they were in their titles or military heroics. The most productive husband and wife team were the 5th Duke, John Manners (1778–1857) and Duchess Elizabeth (1780–1825). The duchess is remembered as the builder of Belvoir Castle as it appears today. Born Elizabeth Howard of Castle Howard, she had married John Manners at eighteen. With a passion for architecture, she immediately saw the potential of Belvoir when she arrived in 1799. She was a dynamic and determined personality, even persisting through the setback of a major fire that destroyed much of her work, and continuing to mastermind the construction of a fairytale castle. She worked closely with her husband's chaplain, who was an amateur architect, to create a mock medieval fortress that could sit alongside the real thing that they had at Haddon.

Around the same time that his wife was building Belvoir, the 5th Duke was attempting to transform the little town of

Bakewell on the Haddon Hall estate. His plan was to turn it from a provincial market town into a fashionable Georgian spa. This was partly to accommodate the growth in the Derbyshire population; the Industrial Revolution was born in the Derbyshire valleys where Richard Arkwright was busy building cotton mills. The duke built several grand houses in Bakewell for the professionals being drawn into the Peak District. He also began construction of a large coaching inn in Bakewell to take advantage of the numbers of travellers passing through the town. The Rutland Arms Hotel, which still stands today, opened in 1805 complete with stables for travellers' horses. (Jane Austen reputedly wrote part of *Pride & Prejudice* while staying at the Rutland Arms during her Derbyshire travels; Pemberley – the home of Mr Darcy of Derbyshire – was based on a view she obtained of nearby Chatsworth.) The duke had built the inn at the top of what would be a new town square. His dream to turn Bakewell into a fashionable spa to compete with Matlock Bath and the Duke of Devonshire's spa at Buxton, never succeeded. Though Bakewell did become famous around that time for the Bakewell Pudding and the Bakewell Tart (enjoyed today in its iced variant, the Cherry Bakewell).

Duchess Violet: the artist aristocrat

There is another Rutland who, in her time, brought fame, and not a little notoriety, to the Manners name. Her legacy can be seen at Belvoir Castle and at Haddon Hall. In the chapel at Belvoir is a beautiful and melancholy sculpture of a child lying as if asleep on an altar. It depicts Robert Manners, Lord Haddon, son of the 8th Duke of Rutland, who died in 1894 at the age of nine. It was sculpted by the boy's bereft mother, Violet, Duchess of Rutland, whose skill was clearly immense, but whose work is not widely known today, despite some of her works being held by the Louvre.

The Manners of Belvoir Castle

Violet was a member of late Victorian bohemian set known as the Souls. The purpose of the Souls was best summed up by their club activities of 'playing tennis, the piano, the fool and other instruments of gaiety'. The Souls were regular guests at Belvoir, where the classic country house weekends were marked not by parties and dinners but by nude tennis doubles matches and intellectual conversation and competitive wit. The Souls revelled in their unconventional behaviour, scandalising polite society. Strange to think her husband the duke was private secretary to the arch-traditional Prime Minister, Lord Salisbury (he was nicknamed 'Salisbury's Manners'). Behind the radical programme, Violet was a highly talented painter and sculptor. Her Pre-Raphaelite style owed much to Burne Jones, J. W. Waterhouse and other masters of Victorian medievalism. Her greatest work is surely the sculpture of her son, her grief etched in marble. A copy can be seen in the chapel at Haddon.

Like many of the Souls, Violet was known to have had extramarital affairs. Her liaison with Harry Cust, editor of the *Pall Mall Gazette*, resulted in a daughter, born Lady Diana Manners (legally daughter of the duke, but widely known to be Harry's). Diana grew up very much like her mother. The 1911 London Season marked her coming out, where she was celebrated as the most beautiful girl of the summer, 'like an orchid among cowslips' according to the Prime Minister's son. Diana was presented at Buckingham Palace by her mother; both could put on a good show of convention where needed. But at home the pair were equally as anarchic. Diana posed naked for her brother's camera and had her own set, rather like the Souls, committed to 'picnic, games ... midnight bathing ... singing and repetition of poetry'. Always at the forefront of new mediums, Lady Diana Cooper – as she became – also became a star of film in the silent era.

The Season
In the eighteenth and nineteenth centuries, the annual London 'Season' brought members of every aristocratic dynasty to the capital. From springtime until the end of June, the nobility left their far-flung country houses to socialise at prestigious events held in and around London. The season coincided with the sitting of Parliament, so peers could engage in politics at the same time, heading off to the House of Lords while their families were busy entertaining themselves.

The social season revolved around balls held by the leading dynasties at their London mansions. All the great families had their own base in the capital, handily named for their title. Perhaps the most famous of these residences was Devonshire House in Piccadilly, where the Cavendish family entertained while in London, but Bedford House, Northumberland House and Rutland House were also up there in glamour stakes. The season was the time for younger members of the ruling class to meet potential wives and husbands. Young ladies would be presented at court and come out into society as marriageable prospects.

The traditional season went into decline after the first World War, becoming an anachronism after the horrors of the trenches. Many of the aristocracy's great urban palaces which had served as centres for season activities were also being sold and demolished. Yet echoes of the season can still be heard today, at events like Royal Ascot, Henley Royal Regatta, and the Wimbledon Championships.

The Bad Manners Sisters: twenty-first-century celebrity
The fame of Lady Diana Manners in the early twentieth century – and for that matter, of Lady Georgiana Spencer in the eighteenth century – is indicative of a public fascination with the private lives of the aristocracy that continues today. As with times past, it is usually the younger female members of the nobility who draw the

headlines. Due to the air of glamour that still clings to the titled classes, this has proven to be the case for the Manners family in the 2000s.

The 11th Duke of Rutland (b. 1959) has five children including his heir, Lord Granby, and youngest child, Lord Hugo Manners. His eldest children are his three daughters who have fascinated the tabloid press in just the way that their ancestors did. Dubbed 'The Bad Manners Sisters of British High Society' by the *Daily Mail*, one article by Richard Kay in the paper on 21 November 2015 went on to elucidate the enduring allure of England's old dynasties even today, when fame as well as government is supposedly won democratically:

> For an age where celebrity grows not on family trees but on social media and reality obsessed TV shows, some will find the aristocratic allure of the Duke of Rutland's glossy daughters quite mystifying. Yet for much of this year Britain's society pages have been filled with accounts of the glamorous and pampered existence of Lady Violet, 22, Lady Alice, 20, and 18-year-old Lady Eliza Manners. Whether it's dancing on the sofa at Tatler's Little Black Book party, hiding under the beds to startle visitors touring the family seat, Belvoir Castle, or upsetting the neighbours with their up-all-night partying, no trifling detail of their lives has escaped attention.

As was the case with their ancestors, the tabloids fixate on the private lives of family members, and neglect to explore their professional achievements. Lady Violet is, for example, a successful businesswoman, founding a digital ticketing platform for visitor attractions. It's a mark of the lasting power of noble titles in Britain that they still have the power of obscuring the complex lives of their owners, whether they be artists in the nineteenth century, or entrepreneurs in the present.

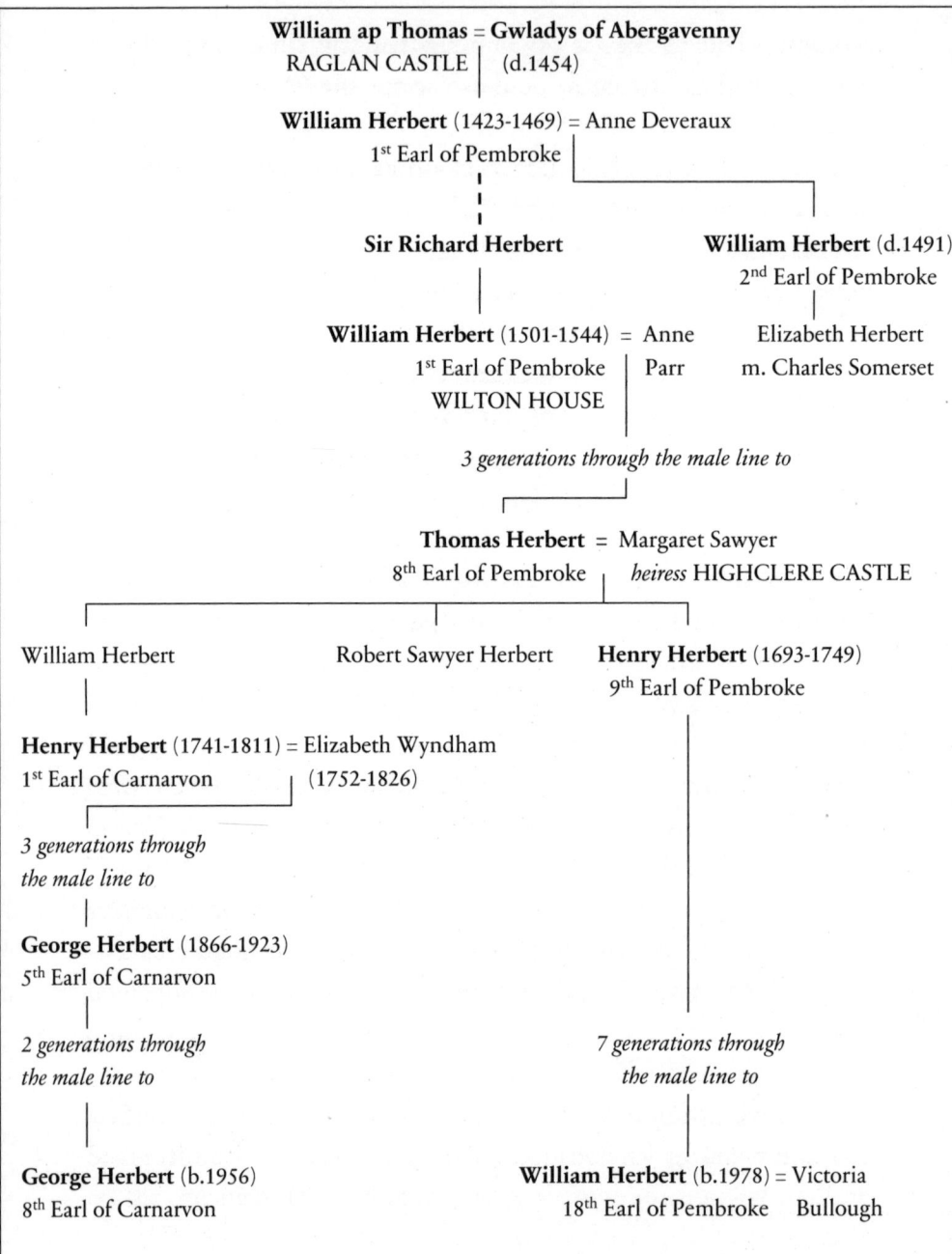

The Herberts of Wilton and Highclere

Earl of Pembroke
Earl of Carnarvon

Earldoms created	1551 (Pembroke); 1793 (Carnarvon)
Monarch	Edward VI (Pembroke); George III (Carnarvon)
Subsidiary titles	Baron Herbert; Baron Porchester

The ancestors of the Herberts were prominent in medieval Wales as warriors and castle builders. Yet their dynastic seats are now two of the most famous genteel country houses in England. The senior branch – the Earls of Pembroke – live at Wilton House near Salisbury in Wiltshire. The junior – the Earls of Carnarvon – are seated at perhaps the most instantly recognisable of English houses today, Highclere Castle in Hampshire, setting for the TV and film series *Downton Abbey*.

Henry VIII – also of a family of Welsh descent – looked favourably on the Herberts. After dissolving the Monasteries, the king granted them the lands at Wilton Abbey where they built their new house. Later, Highclere came to the family through marriage before being passed to a younger son and becoming home to the Carnarvon branch. Until the *Downton* era, Highclere was best known as home to the man who funded the sensational discovery of Tutankhamun's Tomb in 1922, the 5th Earl of Carnarvon. Lord Carnarvon died the following year in mysterious circumstances that fuelled the legend of the 'Curse of Tutankhamun'.

The Blue Knight and the Star of Abergavenny

Wales in the fifteenth century was a country firmly under the control of the English Crown. The Celtic kingdoms of the Dark Ages that had flourished in the misty valleys had finally been subdued under the Plantagenet invaders. William Camden described the death of the final native ruler of the Welsh in his *Britannia*, first published in 1586:

> As concerning the Princes of Wales of British blood in ancient times... King Edward the First [of the royal line of England] ... obtained the Crown, and Lhewellin Ap Gryffith, the last Prince of the British race, was slain, and thereby the sinews as it were of the principality were cut ... united the same unto the Kingdom of England.

With the last native (or 'British') Welsh ruler dead, King Edward I made his own son the new Prince of Wales, a title held by heirs to the throne to this day.

By the time of the Lancastrian kings, many of the old Welsh families had become loyal servants of the English Crown. One such – which had its origins in the Celtic royal family of Gwent – was represented in the early 1400s by Sir William Thomas. The Herbert story begins with William Thomas and his second wife Gwladys, parents of the man who first took the name of

'Herbert'. William had already set about the process of dynasty-building. He purchased a small castle at Raglan and began expanding it into a magnificent fortress. Establishing himself as a power in south Wales, he was knighted by Henry VI. Thomas seems to have been a flamboyant character, for he famously wore blue armour, an affectation that led to his epithet: *Y marchog glas o Went* (the Blue Knight of Gwent).

After the death of his first wife, Thomas married Gwladys, daughter of Dafydd Gam, another loyal knight who died fighting for Henry V at the Battle of Agincourt. Gwladys was renowned in her time, and the subject of attention from the Welsh poet Lewys Glyn Cothi (*c.* 1420–1490). It is believed this man contributed many tales to the *Mabinogion*, the manuscript that preserved much of the pre-Christian Celtic mythology of Wales. He also described Lady Gwladys, Mother of the House of Herbert, as the 'Star of Abergavenny' due to her ethereal, even unnatural beauty. The Lady of Raglan Castle, as she became, was also a passionate supporter of Welsh culture, particularly of the bards and minstrels. They in turn sang not just of her beauty, but of her generosity and concern for the needy, and her steadfast support of the people of Gwent. Gwladys became an immensely powerful figure, not far from a ruling princess in the old Welsh tradition. It is said that when she died in 1454, over 3000 people walked in procession to her burial. These included the peasantry, weeping for the loss of their Lady of Raglan. The size of her funeral entourage may be exaggerated, but there is no doubt that Gwladys was a ruler who eclipsed her husband in popularity. Gwladys and her Blue Knight were buried in Abergavenny Priory where their alabaster tombs can still be seen today. Their son inherited Raglan Castle, adopted the English surname 'Herbert', and became founder of this most notable of Anglo-Welsh families.

The first Herbert: William, Earl of Pembroke

The first Herbert was a staunch Yorkist during the Wars of the Roses. Edward IV made him a Knight of the Garter, Baron Herbert, and after the Battle of Towton in 1461 Earl of Pembroke. Until then, that castle and earldom had been in the possession of a member of a Lancastrian Welsh family, Jasper Tudor. It is interesting that the Herberts and Tudors were on opposite sides in the Wars of the Roses. At the time, Jasper was guardian of his young nephew Henry Tudor. After Towton, he was forced to yield the Pembroke title to his Yorkist rival Herbert, and with it the wardship of Henry Tudor. This proved a precarious appointment. Herbert's undoing came after he found himself on the wrong side of the fickle Warwick the Kingmaker, who turned against the Yorkists and fought them at the Battle of Edgcote in 1469. Here, Herbert was captured and executed by Lord Warwick.

The Pembroke title did remain with the family, Herbert's son William becoming the 2nd Earl. But he was the last of the legitimate Herbert line to hold it. When he died in 1491, he left a daughter, Elizabeth. As a sole heiress, she was sought after by many suitors and married Charles Somerset (of the family that became dukes of Beaufort). Raglan Castle went to the Somersets, and the earldom of Pembroke became extinct.

There were, however, descendants of the 1st Earl remaining, those born not to his wife but to two ladies whose identities remain mysterious. One of these descendants was the earl's grandson, William, and with him the Herbert family reemerged.

The other first Herbert, Earl of Pembroke

The Herberts of today are therefore unusual, in that they descend from an illegitimate son of the founder, whose line not only retained the original family name (rather than being handed a 'bastard' alternative), but was re-granted the family title. The only way in which the line lost out was in the transfer of Raglan Castle to the Somersets (ironically, an illegitimate line themselves). It left the House of Herbert without a seat.

The 1st Earl of Pembroke in the new creation (granted in 1551 by Edward VI) was a man who belied the circumstances of his birth to ingratiate himself with the most powerful in the land. William Herbert (1501–1570) not only married a Parr (sister to Henry VIII's last wife) but became a Knight of the Garter to boot. He was something of an oddity and had nearly ended his court career before it began when he got himself into a fight, killed his opponent, and was obliged to flee to France to evade justice. 'Black Will Herbert', as he was dubbed, joined the French army where he did so well as a soldier of fortune that he managed to convince King Francis I to speak up on his behalf to Henry VIII. Herbert was then allowed to return to England, where he behaved as though nothing had happened. He would take his position very seriously, his head swelling when the king married his sister-in-law, Catherine Parr. He later had himself painted with his staff of office and the Garter at his knee. Herbert clearly liked himself very much, even though one contemporary did not think much to his appearance: 'very cholerique … strong set, but bony, reddish-favoured, of a sharp eye, stern look'.

He was right, nonetheless, that as an in-law of the king, honours and riches would surely come his way. It certainly sorted out the problem of being without a family seat, for Henry VIII granted Herbert the former monastic estate of Wilton Abbey in 1544.

Family seat: Wilton House

Upon arriving at Wilton, Herbert immediately began plans for a new house on the site. It isn't known just how many of the 800-year-old monastic buildings remained, or in what condition, upon the Dissolution of the Monasteries. Whatever was left standing was quickly demolished by Herbert, and his new house was built between 1544 and 1563. A lot happened in England over those years (Herbert reportedly had to throw out a group of nuns who had briefly returned to Wilton during the reign of Queen Mary. Upon Mary's death, Herbert rushed to Wilton like a tiger to turf them out, calling them some choice names as they ran.) But Herbert had already constructed a house splendid enough to receive a visit by Edward VI in 1552, and the Spanish Ambassador Marquis de las Navas in 1554.

Very little remains of Herbert's house which was largely destroyed by fire in 1647 and subsequently rebuilt. The 4th Earl had already begun remodelling the house before the fire, employing Inigo Jones who followed his early form of English Palladian design. Jones is credited with the creation of the state rooms, which include the Single Cube Room (a perfect cube, 30 feet long, wide and high) and next door, the Double Cube Room (a rectangle double the length).

Wilton was extended several times, with work undertaken by James Wyatt beginning around 1801. The grounds are magnificent and include a huge number of distinctive features added by successive earls. These include the Palladian Bridge designed by the 9th Earl in the 1730s. The bridge, based on a rejected design for the Rialto Bridge in Venice by Palladio himself, spans the River Nadder, a small tributary of the Avon, which flows just south of Wilton House.

The Wilton Circle

It was upon the death of Henry VIII that Herbert achieved his greatest honours. He became one of the guardians of Edward VI, who made him Master of the Horse, President of Wales and earl of Pembroke. He remained both important and unpredictable. A supporter of William Cecil, Herbert was one of the nobles sent to Hatfield to greet Queen Elizabeth upon her accession. But the Venetian Ambassador reported to the Doge that Herbert, 'one of the chief noblemen of England', was to be found living in retirement at Wilton when great events required his presence. Lord Pembroke died in 1570, bequeathing Wilton to his son.

The 2nd Earl is not so well remembered as his wife, the former Mary Sidney (1561–1621). As Countess of Pembroke, she was described as 'the Patronesse of wit and learning'. She outlived her husband by two decades, during which time she held court at Wilton alongside her son the 3rd Earl. Mary was a polymath: a poet, translator and scientist, she kept a laboratory at Wilton where she conducted experiments in chemistry. She could read Latin, French and Italian, and with her brother Philip Sidney she translated the Psalms of David. It was said that under Mary Herbert, Wilton House – at this point a Renaissance Prodigy House – was something like 'a College, there were so many learned and ingenious persons' found there.

These ingenious persons included a group of poets and dramatists who were arguably the most important in England's literary history. Assembled by Mary, and based at Wilton, the so-called 'Wilton Circle' included Edmund Spenser (author of *The Faerie Queene*). At Christmas in 1603, King James I stayed at Wilton, holding his court there while an outbreak of plague was ravaging London. Shakespeare's theatre company, the King's Men, attended to perform (possibly a production of *As You Like It*).

Mary's passing in 1621 was marked by suitably dramatic ceremony. Her body was taken by torchlight procession from Wilton to be buried in the family vault at Salisbury Cathedral. Her epitaph read:

> Underneath this sable hers
> Lyes the subject of all verse
> Sydneyes sister, Pembrokes mother
> Death ere thou hast slain another
> Faire & learned & good as she
> Tyme shall throw a dart at thee

'Pembroke' was of course her son. Like his mother, the 3rd Earl, William Herbert (1580–1630) was a scholar and lover of poetry. When he was a child, his mother had him tutored by the learned poets who frequented Wilton. As an adult he took part in masques and mock tournaments. Since then, there have not been many earls of Pembroke who have left a huge impression on history. The title itself is more famed than its owners.

Title: Earl of Pembroke
There have been at least ten separate creations of the earldom of Pembroke. The most notorious of all holders of the title was the man known to history as 'Strongbow', Richard de Clare (1130–1176). As instigator of the Anglo-Norman invasion of Ireland, he is right at the root of the centuries of trouble that followed between the English and Irish. De Clare was the 2nd Earl of Pembroke in a creation made by King Stephen in 1138. A lord of the Welsh Marches, it was at home in Wales that de Clare received a fateful visit from a deposed king of the Irish kingdom of Leinster. Dermot MacMurrough was on his way back from an audience with the English king, Henry II. MacMurrough had pleaded with Henry for military assistance to help him regain his throne from the usurper Rory O'Connor by then High King of Ireland. Henry had not been forthcoming, however, so MacMurrough now decided to try his luck with de Clare. He offered the earl his daughter's hand in marriage and to make him heir to Leinster's throne if le Clare helped him retake it. Le Clare liked the sound of coming into his own kingdom, but first he sought permission from King Henry to raise an army and sail to Ireland with MacMurrough. This was fine by the king so long as his 'imperial' status in the region was recognised, and Strongbow soon set off, taking control of the towns of Dublin, Wexford and Waterford. King Henry crossed to Ireland in 1172 to receive his homage as overlord – and thus began the grim narrative of the English Crown in Ireland.

Other notable creations include those made for the Marshal family (extant between 1199–1245), and that conferred jointly on William de la Pole and his wife Alice Chaucer (granddaughter of Geoffrey Chaucer, author of *The Canterbury Tales*) in 1447. William de la Pole – better known as a duke of Suffolk and nicknamed Jackanapes – was killed by an angry mob in 1450. Then of course there was Jasper Tudor, created earl by Henry VI, whose forfeiture sent Pembroke into the arms of the Herberts.

The Herberts of Highclere

More famous in modern times have been a junior branch of the Herberts who descend from a younger son of the 8th Earl of Pembroke. That earl, Thomas Herbert (1656–1733) had been married in 1684 to Margaret Sawyer, heiress of Highclere Castle in Hampshire. The earl saw no need for the Pembrokes to look after two great mansions, so bequeathed Wilton House to his eldest son (who carried on the Pembroke earldom) and gave Highclere to his second son, Robert Sawyer Herbert. Highclere eventually ended up with his third son's offspring; Henry Herbert (1741–1811) was then created Baron Porchester and 1st Earl of Carnarvon in 1793.

The Herberts of Highclere took part in some diverse international events in the nineteenth and twentieth centuries. In the 1860s, the 4th Earl of Carnarvon was closely involved in the creation of modern Canada. He drafted the bill that established Canada in its current confederated form and introduced it to Parliament. In so doing, the earl had the help of John A. MacDonald, who would become the first Prime Minister of Canada during a summit at his home in Hampshire. The signature of MacDonald appears in the visitors book at Highclere Castle.

Family seat: Highclere Castle
Instantly recognisable today to many through its use as Downton Abbey, Highclere Castle has had its own history worthy of

any costume drama. Long before Domesday Book, the land at Highclere was granted to the bishops of Winchester who ran it as their personal fiefdom. The 'castle' there began its life as a bishop's palace, built by one of the bishops, William of Wykham, in the fourteenth century. The palace was taken from the Catholic Church at the Reformation and sold off, passing through various owners until purchased in 1679 by Sir Robert Sawyer, Speaker of the House of Commons and friend of the diarist Samuel Pepys. The house had been adapted and remodelled several times by the time of the Sawyers, and when it was inherited by the Herberts it was a fairly unremarkable building, square with standard classical adornments. The Earls of Carnarvon did not do much the house initially, though the 1st Earl did employ Capability Brown to create the parkland around it. This park and its cedars are now internationally famous thanks to *Downton*.

The current appearance of Highclere Castle is the legacy of the 3rd Earl (1800–1849) who rebuilt it almost entirely, to designs by Sir Charles Barry, between 1842 and 1849. Barry was at that time working on construction of the Houses of Parliament in Westminster, and it shows. The house he produced for the Carnarvons looks like a miniature of Parliament, minus a clocktower. The 'Jacobethan' – or Jacobean Revival – design did not have the input from the neo-gothic master, Pugin, that Parliament had. But Highclere does still have the stylised silhouette of a castle, in the sense of having a central keep rising high above outer walls. In that, it emulates the Renaissance Prodigy Houses of which Barry was an admirer, which still owed much to the medieval fortresses that preceded them. The interior of Highclere has gothic elements, too. The saloon, with its stone arches and carvings, is built to resemble a medieval great hall. It is all window-dressing though; Highclere is otherwise a classic Victorian country house, built for nineteenth-century sensibilities, and comfort.

Lord Carnarvon and the Curse of Tutankhamun

The 5th Earl of Carnarvon's interest in Egyptology was the result of a motoring accident in 1903. The earl's doctor advised him to spend the winter outside England, somewhere warmer and better for his constitution. He chose Egypt. Every winter he travelled there, becoming enchanted by its exotic monuments. He began buying antiquities for his collection and grew ever more fascinated by what the various pioneer archaeologists were doing around the old royal capitals, excavating the mysterious palaces and tombs of Egypt's ancient Pharaohs.

In 1907, he decided to get involved himself and hired the archaeologist Howard Carter, sponsoring his tomb excavations. Their relationship continued, and work intensified after 1914 when Lord Carnarvon was granted permission to dig in the Valley of the Kings. Howard Carter was convinced that tombs as yet undiscovered lay in the valley, particularly that of the 18th Dynasty Pharoah, Tutankhamun. The First World War interrupted the initial surveys, but Carter and Carnarvon grew increasingly obsessed with finding the tomb of Egypt's boy-king. Years passed and nothing of substance was found. Lord Carnarvon grew despondent and informed Carter that 1922 would be the last year he would finance excavation in the valley.

Carnarvon was at Highclere on 4 November 1922 when he received a telegram from Carter. It read, 'At last we have made wonderful discovery in Valley; a magnificent tomb with seals intact; re-covered same for your arrival; congratulations.'

Later that month Carnarvon landed in Egypt with his twenty-one-year-old daughter, Lady Evelyn Herbert. On 24 November, with Carnarvon and his daughter watching, Carter descended the staircase to the tomb and discovered the intact seal containing Tutankhamun's cartouche on the doorway. Two days later, after accessing the entrance corridor, Carter made an opening in the corner of the tomb chamber doorway itself. Carnarvon famously called to Carter, 'Can you see anything?' Carter replied, 'Yes, wonderful things!'

Inside was the best-preserved pharaonic tomb ever discovered in the Valley of the Kings. Though nobody was supposed to enter until a representative of the Egyptian government arrived, it is believed that Carnarvon, Lady Evelyn, Carter and his assistant became the first people in over 3,000 years to enter the tomb.

Carnarvon was not to live past the following spring. On 19 March 1923 he was bitten by a mosquito, the bite becoming infected. He died at his hotel in Cairo on 5 April. A media frenzy ensued, partly because the death of Carnarvon seemed to have been predicted a fortnight before by the novelist Marie Corelli, who had published a piece predicting 'dire punishment' for anybody breaking the seal of a sacred tomb. The Curse of Tutankhamun made headlines around the world. It contributed to modern fascination with the Ancient Egyptians. Horror stories about Mummies started to appear, one of the first of which was penned by Arthur Conan Doyle, a noted Spiritualist who believed Lord Carnarvon's death to have been caused by the Pharoah's elementals.

The idea that a king of the Thutmoside Dynasty could visit destruction millennia after his death on a member of England's dynastic elite captured the public imagination. The Herberts seemed to play into it by burying their fallen patriarch in his own 'tomb' in the centre of an ancient hillfort on the Highclere estate.

Downton and descendants

Until 2010, the association with Tutankhamun was Highclere Castle's greatest claim to fame. Then, on 26 September ITV aired the first episode of *Downton Abbey*. The 8th Earl of Carnarvon, George Herbert (b. 1956) and Fiona, Lady Carnarvon were friends of Julian Fellowes, the show's creator, who had stayed with them at Highclere many times. Thus, the house helped inspire the story of the aristocratic Crawley family, the earls of Grantham and their retinue of servants in the early twentieth century.

Downton helped to initiate modern – and international – audiences with the arcane rules and rituals governing England's noble dynasties. Series one dealt with what can happen when a peer fails to produce a male heir. The strange situation where house and title are entailed to a distant male cousin – Mr Matthew Crawley – rather than passing to his eldest daughter, Lady Mary, provided the central drama. We have described many real-life examples of such successions taking place. Indeed, it looked like happening to the two branches of the Herbert family in the twenty-first century.

The current Earl of Pembroke, William Herbert, 18th Earl (b. 1978) was the last remaining male line descendant of the 1st Earl when he succeeded in 2003; the last, that is, save for those descendants of the junior line, the Herberts of Highclere. For several years, the heir presumptive to the earl of Pembroke was therefore his very distant cousin, the 8th Earl of Carnarvon. Without a son, Lord Pembroke would eventually be succeeded by Lord Carnarvon, and the Herbert titles would have been united in a single person. The situation only changed in 2012. Lord Pembroke's wife, Countess Victoria, gave birth to a son: Reginald, Lord Herbert. He is now the heir apparent to the earldom of Pembroke.

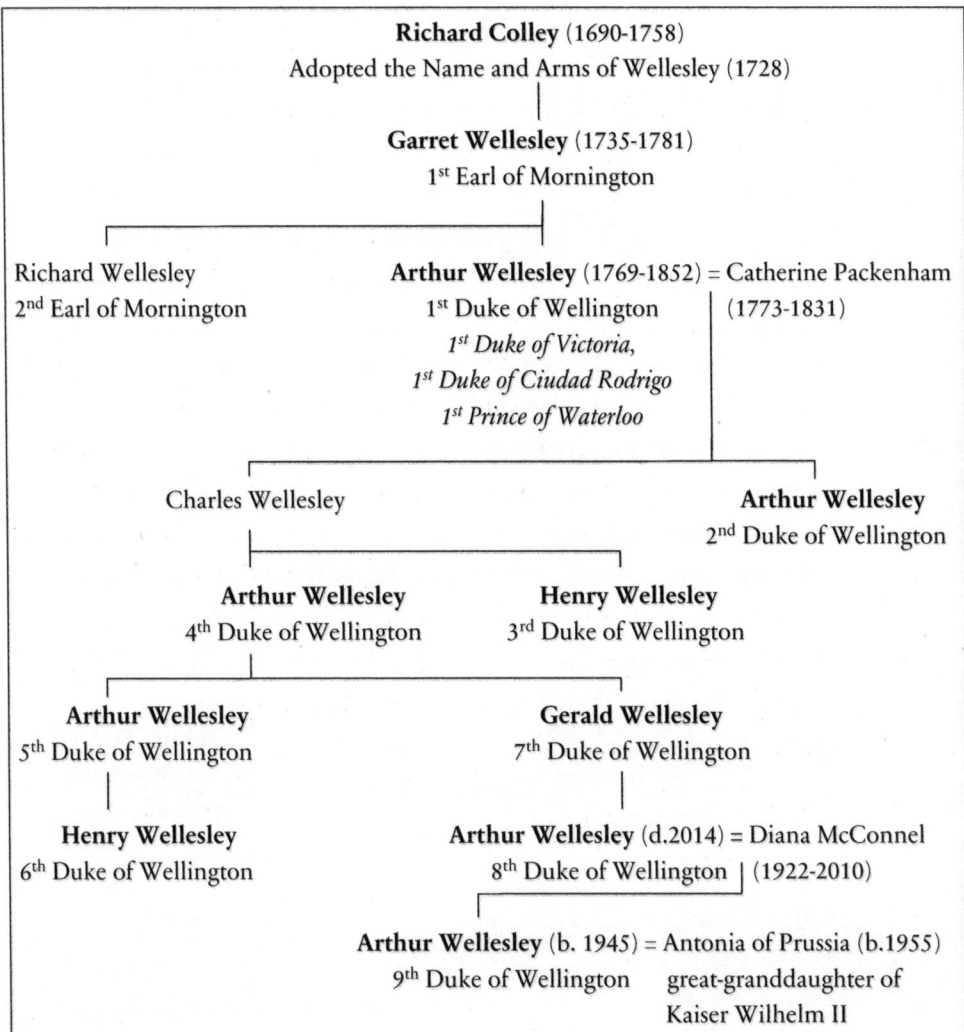

The Wellesleys of Stratfield Saye

Duke of Wellington

Dukedom created	1814
Monarch	George III
Subsidiary titles	Earl of Mornington; Viscount Wellesley; Prince of Waterloo (Dutch); Duke of Ciudad Rodrigo (Spain); Duke of Victoria (Portugal)

The story of the Wellesley family is utterly dominated by the singular figure of Arthur Wellesley (1769–1852): Napoleon's nemesis, army general, twice Prime Minister, the 'Iron Duke' of Wellington. Wellesley was granted his dukedom in 1814, and all subsequent members of his family have lived in the long shadow that he has cast. The current Duke of Wellington – 9th in line of descent from the hero of Waterloo – had his most prominent media moment in 2015 during the 200th anniversary of the battle. The duke attended bicentennial celebrations in Belgium where he was photographed shaking the hand of Charles Bonaparte, descendant of his ancestor's enemy that day in 1815. It is also a result of the Iron Duke's achievements that the Wellesleys hold any number of European titles in addition to their English peerages, dished out by the grateful nations which he had helped liberate from the Napoleonic empire.

Origins of the Iron Duke

Much like the defeat of Adolf Hitler in 1945, the victory over Napoleon in 1815 represented not just a triumph of military strategy and national determination – a successful defence of king and country – it also represented to many a 'moral victory' against a megalomaniac aggressor who had sought to make himself the master of Europe.

Napoleon Bonaparte – self-styled emperor with delusions of reviving imperial Rome – is forever associated with Arthur Wellesley, 1st Duke of Wellington, the man who put an end to his ambitions at Waterloo, just south of Brussels in modern-day Belgium. Since the battle, the small municipality where it took place has entered British popular culture, reflected in the names of a London railway station, a road and bridge, as well as through pop songs by groups as diverse as The Kinks and ABBA.

Both Wellesley and Bonaparte were born in the same year, 1769. Arthur Wellesley came from an old Anglo-Irish family that had once gone under the name of Colley, or Cowley. Arthur's grandfather, Richard Colley (1690–1758) had changed his surname to Wellesley in honour of his Wellesley cousins, from whom he inherited the estates of the old Wellesley family at Mornington, County Meath near Dublin. Before adopting the Name and Arms of Wellesley, the Colley family had been relatively successful landowners, having come to Ireland from England in around 1500. They held various administrative offices under the Tudors and became MPs for Trim, the town in County Meath. Their Wellesley relations were a much older family. That name had been in Ireland since the Anglo-Norman invasion and held an ancient feudal status. Taking the identity of the Wellesleys gave the Cowley family an instant noble sheen. Arthur's father, Garret, was born at Dangan Castle, the grand old Wellesley seat near Trim, and was created Earl of Mornington. His son was also to grow up at Dangan.

Arthur Wellesley was born a younger son of Lord Mornington. Like any younger son, not in direct line to inherit, Arthur would have to make his own way in the world. He spent his childhood at Dangan and at Mornington House, Dublin (the Anglo-Irish elite kept their city mansions for the Dublin season). Arthur was schooled in Trim and later at Eton, but did not distinguish himself academically, and was considered aloof and idle by his mother. Generous and kind-hearted, but a rather aimless young man, for a while it appeared Arthur would amount to nothing in life. Ironically, it was in France that he found his calling. After spending time at the Royal Academy of Equitation, Arthur became a highly proficient horseman. He developed confidence in himself at last, and he returned home to Ireland in 1787 to join the British Army.

What followed could easily have been a distinguished but ultimately unremarkable military career, typical of many thousands of younger sons of the nobility. The name of Arthur Wellesley could have faded quickly into historical obscurity. That it didn't was due to the cataclysmic events about to engulf Europe: decades-long wars that gave Wellesley a chance to make his name.

Arthur, India, and the French Wars

The French Revolution, which began in 1789, was at the root of the wars that dogged Europe from 1793 right up until the Battle of Waterloo in 1815. The revolution did not directly affect Britain until after the execution of Louis XVI, when France's revolutionary leaders sought to unify their nation through foreign wars and began invading neighbouring countries. Britain could not stand idly by. In fact the nation was not permitted to do so; France declared war in 1793.

The French Revolutionary Wars saw Arthur Wellesley in the early stages of his career learning lessons that would inform his military strategy in years to come. During the disastrous Flanders Campaign in 1794–1795, he learned a great deal about what *not* to do in battle, observing the poor leadership of British commanders.

He was then sent to India where his elder brother Richard – now 2nd Earl of Mornington – was set to be made Governor-General. There, Arthur honed his military skills, learning the value of discipline, good intelligence and organisation, during the war for control of the central Indian kingdom of Mysore. Here Arthur was pitted against his first worthy enemy, the sultan known as the Tiger of Mysore. Here was a military foe of unusual cunning, an early proponent of rocket artillery. During an operation in April 1799, Arthur's company was attacked by the sultan's rockets. The then Colonel Wellesley was forced to flee, losing his way in the jungle before regrouping. The very next day, Arthur launched a counterattack with reinforcements that overwhelmed the Indian defence. A month later, he helped British forces capture the Mysore capital of Seringapatam. The sultan was killed in the battle. The kingdom of Mysore fell to the British East India Company.

Unsurprisingly, Arthur had won quite a reputation by the end of his time in India. His talents would naturally be called upon in the war with France. Circumstances in France had changed in 1802 when a military commander of enormous popularity and renown had come to power. General Bonaparte had swept away the revolutionary government and declared himself 'First Consul for Life'. Napoleon seemed intent on dominating Europe. After a brief period of peace, Britain declared war on Napoleon in 1803.

Arthur and Napoleon

The Napoleonic Wars (1803–1815) provided the stage on which Arthur would become a superstar of British history. In Napoleon he found his military match. Both men were extraordinary leaders, though of very different personality and temperament. Napoleon saw himself as ruler of a continent, heir to the military *imperator* Julius Caesar, and crowned himself Emperor of the French in Notre Dame Cathedral in 1804. By contrast, Arthur was a modest man who did not seek self-aggrandisement but fought from a sense of duty to king and country. His fame was a consequence of his actions, not his ambition.

The fame grew rapidly nonetheless during the Peninsular Campaign in Spain and Portugal. Napoleon had invaded Spain in 1808, overthrowing King Ferdinand VII, and installing his own brother, Joseph Bonaparte, as the new ruler in Madrid. Arthur was sent to Portugal where he was appointed Commander-in-Chief of the British and Portuguese armies attempting to liberate Spain.

The war for the Iberian Peninsula lasted several years, Commander Wellesley mounting a relentless campaign, winning numerous tactical victories that slowly wore the enemy down. One of his early triumphs, at the Battle of Talavera in 1809, earned him a peerage as Viscount Wellington. The name was chosen by Arthur's brother William (Arthur himself would not have been interested in the matter). William had discovered a market town in Somerset called Wellington, which was reminiscent of the family name, and thus seemed fitting for a family title. 'I trust you will not think there is anything unpleasant or trifling in the name of Wellington,' William wrote to his brother. Arthur did not. His eldest brother, Lord Mornington, purchased a manor there on Arthur's behalf, creating a neat territorial link.

Tea and sandwiches

The name 'Wellington' is now lent to, among other things, the capital city of New Zealand, and of course the Wellington boot, a leather riding boot which Arthur popularised among the military, and which later became a staple of English country living. The name survived in the later rubber waterproof version.

The Duke of Wellington is not the only peer to lend their name to an everyday item of course. James Brudenell, 7th Earl of Cardigan (1797–1868) was a Lieutenant-General in the British Army during the Crimean War, and became famous – or infamous – after leading the disastrous 'Charge of the Light Brigade' on 25 October 1854.. Cardigan apparently misinterpreted a command during the Battle of Balaclava and led his cavalry on a hopeless dash against Russian artillery. The resulting slaughter was memorialised by Alfred, Lord Tennyson, whose poem celebrated the valour of the lost soldiers, who'd followed their leader to near-certain doom. (Cardigan himself survived the charge.) The origin of the cardigan is thought to lie with the knitted waistcoats worn by British Army officers, which started to become popular during the Crimean War period.

The 4th Earl of Sandwich, John Montagu (1718–1792) did not make much impact while in government, but he reputedly made a big contribution to Britain's – and the world's – eating habits. Montagu was an early proponent of the 'working lunch'. While running the navy, he was said to have asked his men to bring him some meat inside two slices of bread, so that he could eat at his desk. Some say the earl – a notorious gambler – also asked servants to bring the same meal to the card table. There, his fellow gamblers soon began to order 'the same as Sandwich' and, later on, just 'a Sandwich, please'.

A little folklore no doubt enters these stories. Several apocryphal tales have been proffered to explain why Charles, 2nd Earl Grey (1764–1845) should lend his name to a particular brew of tea. Grey

– he who passed the Great Reform Act and the Slavery Abolition Act – is nevertheless most popularly remembered simply as a lover of a good cuppa! He certainly was a lover (his affair with Georgiana, Duchess of Devonshire, was a tragic love match) but there is no evidence that he popularised, or even liked, what we now call Earl Grey Tea. The blend, which uses bergamot oil, is often said to have been created by a Chinese mandarin. Various reasons are given for its invention: it was blended especially to suit the water at Grey's ancestral home, Howick Hall; Grey saved the mandarin's son from drowning and the grateful scholar presented the earl with a special tea in gratitude; and so on. Whatever the truth, Earl Grey Tea is among the most popular global blends today.

Waterloo

Arthur expelled the French from Spain at last in 1814 after an unrelenting fight. Naturally, his victory made him as famous in Spain as it did in Britain. Having masterminded the liberation of the city of Ciudad Rodrigo in 1812, Arthur was dubbed a duke in the Peerage of Spain by a grateful King Ferdinand. (The dukedom of Ciudad Rodrigo is still held by the head of the House of Wellesley today.) After leading a crushing defeat of the French at the Battle of Vitoria in 1813, the then Viscount Wellington chased his enemy across the Pyrenees and into southern France. The breaking of Napoleon's power in Spain was a significant factor in Napoleon's first surrender and abdication in 1814, when it looked as if the emperor had been defeated for good. It was at this point that Arthur, now hailed a national hero, was promoted as 1st Duke of Wellington in the Peerage of the United Kingdom. He didn't know it then, but his greatest victory still lay ahead of him.

In March 1815, Napoleon escaped from his exile on the Isle of Elba and set about reconquering Europe. He marched into Belgium, trying to cut off the British coalition forces – led by

Wellington – from their Prussian allies. Wellington dug his soldiers in near the village of Waterloo, fortifying the various farmhouses along a ridge concealing and protecting his army. It was a tactic he had used successfully in Spain, and it worked effectively now. The battle, when it came, was long and arduous, with Arthur attempting to hold his line long enough for the Prussian army to arrive. It was almost too late: a strategic farm in the centre of the coalition defence was taken by the French, leading to a desperate struggle by Arthur and his men to outlast Napoleon. The emperor had, however, made one crucial tactical error: he had delayed the start of the battle after heavy rain had waterlogged the fields at Waterloo. It gave the Prussians just the extra time they needed. Their arrival, combined with Arthur's final order for the British Guards – still concealed behind the ridge – to suddenly attack the approaching French Imperial Guards, led to the collapse of French morale and of Napoleon's entire battle plan. The emperor fled the field, abdicated again, and was exiled again. This time he was sent to St Helena where he lived out his days.

Prince and Prime Minister

Not since John Churchill had a duke of the realm been so feted by the public for a military victory. Like Churchill, Arthur Wellesley was presented with a great estate upon his return, purchased for him by a grateful nation. Also like the Duke of Marlborough, who had a palace built for him and named after his famous victory at Blenheim, Arthur was to have a spectacular 'Waterloo Palace' constructed. The palace was to be built on his new estate at Stratfield Saye in Hampshire. That plan was soon abandoned as too expensive. No Waterloo Palace ever rose as a twin for Blenheim; the duke simply improved the existing house at Stratfield instead.

As in 1814, after the Iberian victory, the celebration of Arthur Wellesley became an international affair. In Belgium, where the

Duke of Wellington had helped vanquish the invaders, he was even created a prince. Belgium was at that time still part of the Kingdom of the Netherlands, and it was the Dutch king, William I, who made Arthur Wellesley the 1st Prince of Waterloo. There were some difficulties surrounding the succession of this title when Belgium became an independent kingdom in 1831. (The title had been granted by the Dutch Crown, but Waterloo was on Belgian land.) Compromises were reached, however, and all the dukes of Wellington to this day retain the grand title of 'His Serene Highness the Prince of Waterloo'.

Family seat: Stratfield Saye House
It was perhaps a relief to Arthur Wellesley that no Waterloo Palace was ever built for him. He was not a vain man and would probably have been embarrassed to live in a place as enormous and ostentatious as Blenheim Palace (a house which suited John Churchill very nicely). Instead, Stratfield Saye is a relatively modest seat, described by Queen Victoria as 'a low and not very large house, but warm and comfortable'. The house was built originally for the Pitt family (ancestral relations of Prime Ministers Pitt the Elder and Younger) in the early 1600s. The Jacobean house was altered and improved by Wellington upon his arrival there in 1817.

Unlike many ducal seats today, Stratfield is not a major tourist attraction, only opening to the public on select days each year. It is still the family home of the Wellesleys. The memory of the 1st Duke hovers, quite literally, over the building, as it does figuratively over the family who live there. A triumphal column standing at its entrance is crowned with a statue of Arthur Wellesley. The Stratfield Saye stables now contain an exhibition about the 1st Duke. Visitors can view the gigantic carriage that carried the duke's body to his funeral in 1854, made from melted down cannons captured at the Battle of Waterloo.

Prime Minister

The esteem in which the Duke of Wellington was held led to his invitation to become Prime Minister, an office he undertook from 1828 to 1830 and briefly again in 1834. Arthur was not a natural political leader. He treated the premiership as a military officer would, simply commanding and expecting his orders to be obeyed. There was little attempt at debate. A natural Tory, whose experience against the French made him wary of radicalism or revolutionary change, Arthur was conservative and resistant to even the most moderate reforms. Nevertheless, as Prime Minister, Wellington was responsible for a truly landmark piece of reforming legislation in the form of the Catholic Emancipation Act of 1829. This law removed most of the restrictions that had prevented Roman Catholics from sitting as MPs and holding many other public offices. The Act reversed the direction of travel prevalent since 1688, and the Protestant Ascendancy. It was largely as a result of agitation in his native Ireland that Wellington put aside any personal misgivings he may have felt as a member of the Anglo-Irish Protestant elite and lifted the ban on Catholics in public office. His fear of a popular uprising convinced him of the need for change in order to conserve, a philosophy that would become the cornerstone of modern conservatism.

A dynasty in the shade

The funeral of the 1st Duke of Wellington took place on 18 November 1852. It was an enormous affair. Crowds thronged the Royal Hospital Chelsea at the duke's lying in state. His body was transferred by carriage to St Paul's Cathedral, which was crammed with thousands of mourners. Queen Victoria wrote of Wellington: 'He was the pride and the bon génie, as it were, of this country! He was the GREATEST man this country ever produced, and the most devoted and loyal subject, and the staunchest supporter the Crown ever had.'

The Wellesleys of Stratfield Saye

It would have taken a later statesman of the renown of Winston Churchill for any subsequent Duke of Wellington to compete with the fame of the illustrious founder. Instead, the 5th Duke of Wellington (1876–1941) was known as an advocate for appeasing Hitler and active in antisemitic organisations. Other dukes were not so controversial but still did not make waves beyond holding minor political offices. The 7th Duke (1885–1972) made a contribution to heritage by presenting Apsley House, the family residence in London, to the nation, and opening it and its art collections to the public. Apsley had been purchased by the 1st Duke's brother, Lord Mornington, as a political base for Arthur. The Mornington title actually came to the 2nd Duke of Wellington after his uncle's line failed, and it is still held by the present duke along with other titles gathered by his illustrious ancestor. The present duke's coat of arms (the quartered arms of Colley, the old family name, and Wellesley, which they adopted) is surmounted by a Union flag, yet another rare honour granted to the Iron Duke.

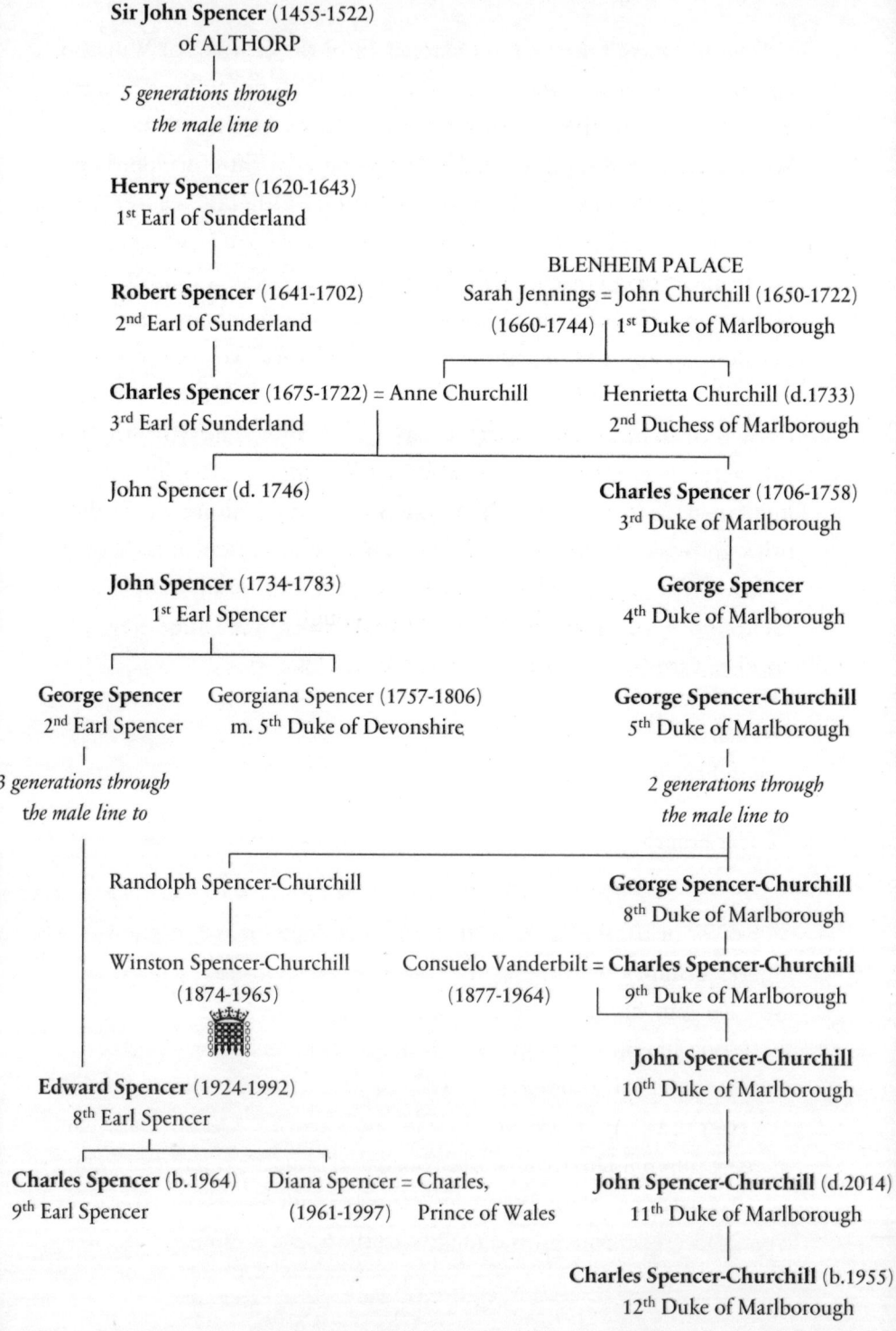

The Spencer-Churchills of Blenheim Palace

Duke of Marlborough

Dukedom created	1702
Monarch	Anne
Subsidiary titles	Marquess of Blandford; Earl of Sunderland; Baron Spencer
Cadet branch	Spencers of Althorp (Earl Spencer)

For most of us, the name 'Churchill' evokes the image of one iconic figure: Britain's wartime Prime Minister, Sir Winston (1874–1965). To give him his full name, he was Winston Spencer-Churchill, one of a long line in the House of Spencer, whose ancestor had married the daughter of another great war leader, General John Churchill (1650–1722). As a reward for famous victories, Queen Anne had made Churchill Duke of Marlborough and built him Blenheim Palace in Oxfordshire. With no male heir, the dukedom was passed by special decree through his daughter to the Spencer family. Thus were combined two great inheritances: the Churchill seat at Blenheim, and

Althorp House (the Spencer ancestral home since 1508). It proved too great an inheritance for any one man, so the heir, Charles Spencer, 3rd Duke of Marlborough, divided it up. He kept Blenheim as the Marlborough seat (with 'Churchill' later added to the surname) and handed the old Spencer seat at Althorp to his younger brother. The brother's descendants became the Earls Spencer, a line that produced Lady Diana Spencer, the Princess of Wales.

The twin houses of Spencer

In the eighteenth century, the Spencer family tree sprouted a pair of eminent branches. Each is peopled with characters so renowned they can often be identified by their first names only: Winston in the case of the Blenheim branch, Diana (1961–1997) in the case of Althorp. There are many more notables, particularly when it comes to the women of the House, who have, among other things, saved the family from destruction (Consuelo Spencer-Churchill) and gained such popularity with the public that they hold a lasting celebrity that none of the dukes or earls can rival (Lady Georgiana Spencer, Lady Diana Spencer).

Unusually, it is the junior branch of the family which today occupies the original ancestral seat, Althorp in Northamptonshire, where the Spencers emerged in the fourteenth century as sheep farmers. The senior branch, meanwhile, reside at the far larger and grander Blenheim Palace (the only non-royal or non-episcopal residence in England to be named a 'palace') which they inherited by marriage in the eighteenth century. They added Churchill to their name, becoming the Spencer-Churchills. But though that double-barrel is still scrawled on birth certificates, it has popularly been shortened to 'Churchill'. The senior line of Spencer is therefore better known as Churchill (as Sir Winston knew very well).

The origins of the Spencer story lie, nevertheless, in the centuries before the Churchill connection was made, between 1508 and 1733, when the family started to climb the ladder of nobility.

From Farmer Spencer to the Sunderland Spencers

The first Spencer to create a stir in the historical records was Sir John Spencer (1455–1522). He purchased the 300-acre estate at Althorp, establishing a dynastic seat. John had made his money from rearing sheep, an occupation his ancestors had apparently been pursuing for a century or more, both in Warwickshire and later in Northamptonshire. An ambitious man, John obtained a knighthood and a coat of arms from Henry VIII. He also built an early iteration of Althorp House. The Spencers were therefore of the new Tudor-era breed of landed gentry on the rise. Wealth was their springboard, and they became very rich indeed from their lands.

In 1603, Robert Spencer (1570–1627) was heading one of the richest landed families in England, a fact recognised by his elevation to the Peerage that year as the 1st Baron Spencer. King James I also gave Lord Spencer a diplomatic posting befitting his new status, sending him to the court of Frederick, Duke of Wurttemberg. Robert became a Knight of the Garter and married Margaret Willoughby of Wollaton Hall, that spectacular Prodigy House built for another family of rising stars. Sheep continued to be farmed at Althorp, but by tenant farmers.

In 1643, in the midst of the Civil War, the 3rd Baron Spencer, a staunch Royalist, was promoted to earl of Sunderland by King Charles. Henry Spencer was loyal to the end, just twenty-two years old when he fought and died at the First Battle of Newbury. The king was in personal command when Lord Sunderland was hit by cannon fire.

It was with the 3rd Earl of Sunderland, Charles Spencer (1675–1722) that the connection with the Churchill family arose. Charles married three times. His first wife was a Cavendish with whom he had a daughter. His third was an Irish heiress but no children survived from that marriage. His second wife, however, was Lady Anne Churchill, one of many daughters of His Grace, the 1st

Duke of Marlborough, whose only son and heir was to die three years later of smallpox, at the age of seventeen. The marriage of Charles Spencer and Anne Churchill produced not only an heir for Althorp, but for the celebrated Duke of Marlborough.

The hero of Blenheim: John Churchill, 1st Duke of Marlborough

The writer William Makepeace Thackeray did not think much of John Churchill. In his historical sketches Thackery wrote:

> Here is my lord Duke of Marlborough kneeling too, the greatest warrior of all times; he who betrayed King William – betrayed King James – betrayed Queen Anne – betrayed England to the French, the Elector to the Pretender, the Pretender to the Elector ... and you, my lord Duke of Marlborough, you would sell me or any man else, if you found your advantage on it.

It's true that Churchill was a great warrior. He began his soldiering career aged seventeen in 1667, revealing a military genius during the Franco-Dutch War that earned him rapid promotion. It's also true that Churchill was self-interested, and as Thackeray suggested, would readily switch sides, simply abandoning former allies whenever it served his designs. Churchill fought for James II against the Monmouth Rebellion. He then defected to support William of Orange in his coup against James (and was created Earl of Marlborough in reward). Later, he was suspected of plotting to restore James to the throne and was imprisoned in the Tower in 1692. Regaining favour, at the accession of Queen Anne she made him Captain-General of the English forces. He led the allied nations during the War of the Spanish Succession (1701–1714) during which he achieved a string of stunning victories over the French. The most famous was at the Battle of Blenheim in 1704.

Queen Anne rewarded him with a brand-new palace. But he then fell from favour again, was outmanoeuvred by political rivals, and went into self-imposed exile on the continent until the queen's death in 1714. To say the 1st Duke of Marlborough was a complex figure is to put it mildly.

John Churchill was born into a landed gentry family in 1650, the son of Sir Winston Churchill and Elizabeth Drake, a grandniece of George Villiers, Duke of Buckingham. In 1677 Churchill married Sarah Jennings (1660–1744), the woman who was largely responsible for his political rise. Disliked by many at court due to an infamous temper (her nickname was 'Vesuvius'), she was nevertheless very well connected and able to promote her family's interests. A close friend and confidante of the then Princess Anne, Sarah became immensely powerful when Anne succeeded as queen. By then the couple had joined the Peerage as earl and countess of Marlborough. (That title was chosen to honour Churchill's maternal descent from the Ley family, earls of Marlborough a century before.) Queen Anne then made her friends marquess and marchioness of Blandford, and Duke and Duchess of Marlborough in 1702, completely at her own discretion.

Churchill's military career progressed alongside his peerage promotions. He had ample opportunity to win further glory in the theatres of war in Europe. And he did just that in 1704 in a battle that made his name, at Blenheim in southern Germany.

The Battle of Blenheim

Blenheim was a key episode in a war few people today are that familiar with. The War of the Spanish Succession (1701–1714) may sound like Spain's eighteenth-century version of the Wars of the Roses, of little interest to Great Britain, but it actually affected the entire balance of power across Europe and marked the start of Britain's rise to becoming the world's preeminent superpower.

The initial cause was the death of the king of Spain without an heir, leaving one of the world's greatest empires without a leader. A possible successor was a grandson of the powerful 'Sun King' of France, Louis XIV (who had married a Spanish princess). The British, Austrians and Dutch were aghast at the idea of a union of France and Spain that could potentially dominate the globe. Thus, they formed an alliance to fight the French succession in Spain. In 1704, King Louis set his sights on knocking Austria out by conquering its capital, Vienna. The seat of the Austrian emperors was in serious danger of falling. That it didn't was down in no small part to John Churchill.

The Duke of Marlborough led a highly secretive march of troops all the way from the Netherlands to confront the French forces threatening Vienna. He met up with the Austrian commander, with whom he developed a daring plan. They would use diversionary tactics, attacking the edges of the French position at the village of Blenheim by the Danube River, and Lutzingen in the hills. This, they hoped, would lure the centre of their enemy's army towards the flanks, at which point Marlborough would suddenly attack, leading a massive cavalry charge to rout the French centre. The audacious plan worked. Many of the French who did not surrender drowned in the Danube attempting to escape.

This important victory smashed the illusion of Louis XIVs invincibility. It marked the beginning of the decline of French dominance in Europe, and the arrival of Britain as the new power, soon to grow into an imperial behemoth. The Spanish question was settled by a treaty that prevented unification of France and Spain (though did create a Spanish Bourbon monarchy which sits on the throne in Madrid today).

For his part in saving Vienna, John Churchill was honoured by the Austrian emperor who made him a Prince of the Holy Roman Empire. The duke was also granted more land in England by

Queen Anne – the manor of Woodstock – and the funds to build a palace worthy of commemorating the triumph at Blenheim.

There is no doubt John Churchill was a towering military talent. His reputation as one of the world's greatest generals spread across Europe, enhancing Britain's reputation still further. But Churchill's motivations were not loyalty to Queen or country, but desire for fame and renown. He was as egotistical as he was brave, and the building of a great palace in his honour was probably the least he expected.

The building of Blenheim Palace was overseen by Duchess Sarah, who had a fraught relationship with its architect John Vanbrugh. Employed after his impressive work at Castle Howard, Vanbrugh called Sarah 'that wicked woman of Marlborough', and the pair had furious rows. The building work was initially funded by the Treasury. But by 1712, Sarah's famously close relationship with Queen Anne had turned sour. The money dried up when the Marlboroughs fled into exile in Europe, and Vanbrugh found it near impossible to obtain payment. Only after Anne's death, when the Marlboroughs returned, did building work continue. Some was paid by the government, but most came from the duke's own pocket.

The Churchills also had a succession problem to deal with. Sarah and John had been greatly affected by the death of their only son, Lord Blandford, in 1703. But if the Peerage law governing their titles remained unaddressed, the death also meant the end of both the dukedom and the Churchill name. It was generally agreed that John Churchill's achievements were such that his honours should not be allowed to die with him. So, in 1706, Parliament passed a special Act allowing the Marlborough dukedom to pass to John and Sarah's eldest daughter, Henrietta Churchill.

Henrietta Churchill, 2nd Duchess and Charles Spencer, 3rd Duke of Marlborough

The *suo jure* Duchess of Marlborough inherited the title upon the death of her illustrious father in 1722. Henrietta (1681–1733) married Francis Godolphin in 1698. But history was to repeat itself in 1731 with the death of yet another Lord Blandford: their son William Godolphin. Henrietta was apparently not too saddened by her son's demise. Blandford was a libertine whose end came after a drinking bout in Oxford. The duchess is reported to have said, 'Anybody who had any regard for papa's [the 1st Duke's] memory must be glad that the Duke of Marlborough was not now in danger of being represented in the next generation by one who must have brought any name he bore into contempt.'

The death of Lord Blandford meant that the succession was once again thrown into doubt. But the Act allowing Henrietta to become duchess in her own right, had also allowed the dukedom to pass through any of John Churchill's daughters (though it would afterwards continue in the male line). So it was that the Marlborough title passed to the son of Anne Churchill by Charles Spencer.

Born in 1706, Charles Spencer did not expect to inherit either his father's Spencer estates or the properties of his mother's family. He was a younger son – so not in line for Althorp and the earldom of Sunderland – while the Churchill estates had long been expected to pass to Henrietta Churchill's son, Lord Blandford. Then, in 1729, his elder brother the 4th Earl of Sunderland died childless, making Charles earl and master of Althorp. Five years later, his cousin Lord Blanford died, making him heir to the dukedom of Marlborough. In 1733 Charles Spencer, 5th Earl of Sunderland, succeeded his aunt Henrietta as the 3rd Duke of Marlborough, and moved into Blenheim Palace.

Family seat: Blenheim Palace
The house of the Duke of Marlborough was not built only to be a family home, but to act as a lasting monument to his great victory at Blenheim. John Vanbrurgh designed the palace on a scale to

awe visitors, a massive English Versailles, in an extravagant style dubbed the English Baroque. Vanbrugh never saw his masterpiece completed. He departed the project in 1716, in a furious temper with Duchess Sarah's 'intolerable treatment' of him. The pair had clashed repeatedly over both cost and design. In 1725, the Vanbrugh tried to catch a glimpse of the finished palace while the duchess was away but was apparently refused entry to the grounds.

Blenheim is genuinely breathtaking in its size and splendour. From a distance the palace looks like a town, glittering with gold-tipped gables and towers. The interiors are just as splendid. Ceilings painted by Louis Laguerre and James Thornhill (who also decorated Chatsworth) adorn the Great Hall and the Saloon. The murals depict John Churchill presenting his battle plans to the mythic Britannia, and his triumph. The Anglo-Dutch sculptor Grinling Gibbons created the massive marble door frames which include the 1st Duke's crest as Prince of the Holy Roman Empire (in truth he created just one, and the duchess had cheaper copies made to fit the rest of the doors). The stunning Long Library was designed by Nicholas Hawksmoor.

It seems unfair that Vanbrugh never got to see it (he died the year after his final attempt). The importance of his design, which gave birth to English Baroque, is today recognised by the United Nations which designates Blenheim Palace as a UNESCO World Heritage Site.

The Spencers of Althorp

With Blenheim as his home, the 3rd Duke of Marlborough gave his old ancestral seat to his brother, John Spencer. John's son – also John – was created the 1st Earl Spencer in 1765, and his descendants remain at Althorp to this day.

Prominent Whigs from the start, the Spencers of Althorp produced several notable political figures. But they are best represented by two women born two centuries apart, whose lives followed eerily – and tragically – similar paths: Lady Georgiana Spencer (daughter of the 1st Earl) and Lady Diana Spencer (daughter of the 8th Earl).

Georgiana was born at Althorp in 1757. She grew up to become the celebrity it girl of her day. Socialite, fashionista and gossip-column favourite, Georgiana was a friend of Marie Antoinette and called a 'phenomenon' by Horace Walpole. Georgiana's enormous ornamental wigs and elaborate outfits became the sensation of London society. She threw riotous balls, was painted by Gainsborough and Reynolds, and caused scandal through her affairs. Underneath the glittering surface, Georgiana was extraordinarily intelligent: a political activist for the Whigs (and early proponent of women's rights), a literary star who published several novels, a musical composer, and an amateur scientist who conducted experiments in chemistry and amassed a huge collection of minerals and natural history specimens. Georgiana was hugely popular with the public for her generosity and her 'common touch'. But her life was marked by a deeply unhappy marriage that probably contributed to her addictions to alcohol and gambling.

At the age of seventeen, Georgiana had been married to William Cavendish, 5th Duke of Devonshire, who was – like her father, Earl Spencer – a leading Whig grandee. As Duchess of Devonshire, Georgiana became chatelaine of a vast number of estates, from Chatsworth in Derbyshire to Devonshire House in Picadilly, where she threw spectacular parties. Her husband was, by all accounts, a cold and distant man who grew envious of his wife's popularity. His mistress, Lady Elizabeth Foster, lived with the duke and duchess in a notorious *ménage à trois*, while Georgiana, desperately unhappy in her marriage, began an affair with the Whig politician Charles Grey (later, Prime Minister Earl Grey). Having given her husband a male heir in 1790, her health declined, and she succumbed to gambling. She died in 1806 aged forty-eight.

In 2008, publicity for a film about Georgiana (*The Duchess*, with Keira Knightley in the starring role) made much of the similarities between her life and that of Diana Spencer. Like Georgiana, Diana made an impressive marriage, in this case to the heir to the throne, the Prince of Wales. Like Georgiana, Diana became a popular icon, fashion star, and a focus of tabloid attention. And, like Georgiana, Diana's marriage was an unhappy one, with her life being cut tragically short.

The marriage of a future king to a Spencer provoked some dynastic snobbery from above and below. Traditionally, British Monarchs had married foreign royals, so marrying a member of an English aristocratic dynasty was deemed inappropriate by some in the establishment (even in 1981). Yet for some people, the royals were seen as not changing fast enough. Diana was of an old noble family, representing England's past, not its future.

Dynastic debates did not worry the public at large, in England or around the world. The 'fairytale wedding' of then Prince Charles to Lady Diana Spencer was watched by an estimated 750 million television viewers. Diana was walked down the aisle of St Paul's Cathedral by her father, the 8th Earl Spencer, and after the ceremony she appeared on the balcony of Buckingham Palace to a rapturous reception. In 1982, Diana gave birth to a son, Prince William, with a second, Harry, born in 1984 (their personal coats of arms included seashells taken from the Spencer shield). Less than ten years later, Diana and Charles' marriage very publicly fell apart. She remained a target for paparazzi after her divorce, an encounter with chasing photographers leading to her untimely death in a car crash in Paris in August 1997. At her funeral in Westminster Abbey, Diana's brother the 9th Earl Spencer gave a controversial eulogy that criticised the royal family, while reminding listeners that the Spencers were also the 'blood family' of Princes William and Harry. Diana's coffin was then taken to Althorp, her ancestral home, where she was buried on an island in a lake in the grounds.

The American duchess

It could be said that the Blenheim branch was overshadowed by the fame of the family at Althorp in the nineteenth and twentieth centuries. The dukes of Marlborough were hardly household names beyond their estates, and they were further outshone by their wives. One duchess in particular stood out, both for her nationality and for her legendary wealth, which came to the rescue of the Marlborough's palace. Like all great houses built in the centuries before, Blenheim was feeling its age by the late Victorian era, requiring urgent upkeep. Unfortunately, this was also the time that the British aristocracy was entering its financial decline. The 1880s saw the agricultural depression start to bite. Now, more than ever, wives were chosen for money. The 9th Duke of Marlborough was not the only patriarch of an old English dynasty to go in search of wealthy American heiresses.

In 1895, the famously loveless marriage began between the 9th Duke and the New York heiress, Consuello Vanderbilt (1877–1964). She was the great-granddaughter of the legendary Cornelius Vanderbilt (1794–1877) whose railroad and shipping empire had made his family the richest in America. Consuello was born in Manhattan amid the splendour of the city's Gilded Age. Her parents, like most Americans with huge wealth but no old-world rank, were as eager to marry their daughters into the British aristocracy as the aristocrats were eager to have them and their money. Consuello's social-climbing mother, Alva, was the driving force in contriving her daughter's marriage to the Duke of Marlborough. Consuello had been in love with someone else when she was forced into the arranged marriage, locked in her rooms with no contact with the outside world, until the ceremony in St Thomas Church in Manhattan. The bride and groom didn't like each other from the start. But that was incidental: the marriage settlement gave the duke $200,000 a year from Vanderbilt funds. The couple divorced in 1921, but the American duchess had saved Blenheim Palace.

Winston

If you visit Blenheim Palace today, you can visit the small bedroom where Winston Leonard Spencer-Churchill was born on 30 November 1874. His mother was also an American-born socialite, Jenny Jerome. His father was Lord Randolph Spencer-Churchill, third son of the 7th Duke of Marlborough. His name was chosen to emphasise dynastic continuity (Winston, the 1st Duke's father, had been a Civil War Cavalier). A long way from the dukedom himself, young Winston had to make his own way in the world, albeit with the very useful family name and connections that always assisted members of the upper classes. Like many in his position, he fixed on a military career, and after public school attended the Royal Military Academy, Sandhurst. He was commissioned into the army in 1895.

At first, Winston did not look like following in the footsteps of his celebrated ancestor John Churchill. Where John's battle strategy was legendary, Winston oversaw the utterly disastrous Gallipoli campaign during the First World War, leading to his resignation as head of the Navy. What he did have in common with John was an ability to switch sides where required (as an MP he moved from the Conservatives to the Liberals and back again) and his long years in the political wilderness.

John Churchill had gone into exile while out of favour. Winston Churchill did not. He spent his time loudly opposing the Nazi regime rising in Germany and arguing that Britain should be ready for war. It made him unpopular. But he was vindicated upon the outbreak of war with Germany in 1939, and in 1940, perfectly placed to take over from the failing Prime Minister Neville Chamberlain.

The wartime leadership of Winston Spencer-Churchill may be the last great example of a member of one of England's old dynastic class steering the nation towards its destiny from the highest office in the land. The descendant of a man knighted by

Henry VIII, and of another ennobled by Queen Anne, who bore the names of both, led the country through its darkest hour in the middle of the twentieth century. It's not a part of the story often commented upon, but the soaring oratory and bullish spirit that helped Britain to victory in 1945 flowed in part from Winston's love of drama (and from an ego that desired fame) that was clearly evident in his ancestor the 1st Duke of Marlborough. Historians continue to debate the legacy of Winston Churchill today – hero or imperialist? Saviour of the nation, or warmonger?. Churchill's birthplace is today overseen by Jamie Spencer-Churchill, 12th Duke of Marlborough. Althorp is overseen by Charles Spencer, 9th Earl Spencer.

Bibliographical Note

There are numerous routes deeper into dynastic history. Volumes of family history exist in some form for each of the dynasties covered in this book. There are far too many to list, but some of the most informative include: *The Cecils: Privilege and Power Behind the Throne* by David Loades; *The House of Beaufort* by Nathan Amin; *The Devonshires* by Roy Hattersley; *The Grosvenors of Eaton* by Diana Newton; and *The Dukes of Norfolk, a Quincentennial History* by John Martin Robinson. Some of the best dynastic histories are actually 'country house biographies', many written by the owners themselves: *Harewood, a New History* by David Lascelles; *Althorp, the Story of an English House* by Charles Spencer; *Capability Brown and Belvoir* by Emma Manners; *Chatsworth, the House* by Deborah Devonshire; *Longleat from 1566 to the Present Time* by Daphne Thynne; *Wellington, a Journey Through My Family* by Jane Wellesley. There are also countless biographies of individuals mentioned in this book. To name a popular handful: *Tudor King in All But Name, the life of Edward Seymour* by Margaret Scard; *Bess of Hardwick* by Mary Lovell; *Georgiana, Duchess of Devonshire* by Amanda Foreman; *The Man behind the Tudors, Thomas*

Howard, 2nd Duke of Norfolk by Kirsten Claiden-Yardley; and *The High-Flying Duchess* by Meriel Buxton.

Historical studies of the aristocracy as a class often neglect the family histories behind high politics, but indispensable works include Cannadine's *The Decline and Fall of the British Aristocracy* and the many classic works of F. M. L. Thompson. Books that do take a dynasty-centric approach are few but include Christopher Lee's *This Sceptred Isle: the Dynasties*, which covers historic as well as extant dynasties like the Saxon-era Godwins and medieval Despensers, both long since vanished, and Brian Masters' *The Dukes*, which examines ducal families (including Scottish and Irish). It also contains a bibliography of primary and secondary sources and references.

For comprehensive genealogy, *Burke's Peerage and Baronetage* is the go-to, while *Debrett's* has published lavish guides to stately homes which contain a wealth of information on those who built them. Today's guidebooks to country seats are also authoritative introductions to the families who owned and often still own them.

Index

Adam, Robert 142, 148, 219
Alnwick Castle 48, 90, 137, 141–42
Anne (queen regnant) 233, 265, 268, 269, 271, 278
Arundel Castle 69–70, 75, 149
Arundel, Henry, 12th Earl of 67
Arundel, St Philip, 13th Earl of 69, 71, 73, 74
Attainder, Acts of 29, 53, 68, 69, 79, 88, 93, 98, 183

Badminton House 124, 132–34, 135
Barry, Charles 219–20, 248
Bath, Alexander, 7th Marquess of 100, 106, 107
Bath, Ceawlin, 8th Marquess of 106–07
Bath, Emma, Marchioness of 107
Bath, Henry, 6th Marquess of 104–06
Bath, John, 4th Marquess of 100
Battle of Agincourt 18, 228, 241
Battle of Blenheim 268, 269–70
Battle of Bosworth 53, 57, 63, 109, 113–14, 115, 116, 117, 144, 145
Battle of Hastings 14, 19, 26, 124, 218
Battle of Waterloo 253, 254, 255, 259–61
Beaufort, Henry, 1st Duke of 132, 133, 134
Beaufort, Henry, 12th Duke of 134
Beaufort, Margaret 18, 85, 113, 126
Bedford, Andrew, 15th Duke of 193
Bedford, Hastings, 12th Duke of 192
Bedford, Henry, 14th Duke of 193

Bedford, Herbrand, 11th Duke of   192
Bedford, John, 1st Earl of   182–83
Bedford, John, 13th Duke of   193
Bedford, Mary, Duchess of   193–95
Bedford, William, 1st Duke of   184–86
Bedford, William, 5th Earl of   122
Belvoir Castle   48, 225, 226–27, 229, 233, 234, 235, 237
Berry Pomeroy Castle   88, 93–4
Bigod family   14, 15, 55, 58, 227
Blenheim Palace   9, 25, 47, 206, 260, 261, 265–66, 271, 272–73, 276–77
Boleyn, Queen Anne   52, 61, 63, 82–3
Bonaparte, Napoleon   253, 254, 256–57, 259–60
Boyle, Charlotte   36, 208–09
Bradley House   79, 88, 93, 94
Brown, Capability   48, 100, 133, 148, 150, 168, 189, 207, 219, 248
Burleigh House   163–65, 167–68, 170, 171, 172, 177–79
Burleigh, William, 1st Baron   12, 19, 45, 67, 118, 146, 163, 165–70, 177, 244
Burlington, Laura, Countess of   214
Burlington, Richard, 3rd Earl of   47, 189, 209, 210

Cannadine, David   15, 44, 121
Cardigan, James, 7th Earl of   258
Carnarvon, George, 5th Earl of   240, 249–50
Carnarvon, George, 8th Earl of   251
Carnarvon, Henry, 1st Earl of   247, 248
Carnarvon, Henry, 3rd Earl of   248
Carter, Howard   249–50
Cavendish, Sir William   20, 197–201
Chanel, Coco   158–59
Charles III   42, 161, 213, 275
Chatsworth   25, 27, 46, 47, 48, 102, 150, 177, 197–202, 204, 205–15, 230, 234, 273, 274
Chippendale, Thomas   219
Civil War, English   22–3, 46, 75, 119, 132, 184, 202, 204, 218, 227, 267, 277
Cooper, Lady Diana   235–36
Coronets   40, 41
Crusades   18, 56, 116, 140

Davies, Mary   156
De Louvain, Jocelin   140, 141
De Montford, Simon   16
De Mowbray, Margaret   54
De Ros, Eleanor, Baroness   226
De Ros, George, 11th Baron   226, 227
De Todeni family   226, 227

Index

De Vere family 14, 15, 30
De Warenne family 14
Derby, Caroline, Countess of 121
Derby, Edward, 13th Earl of 119–20
Derby, Edward, 14th Earl of 120–21
Derby, Edward, 19th Earl of 121
Derby, Edward John, 18th Earl of 121
Derby, Ferdinando, 5th Earl of 117–18
Derby, James, 7th Earl of 119
Derby, James, 10th Earl of 119
Derby, Thomas, 1st Earl of 109, 112–15, 120, 145
Devonshire, Amanda, Duchess of 215
Devonshire, Andrew, 11th Duke of 27, 37, 211–13
Devonshire, Deborah, Duchess of 27, 37–8, 211–14
Devonshire, Georgiana, Duchess of 208, 209, 236, 259, 266, 274–75
Devonshire, Louise, Duchess of 209
Devonshire, Peregrine, 12th Duke of 33, 37, 215
Devonshire, Spencer, 8th Duke of 208, 209
Devonshire, William, 1st Duke of 13, 46, 47, 186, 197, 204–08
Devonshire, William, 4th Duke of 36, 48, 208
Devonshire, William, 5th Duke of 208, 209, 210, 275
Devonshire, William, 6th Duke of 207, 209
Devonshire, William, 1st Earl of 201–02
Diana, Princess of Wales 9, 266, 274, 275
Downton Abbey 27, 48, 220, 239, 240, 247, 248, 250–51

Earl Marshal 38, 41, 51, 52, 57, 58, 67, 76, 201
Eaton Hall 153, 154, 159, 160
Eaton, Joan of 154, 160
Edward IV 54, 55, 57, 113, 183, 225, 228, 229, 242
Edward V 55, 57
Edward VI 65, 79, 83, 85, 88, 145, 183, 243, 244
Elizabeth I 12, 67, 68, 82, 87, 89, 99, 117, 118, 146, 163, 165, 170, 171, 172, 198, 201
Elizabeth II 27, 42, 45, 124, 134, 163
Exeter, David, 6th Marquess of 178–79

Ferrers family 116
Field of Cloth and Gold 128, 165, 227
Fitzalan family 14, 67, 69–70, 75
Flitcroft, Henry 48, 189

Freud, Lucian 27, 214

Gaunt, John of 124–27, 155
Glorious Revolution 24, 47, 103, 184, 186–87, 188, 204, 207, 262
Granby, John, Marquess of 233
Grand Tours 100, 177, 188, 219
Grey, Charles, 2nd Earl 120, 190, 258–59, 274
Gros Veneur, Gilbert 151, 153–54, 162
Gunpowder Plot 71, 72, 146
Gwladys of Abergavenny 240–41

Haddon Hall 226, 230, 231–34
Haddon, Robert, Lord 234–35
Hardwick, Bess of 43, 45, 46, 197, 198–02, 204, 206, 211, 230
Hardwick Hall 43, 45, 197, 201–02, 206, 211
Harewood, David 223
Harewood, David, 8th Earl of 222–23
Harewood, Edward, 1st Earl of 220
Harewood, Edwin, 1st Baron 218–20
Harewood, George, 7th Earl of 221–22
Harewood, Henry, 6th Earl of 221
Harewood House 217, 219–20, 221, 222, 223

Harewood, Princess Mary, Countess of 221–22
Hatfield House 163, 171–72, 211, 244
Henry VIII 19, 20, 21, 51, 59–65, 77, 79, 82, 83–4, 85, 86, 89, 97, 118, 128, 145, 156, 159, 165, 177, 181, 183, 225, 227, 228, 239, 243, 244, 267, 278
Heraldry 38–42, 51, 58, 64–5, 89, 110, 111, 124, 127, 141, 154–56, 198, 203, 209, 228, 263, 267, 275
Herbert, Elizabeth 127–28
Herbert, Lady Evelyn 249–50
Highclere Castle 48, 239–40, 247–48, 249–50
Hitler, Adolf 214, 222, 254, 263
House of Lords 10–11, 13, 16, 17, 21, 22–3, 24, 26, 28, 32, 72, 74, 89, 93, 106, 158, 161, 163, 172, 174–75, 190, 191, 192, 204, 208, 236
Hundred Years War 18, 32, 80, 125–26, 176, 203

Jones, Inigo 47–8, 72, 171, 184, 244

Kennedy family 28, 198, 211, 213
Kent, William 48, 133, 209
Knowsley Hall 49, 105, 110, 118–19, 121

Laguerre, Louis 47, 206, 273
Lathom family 110–11, 116, 118–19
Lear, Edward 119
Letters Patent 29, 32, 34–6, 55, 85, 91, 102, 184, 233
Longleat 9, 48, 49, 88, 94, 95, 98, 99–100, 101, 102–07, 121
Lupus, Hugh 139, 153

Magna Carta 15, 16, 32, 54, 56, 82, 140, 185, 188, 226
Manners, Lady Alice 237
Manners, Lady Eliza 237
Manners, Lady Violet 237
Manners, Lord Hugo 237, 226
Manners, Sir John 230–31
Manners, Sir Robert 225, 226
Marlborough, Charles, 12th Duke of 278
Marlborough, Consuelo, Duchess of 266, 276
Marlborough, Henrietta, 2nd Duchess of 271–72
Marlborough, John, 1st Duke of 233, 260, 261, 265, 268–72, 277
Marlborough, Sarah, Duchess of 269, 271, 273
Mary I 20, 66–7, 118, 145–16, 166, 167, 199
Mary II 24, 184, 186
Mary, Queen of Scots 67–9, 84, 146, 169, 170, 201

Mornington, Garrett, 1st Earl of 255
Mornington, Richard, 2nd Earl of 256, 257, 263
Mortimer, Roger 17

Newcastle, Henry, 2nd Duke of 203
Newcastle, Margaret, Duchess of 202–03
Newcastle, William, 1st Duke of 202–03
Norfolk, Edward, 18th Duke of 52, 76
Norfolk, Henry, 15th Duke of 74–5
Norfolk, John, 1st Duke of 35, 51, 52–8, 144
Norfolk, Thomas, 1st Duke of 54, 55, 56, 70, 176
Norfolk, Thomas, 2nd Duke of 53, 59
Norfolk, Thomas, 3rd Duke of 52, 60–7
Norfolk, Thomas, 4th Duke of 67–8, 69, 74, 146, 201
Norfolk, Thomas, 5th Duke of 74
Northern Earls' Rebellion 67–8, 146, 168
Northumberland, Elizabeth, Duchess of 147
Northumberland, Henry, 1st Earl of 143
Northumberland, Hugh, 1st Duke of 147–48

Northumberland, Jane, Duchess
of 149-50
Northumberland, Ralph, 12th
Duke of 149

Order of the Garter 27, 40-1, 84,
111, 117, 121, 127, 171, 176,
227, 242, 243, 267

Palatinates 154
Paxton, Joseph 150, 209, 210
Pembroke, Mary, Countess
of 245-46
Pembroke, Thomas, 8th Earl
of 247
Pembroke, Victoria, Countess
of 251
Pembroke, William, 1st Earl of
(d.1469) 241-42
Pembroke, William, 1st Earl of
(d.1570) 242-44
Pembroke, William, 18th Earl
of 251
Percy, Henry 'Hotspur' 143-44
Percy, Richard 140
Percy, William 137, 139-40
Pilgrimage of Grace
(1536) 145-46
Privy Council 19, 98, 166, 170
Protestant Reformation 19-21,
23, 60-3, 65-6, 79, 85,
145-46, 166, 168, 177, 199
Primogeniture 33-4, 36, 201

Richard II 56, 111, 155

Richard III 39, 51, 55, 57-9,
113, 145
Ridolfi Plot 68, 169
Royal forests 81, 116
Russell, Bertrand, 3rd Earl 191
Russell, John, 1st Earl 190
Russell, William, Lord 23,
181-82, 184-86, 207, 232
Rutland, Elizabeth, Duchess
of 227, 233
Rutland, John, 1st Duke of 232,
243
Rutland, John, 5th Duke
of 233-34
Rutland, Thomas, 1st Earl
of 227-28
Rutland, Violet, Duchess
of 234-35
Rye House Plot 185

Salisbury Convention 174-75
Shrewsbury, George, 6th Earl
of 200-01
Salisbury, Robert, 1st Earl
of 170-71
Salisbury, Robert, 3rd Marquess
of 26, 163, 172-74, 235
Salisbury, Robert, 7th Marquess
of 175
Sandwich, John, 4th Earl of 258
Seymour, Queen Jane 64, 77,
82-4, 88
Seymour, Sir Thomas 77, 85,
86-7

Index

Shakespeare, William 54, 65, 101, 110, 114, 115, 118, 143, 229, 245
Slavery 120, 149, 217–18, 219, 220, 222–23
Smythson, Robert 45–46, 99, 202
Social season 235, 236
Somerset, Algernon, 7th Duke of 147
Somerset, Charles, 6th Duke of 90–1, 101, 147
Somerset, Edward, 1st Duke of 62, 64–5, 79, 83, 84–8, 89, 91, 95, 97–8, 131, 145, 166, 168
Somerset, Elizabeth, Duchess of 90, 101–02, 147
Somerset, John, 19th Duke of 79, 93
Somerset, Lord Henry 134–5
Somerset, William, 2nd Duke of 89–90
Spencer, Charles, 9th Earl 275, 278
Spencer, Edward, 8th Earl 275
Spencer, John, 1st Earl of 273, 274
Spencer, John of Althorp 267
Stanley, John I of Man 111, 112, 118
Stanley, John II of Man 112
Stanley, Thomas, 1st Baron 112
Strange, George, 9th Baron 113, 114, 116–17

Strange, Joan, 9th Baroness 116–17
Stratfield Saye 260–61
Suffolk, Katherine, Countess of 71–3
Sunderland, Charles, 3rd Earl of 267–68
Sunderland, Henry, 1st Earl of 267
Surrey, Henry, Earl of 63–6
Swynford, Katherine 125–26

Talbot family 76, 186, 200–01, 202, 203–04
Thomas, William 240–41
Thynne, Sir John 88, 93, 95, 97–100, 166, 168
Thynne, Thomas of Longleat 101–02, 147

Vanbrugh, John 47, 73, 271, 273
Vernon family 230–32
Villiers family 269, 103, 129

Warbeck, Perkin 80, 115
Wars of the Roses 18, 19, 53, 54–5, 109, 112–15
Warwick, Richard, 16th Earl of 113, 114–15, 176, 183, 242
Waugh, Evelyn 42, 73, 213
Wellington, Arthur, 1st Duke of 253–63

Wellington, Arthur, 5th Duke of 263
Wellington, Arthur, 9th Duke of 253, 263
Wellington, Gerald, 2nd Duke of 263
Wentworth Woodhouse 48, 189
Westminster, Gerald, 6th Duke of 161
Westminster, Hugh, 1st Duke of 32, 157–58, 160
Westminster, Hugh, 2nd Duke of 158–59
Westminster, Hugh, 7th Duke of 161–62
Westminster, Olivia, Duchess of 161–62
Westminster, Robert, 1st Marquess of 157, 160

Weymouth, Thomas, 1st Viscount 102–03
William, Prince of Wales 121, 161, 275
William the Conqueror 13, 14, 30, 32, 53, 80, 81, 124, 140, 151, 153, 154, 232
Wilton House 239, 243–46, 247
Woburn Abbey 181, 183, 185, 189–90, 192, 193, 194, 195
Wollaton Hall 46, 267
Worcester, Charles, 1st Earl of 127–28
Worcester, Edward, 2nd Marquess of 131
Worcester, Edward, 4th Earl of 131–32
Writs of Summons 15, 112, 116, 175